Marvels of Our Blessed G-d's Torah

By **HaRav Tzvi Hersh Shlez**

Translated and Abridged by

Rabbi Yitzchak Goodman

Copyright© 2013 Rabbi Yitzchak Goodman

ISBN: 978-0615838748

All rights reserved.
No part of this book may be reproduced, stored in a retrieval system, or transmitted by any means, electronic, mechanical, photocopying, recording or otherwise without the express written consent of the author and publisher.

Ish Tov Publications
737 Empire Avenue
Far Rockaway, NY 11691

Comments may be sent to RavIzzy613@gmail.com

Printed in the United States of America

בס"ד

RABBI ARYEH MALKIEL KOTLER	בע"ה	ארי' מלכיאל קוטלר
BETH MEDRASH GOVOHA		בית מדרש גבוה
LAKEWOOD, N.J. 08701		לייקוואוד, נ. דז.

ב"ה סיון תשע"ב

(דברים ו-ז) ושננתם לבניך ודברת בם, ואמר רבנן מאי ושננתם שיהיו דברי תורה מחודדים בפיך שאם ישאל אדם דבר אל תגמגם ותאמר לו אלא אמור לו מיד. ודרשא סמוכה לבניך, ולבניך בניך זה אשר תחת לבן הארוכה של הדור ודור מיום שנתנה התורה לישראל עד סוף כל הדורות וכנופש מקצרת להשיאה מפת ה' לישראל במקום של תלמוד תורה והתלמדות שגם אם יודעים הענין לטוב יש לבקש ולרדוף אחריה גדולות בלימוד התורה וחיי תורה מאמצ מאד עיין וכל אשר אפשר ל' שאותה התורה וטעם ולעסוק לימוד התורה בכוונתה ואין אפשר כאן לבאר כל ספרי ...

הכו"ח לכבוד התורה

אריה מלכיאל קוטלר
בלאאמו"ר הגה"צ זצ"ל

דוד קאהן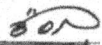

ביחמ"ד גבול יעבץ
ברוקלין, נוא יארק

ערב פסח תשע"ד

בס"ד

The sefer Niflaos MiToras HaShem Yisborach is outstanding in that its novelae are provoking, and it sensitizes the reader to understand Torah in depth where it foretells what the future has in store for Klal Yisroel.

It takes a person of unique ability and originality to undertake a translation of this important and difficult work. I commend my good friend Rav Yitzchak Meir Goodman shlit'a for his presentation in a most readable style that presents the richness of our holy literature to our people.

Yeyasher kocho!

With deep affection,

דוד קאהן

CONGREGATION KNESETH ISRAEL

THE WHITE SHUL
פיק כנסת ישראל

728 Empire Avenue
Far Rockaway, NY 11691

Phone: 718.327.0500
Fax: 718.327.7415

www.whiteshul.org
office@whiteshul.com

בס"ד

Rabbi
Eytan Feiner

Rabbi Emeritus
Ralph Pelcovitz

President
Chaim Leibtag

Senior Vice Presidents
Ed Bloom
Naftali Solomon
Yossie Stern

Vice Presidents
Tom Bauer
Yossi Bennett
Heshy Friedman
Chanan Mittel
William Pearlman

Treasurer
David Alter

Counsel
Gabriel Kaszovitz
Stephen Goldenzweig

Recording Secretary
Lri Katz

Gabbai
Mottie Schwartz

Co-Chairmen of the Board
Nesanel Feller
Tuvia Silverstein

כ״ד שבט תשע״ג
יום ב׳ לשבת פר׳ משפטים\שקלים

לכבוד הרה"ג רב יצחק מאיר גודמן שליט"א:

יישר כוחך for your excellent English rendition of a true masterpiece in the world of Torah classics, Rav Tzvi Hersh Shlez's פסאות מתורת ה'. You have done an exceptional job in abridging a verbose text and elucidating a somewhat difficult work with perfect fidelity to the author's core ideas.

Just as you masterfully displayed in your *Great Torah Lights From Great Torah Minds* – a delightful compilation of various commentaries coupled with your own novel insights – you have now skillfully crafted a clear and carefully curtailed volume of a most important sefer, a vital companion as one journeys through תנ"ך. Kudos to you for presenting the reader with all the brilliance of the original, without dilution of its primary points and compelling messages.

כל הכבוד ותזכה למצוות for successfully making this invaluable sefer accessible to the המון עם, and for providing such a precious gift to our generation and beyond.

הכותב ורהחותם לכבוד התורה – לומדי-ה ומרביצי-ה,
ובברכת כל טוב תמיד

איתן פיינר

Member of

Bais Medrash of Harborview
218 Harborview South
Lawrence, New York 11559

Rabbi Yehoshua Kalish

I was thrilled that my dear friend, Rav Yizchak Meir Goodman Shlit'a has undertaken the difficult task of translating the brilliant sefer *Niflaos MiToras HaShem Yisborach*. When I was a talmid in the Lakewood Yeshivah, I heard that HaRav Aharon Kutler זצוק"ל studied and greatly admired this work. After acquiring it, I was fascinated and overwhelmed by the ingenious way the author shows how the Torah foresaw and left clues for every important event that is related later in the *Nach*.

Rav Goodman has done an extraordinary job of taking a very wordy, flowery, and repetitive work, and condensing it in a lucid and succinct style. He has done a tremendous service for *klal Yisroel* by making this trail-blazing volume accessible to all. I highly recommend everyone to avail themselves of this eye-opening and remarkable sefer.

החותם לכבוד התורה

הרב יהושע הלוי קאליש

Introduction

From the time I first encountered this amazing volume and discovered that it is little-known in the Torah world, I had a powerful urge to translate it someday for the wider Jewish public.

In our shul in Far Rockaway, it served us as the text for study between Minchah and Maariv, and we completed it in about eight years. However, once I began the task, I recognized an extremely overwhelming problem. The author constantly repeats ideas, becomes very emotional at times, and adds many summaries as he goes along.

An exact and literal translation would be an extra burden for the reader and increase the number of pages enormously. The flowery style of the author (a few samples of which I did include) would surely not appeal to the modern reader, and would detract from the brilliance of the ideas he discovered and discussed. I, therefore, took the liberty of creating a less literal, abridged translation. I omitted many ecstatic expressions of delight, and many reviews and repetitions of points made. I added more detail to references which were made in great brevity, but which added important points to the author's thesis. I also noted the sources for many quotes which were not identified.

I do believe that those who will read this liberal translation, and check the original, will find that no important points were left out, and that the author's marvelous insights and astonishing originality were faithfully preserved and presented. I also allowed myself some personal observations and comments, which are found as footnotes at the end of the volume. I believe that the huge number of original insights and interpretations can be usefully integrated by teachers of Tanach in their classes, and will delight their students.

While I could not find significant biographical material about this author, the approbations he received from leading Rabbanim show that he was greatly respected, as was his father, Rav Ben-Tzion, who had moved to Eretz Yisrael. (He does indicate in chapter 57 that he was a descendant of the *Levush*.) Among the great giants of Torah who lavished praise on this work are Rav Yitzchak Elchanan Spector, who was recognized as one of the most outstanding Rabbanim of his day and Mahari'l Diskin, an almost legendary personality of his time.

Rav Shlez lived in a little town called Karsan, near Kiev, and apparently served as its Rabbi. In his introduction, however, laments that he did not even possess basic texts to examine, like the Ramban and the Ibn Ezra on the Torah!

It is very well-known that HaRav Aharon Kotler zt"l praised this book greatly and was often seen carrying it with him in his Yeshivah in Lakewood. He called it a "segulah for Yiras Shamayim."

I firmly believe that, in time, this great classic will be recognized for what it is, and will become a standard volume for study by all who are interested in Tanach. The author's ultimate goal was to show the Divine nature of a work that only G-d Himself could have written, as he emphasizes dozens of times. I believe that he succeeded magnificently. If this translation helps to bring this volume to the attention of the wider Jewish world sooner, and perhaps sways skeptical minds too, my effort of several years will be well rewarded.

PART ONE: Uncovering Hidden Aspects (in the Lives) of our Fathers

---

Chapter 1

Following the feet of Avraham in Eilonei Mamre which is Chevron, and peeking between the slats – that the Torah saw from the beginning that David would attain the kingship over Yehudah and Israel in Chevron, and other details of the Torah's vision of the future . You will see these items when you examine my words.

Note, my brother, a precious stone before your eyes, and without noting you might pass it and not stoop to take it. See a wondrous thing, about G-d's promise to Avraham (*Bereishis 17:6*) "And kings will descend from your loins," and so too about Sarah (*ibid.*) "and kings of nations will descend from her" : That promise was [made] in Chevron, as is written (*Ch.13:18*) "And Avraham took his tent and settled in Eilonei Mamre which is in Chevron, etc.." and we do not find that he left there until after the event at Sodom when he was 99 years old. Note the comment of Rashi (21:34) showing that when the promise of kings descending from him was made by G-d he was in Chevron.

Now note that the fruition of that promise was also in Chevron, for the greatest king, King David, to whom the kingdom was given for all eternity, received his monarchy in Chevron, where he was anointed as king over all Israel. That is where all Israel gathered to crown him, as we find in *Shmuel II* (ch. 5), "And all the tribes of Israel came to David at Chevron... and they anointed David as king over Israel." Lest you say that this [location] was just a coincidence, see that a special message of G-d determined that specifically Chevron should be the site for his attaining the kingdom, as we find (*Shmuel II*, 2), "And David asked G-d, 'Should I go up to one of the towns of Yehudah?' And G-d said, 'Go up.' and David said, 'where to?' and He said, 'to Chevron.'" And it then says that the people of Yehudah came and they anointed David there as king over the House of Yehudah. Thus, it was the specific intent of G-d that he should receive the monarchy in Chevron, over both Yehudah and Israel.

Clearly the choice of Chevron was not by chance. So too, G-d's promise to Avraham that kings would descend from him was not coincidentally made at Chevron. Chevron was not the permanent site of Avraham's habitation, for when he arrived in the land, we find him at "the place of Shechem," and afterwards between Beth-El and Aay. Later, he traveled southward, and made additional journeys until he settled in Eilonei Mamre, where he was told about his royal descendants. Later, he left Chevron for Gerar and other places. Clearly, his settling in Chevron was for the purpose of receiving that promise specifically in Chevron. How amazing are the words of G-d! For the trees, and stones, and soil of Chevron heard this promise of G-d and stood ready to confirm the pledge of G-d many, many centuries (637 years) later.

Thus, with precise intention G-d made this promise in Chevron, the place where [He knew that] the pledge would be kept, so that later generations would understand that the Torah is Divine, so that we should keep the commandments for our ultimate good. As we proceed, you will see in the coming chapters that not only in this case did the accomplishment of a promise take place at the spot that it was originally made, but wherever G-d made His pronouncements, there was a sublime purpose, for generations later, those pronouncements came to fruition in the places where the promises were made. Thus, it is as if the Torah had said that Avraham's royal descendants would rule in Chevron. Only G-d, who foresees the future, could manipulate such events. You will also see in chapter 29, that the Torah already foresaw that Kalev would inherit Chevron, and in chapter 30 I showed that the holy Torah foresaw that Chevron would be a city of refuge.

Yet you might ask: Did not Rashi state on the verse that "kings will descend from your loins" that this refers to both kings of Jews and of Edom? Why would G-d speak of Edom's kings in Chevron, since they never ruled in Chevron? This is no problem, for the primary purpose of this text was to predict about the kings of Israel, while Edom was only hinted at in passing. Hence the promise was made in Chevron for the primary king of Israel would rule there. It is clear that the focus of this section is on Israel as the proceeding verses (7-8) speak of giving the land of Canaan to "your children," which means those who ultimately inherited the land. And the verse immediately following the statement of the kings speaks of the covenant, which is circumcision, clearly meant only for Israel [not Edom]. Furthermore, when G-d made this promise about Sarah in Chevron, He said that kings of "amim" (עמים) [nations] would come from her, and the Tur on Torah quotes from the Ramban that Edom and Yishmael are called "goyim" while Israel is called "amim" as shown in many verses of the Torah (e.g., *Devarim* 33:3 and 19). (1)

It appears there is sound reason why G-d chose Chevron as the site for the prophecy of kingship and for its fruition. For the most difficult aspect of conquering the land of Canaan was the descendants of the giants (*anakim*), as Moshe states (*Devarim* 9:2), "...you knew and you heard 'who can stand against the sons of the *anak*'," and the hearts of the Jews quaked from fear of them at the time of the spies. Their place of habitation was Chevron (*Yehoshua* 15), and Kalev drove out the three sons of the *anak* from there. Therefore, G-d arranged that David should receive his kingship there, and acquire there a staff of power, to demonstrate that his strength is greater than theirs. It further demonstrated that his hand is more uplifted than those giants whose like will never again rise. There, in their home base and center of power, G-d gave the strength and power to another, i.e. David. Thus, He who said in Chevron that kings will descend from you foresaw that Chevron would be the site of the great power of the *anakim*, and He informed us that He will give power to the one He chooses. And in Chevron, G-d repeated His promise to give Israel the entire land of

Canaan, although He had already made that promise earlier. This was to give the extra power to destroy the *anakim* against whom nobody had been able to stand before. You must know that in every place that G-d blessed our forefathers there was a special reason for the choice of that spot as you will see in further chapters and in chapter 80. Also, G-d's statement to Avraham (15:15) that he will die in a good old age was made in Chevron, and that is where he died, and was interred in the Machpelah Cave. G-d, who stands above time, constantly foresees the future and prepares us for it.

How neatly this fits with Rashi's interpretation of the vulture which swooped down upon the cut animals in the "Covenant between the Pieces" (*Bereishis* 15:11). Rashi states that this vulture is David who wishes to devour the nations that drove us into four exiles. It is chased away to symbolize that David cannot do so until the era of Mashiach arrives. This covenant was also made in Chevron where David rules, so this bird is appropriately interpreted as David. (2) Do not question whether this covenant was in Chevron, for the "*Seder Olam*" (who states that the covenant occurred when Avraham was 70 years old [and the Torah is not chronologically recorded], and you might suggest that he was not yet in Chevron), himself writes that Avraham spent 25 years in Chevron before moving to the territory of the Philistines. Further on, in Chapter 4, I will explain a sound reason for David being crowned specifically in Chevron.

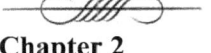
Chapter 2

Following and examining the footsteps of Yaakov in Luz (Beth-El) after he returned from Charan (the reason for skipping from Avraham is because these topics are connected) and looking through the window of the Torah we find that it foresaw that Chevron would be in the territory of the tribe of Yehudah; that Luz would be situated between the descendants of Binyamin and Yoseph; and it foresaw kings of Israel descending from Ephrayim and Menashe; and additional items worthy of your careful attention.

Now, brother, stay with me at Chevron while I take you to another place, Luz, where you will see the glory and fear of G-d. See an amazing thing – that at Luz/Beth-el, G-d said to Yaakov (Ch 35) that "a nation and group of nations" will come from him and kings will descend from his loins. "A nation" meant Binyamin, and "group of nations" meant Ephrayim and Menashe. This is no fanciful interpretation, for Yaakov himself said so clearly when he stated (Ch. 48:3-4), "Almighty G-d appeared to me in Luz...and said, 'I will increase you... and make you a group of nations, and now your two sons... Ephrayim and Menashe will be to me like Reuven and Shimon.'"

Thus Yaakov indicates clearly that he understood the group of nations to refer to Ephrayim and Menashe. And now note this marvel: Where is Luz located? It is precisely between the boundaries of Binyamin and Yoseph, as Rashi records (*Bereishis* 28:17), and clarified in *Yehoshua* (Ch. 18:13), as explained in the commentators there. How amazing that G-d chose Luz as the site to tell Yaakov of Binyamin and of the split of Yoseph into Ephrayim and Menashe, at a town that stood precisely between Binyamin and Ephrayim, with Menashe close by and touching Ephrayim. There was no better site to tell Yaakov of this prophecy than the border of the nations being spoken of.

I will also explain in Ch.5 that another prophecy dealing with Yehudah and Binyamin was given between their borders. Thus the Torah chooses to present future prophecies at a border between those to whom the prophecy applies. So too, in Ch. 6, we will see that a prophecy involving Israel and Yishmael was given at a border that separates them, and similarly in Ch. 18, we will discuss a prophecy about Israel and Eisav that was given at their border. How obvious then that the Torah was given to us by G-d!

How marvelous that of the many places that Yaakov

traversed, G-d specifically chose Luz as the site to inform him of the nations that will descend from him. Clearly this was not a coincidence. For G-d had appeared to him at Shechem and instructed him to go up to Luz. Why did he not immediately give him this blessing then and there, where Yaakov had built an altar? Obviously He wished to give that prophecy at Luz for that is where it came to fruition in later history, in terms of both population and location. In fact G-d had earlier blessed Yaakov to have a great nation, so the primary point about this prophecy was to give it at the perfect spot, Luz, where the blessing for Binyamin, Ephrayim, and Menashe would gain additional power, as I will explain in Ch. 80. What a wonderful treasure this is, that people pass over without noting it at all. This exact boundary of Luz that stood between the "nation" (Binyamin) and the "group of nations" (Ephrayim and Menashe) stood ready to testify about the prophecy given three centuries before and proclaim its truth. There too, not at Shechem, G-d had promised that "kings will descend from your loins", for both from Binyamin (Shaul and Ish-Boshess) and from Yosef (Yeravam, Yeihu, and many of their offspring) came most of the kings of "Israel." We showed earlier that the prophecy about David was given at Chevron, which was the border territory of the tribe of Yehudah, David's tribe. Hence, all the prophecies about the kings of the Jewish people were given in the most perfect locations, which hear the prophecies and later testify to their actualization. All these facts which you see and hear are a logical proof of the first order to demolish the belief of scoffers who deny the Divine origin of our Torah. It is clear that from the very beginning G-d chose to reveal future events in the places where they would eventually take place, for He stood above time and foresaw our history. You will see hundreds of such proofs in this volume, and know without doubt that G-d, Master of the universe, who rewards those who observe His Torah, gave us the Torah.

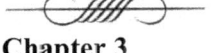
Chapter 3

We follow the footsteps of Avraham to Shechem, after clarifying why G-d chose Mt. Gerizim and Mt. Eival for the [ceremony of the] Blessings and Curses. And why G-d chose Mt. Eival, not Mt. Gerizim, to establish the great stones, and will prove that the Torah foresaw the division of the tribes [into two kingdoms] at Shechem. And that at the south of Shechem would be the border of Yehudah and Binyamin, while at the north of Shechem would be the territory of the Ten Tribes. Also, that near Shechem would be the city of Shomron, and all that would happen there was foreseen. The Torah also saw that Beth-El (Luz) would be in Binyamin's land, near Yehudah, and other items as well will emerge from this chapter.

It is a wondrous thing that the Torah commanded that the

oath (*Devorim* 27), i.e. the Blessings and Curses, be done at Eilon Moreh (Shechem), on Mt. Gerizim and Mt. Eival. Observe that from there emerged the destruction implied in that oath. At Shechem, Yeravam was crowned and the people divided into Israel and Yehudah. Yeravam made the golden calves (idols) which was the ultimate cause of the dispersion of the Ten Tribes, as clearly recorded in Tanach (*Melachim II*, 17:21-23).

A mortal king cannot know who will defy his laws, or where it will happen, hence he cannot issue warnings or threats about such treason at the very place where it later occurs. But the Holy One proclaims His ordinances to the "ears" of the place that He foresees will be the site of the rebellion against His words. From there would be the judgment for the exile of the ten tribes, and the location itself will be the witness to the warning. [Indeed, the first curse is for idolatry!] By sending some tribes upon Mt. Gerizim and others on Mt. Eival, G-d showed that later there would be a division into two kingdoms! This will be further discussed in Ch. 54. It is obvious that this place was chosen for this intention, for when they crossed into Eretz Yisrael, this ceremony could have taken place at Yericho or Aay. They were commanded to go to Shechem, although they should logically have received these admonitions as soon as they came into the land.

It was clearly chosen to serve as a witness in future centuries that the people were warned about the consequences of their backsliding. Therefore, Moshe ordered the Torah to be engraved on stone and placed on Mt. Eival when they enter the land (27:4). This served as a warning to the people of that area not to abandon G-d or

His Torah. We will later demonstrate that the worst kings of Israel were at or near Shechem, ignoring the warnings given at that very place. Again G-d foresaw later history and prepared admonitions at the place where His commandments were broken, to show us that He alone gave the Torah, and rewards the righteous and punishes the wicked. Who could imagine that Moshe wrote the Torah by himself, and just happened to place events and choose places to perfectly coincide with later history, as it took place in those locations? This would be entirely ridiculous.

Know that there is no doubt that Eilon Moreh is synonymous with Shechem, as proven in (*Shoftim*, Ch. 9) [and *Bereishis* 12:6]. Hence what we have recorded in this chapter is ironclad.

Let us discuss these places further. It is known (and recorded in the volume *Emek HaMelech*) that Mt. Gerizim, south of Shechem, is full of beautiful vegetation and olive trees. North of Shechem stands Mt. Eival, totally rocky and barren. Not far from there is the mountain purchased by King Omri, upon which he built the city of Shomron, which became the capitol of the kingdom of Israel. And not far from there was Shilo, in the territory of Ephrayim, as we find (*Yirmiyahu* 41:5) that people from Shechem, Shilo, and Shomron traveled together. Now see how perfectly G-d commanded that the blessing be upon Mt. Gerizim and the curse upon Mt. Eival. The territory of Yehudah and Binyamin, the tribes not associated with Yeravam, and who were not driven into the exile, was south of Shechem, closest to the blessings of Mt. Gerizim. All the other tribes were north of Shechem, closer to Mt.

Eival, the site of the curses. Therefore, the stones that recorded the Torah were placed there as a warning (in vain) to the rebellious ten tribes. Amazing!

Furthermore, Mt. Shomron stood a two-hour journey from Shechem westward, and Shomron, capitol of Yisrael, was the center of the rebellion against the Torah, by Achav and the others. Hence the recital of the blessings and the curses at Shechem, and near Shomron, was the perfect location for these warnings. How appropriate that the first of these warnings was about idolatry! In Chapter 54 I will note other items about this location. In Chapter 14 I will show that Yaakov foresaw the burial of Yosef at Shechem, and that it would be located in Ephrayim's territory. In Chapter 30 I will discuss how the Torah foresaw that Shechem would be a center of murder and that it would be a city of refuge.

I would like to suggest a new idea, that when the Torah says "near Eilonei Moreh" it meant Shomron, west of Mt. Gerizim and Mt. Eival. The term "Moreh" probably indicates the word for rebellion as in "ben sorer umoreh (the rebellious son)," for it was a center for rebellious Jews. It is known that many names of places in the Torah were given long before an event of later history that fashioned that name, as in (*Bereishis* 14:14), "he pursued [them] to Dan," a name from later history, and also in describing the four rivers emanating from the Garden of Eden we find Kush and Ashur already listed (*Bereishis* 2:13-14).

Therefore, it is quite possible that when Avraham passed through Eretz Yisrael "up to the place of Shechem (12:6)," it might actually mean to Mt. Shomron, rather than Shechem itself, since "the place of" is otherwise extraneous. Therefore, foreseeing evil things in the future, he built an altar there to pray to G-d. Even more logical, it may refer to Mts. Gerizim and Eival, and Avraham had visions of the oaths that they would take there, and their acts of idolatry at Eilonei Moreh (Shomron), prompting him to built that altar.

Since the navi Yechezkel (16:2) calls wicked Jews "Emori" and "Chiti", and I found an early commentator who claims that "Canaanim" in Ovadiah (*Trei Asar*, Ovadiah, 1:20) refers to Jews who act like the Canaanites, I might suggest that when the verse describing Avraham's arrival to "the place of Shechem, up to Eilonei Moreh," states "and the Canaani was then in the land," that it means Avraham foresaw the evil that would come forth from Shomron, and "*then*" the (Canaanim = evil Jews) were in the land!

After building that altar, he traveled further and came between Beth-El and Ai, where he built another altar (12:8) and prayed to G-d! Why? We find (*Yehoshua* 18:13) that Beth-El was the northernmost point of Binyamin's territory, with Yehudah to the south of Binyamin. Hence, Beth-El separated the area of the Ten Tribes from the area of the kingdom of Yehudah-Binyamin. How reasonable to suggest that this altar was the site of Avraham's prayer that the idolatry of the Ten Tribes should cease at the border of the kingdom of Yehudah-Binyamin and not spread to it as well. This prayer was efficacious! As we will discuss in Ch. 79, all the travels and altar-building of our forefathers were directed at future events of their offspring in those places. Avraham's altar succeeded exactly the way Aharon's incense later separated the living from the dead (*BeMidbar* 17:12-13). Accordingly, it is noteworthy that when Avraham built that second altar, we find that he pitched "his tent" – *spelled "her tent."* (Rashi has Chazal's explanation here.) Amazingly, Shomron is called "Ahalah" (*Yechezkel* 23:4)! It is as if the Torah tells us that he pitched *ahalah* there and built an altar to block its further expansion to the south where the kingdom of Binyamin-Yehudah stood. Thus, the mis-spelling of *ahalah* tells us both the simple reading of the verse, as well as the extra hidden meaning for future centuries.

I might venture a guess regarding an act of Yaakov near Shechem. We find (*Bereishis,* Ch. 35) that Yaakov was given all the small objects of idol-worship in the hands of his children [souvenirs?], and the earrings they wore, which he buried under a tree near Shechem. It is puzzling why he did not burn them, as some commentators ask. While the Ramban defends him from wrongdoing, he does not answer the ultimate question itself - why not burn them? I believe that for this small error in judgment, HaShem caused that the later idol-worship that occurred amongst our ancestors took place at that place. I believe that this is a reasonable suggestion. (Alternatively, perhaps Yaakov foresaw the future idol-worship at this area, and therefore buried these little idols there as a marker for us to notice!)

Note that Yehoshua judged the people at Shechem (*Yehoshua* Ch. 24), evoked their promise to serve G-d forever, and then erected a great stone "beneath" [under the shadow?] of the *eilah* as the witness to the pledge. Rashi identifies this tree with the one used by Yaakov to bury the idols. Thus, Yehoshua also marked that very location as a testimony to the commitment to worship G-d, at the place where this promise was broken. Avimelech, Gideon's son [who murdered all his brothers and became leader of the people in Shechem], whose three years of rule were marked by idolatry and much killing, was finally killed in battle. All the events in and around Shechem are reflected in Yaakov's original act of burying idols at Shechem.

The term "Shechem" itself (literally, "portion") hints at division, while the root of "Chevron" is attachment. Shechem was the site for dividing into two kingdoms, while Chevron was where David ruled for seven years over a united kingdom. In Ch. 34 we will discuss other names and their meanings.

It is clear that the Torah foresaw from the beginning that Shechem would be the site of 1) the splitting into two kingdoms, 2) the rise of idolatry in Israel, 3) the border area separating from Yehudah-Binyamin to the south, 4) that Beth-El would be in Binyamin's territory, and 5) that Yehudah-Binyamin would separate from the other ten tribes, and would worship G-d in His temple.

Another interesting point: When Avraham arrived in Eretz Yisrael, he received his first message at Shechem that this land would belong to his children. This was a most appropriate place for this information, since, as is evident from reading Tanach (*Yehoshua* Ch. 20), and also discussed in the Talmud (*Makos* 9), Shechem is situated at about the center of the land. When the promise was made, the boundaries were unknown to Avraham, but G-d foresaw the centrality of this city and made the perfect choice for the site of this vision of the future.

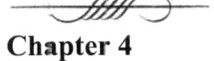

Chapter 4

Following the footsteps of Yosef who went to Shechem and to Dosan, we bring further proofs that the Torah already saw that which was recorded in the last chapter. It also hints at how many years the kingdom of David's House would continue, and that Binyamin would forever be intertwined with Yehudah.

See the amazing chain of events: The tribes sold Yosef near Shechem, and were later "sold" into the hands of Yeravam Ben Nevat, descended from Yosef (*Melachim I*, 11:26), first king of Yisrael, and all the others who followed (as will be explained in Ch. 41, eleven of them descended from Yosef). These kings, collectively, were the cause of the exile of the ten tribes and their "sale" to the king of Ashur, as punishment for the sale of Yosef. As Rashi notes (*Bereishis* 37:14), Shechem is a place marked for punishments: Yosef was sold there; the kingdom was divided there. Just as Yosef ultimately became [like a] king in Egypt, so did his descendant Yeravam become king at Shechem. Later, Yosef is buried in Shechem. It is as if he stands on watch at the location where he was sold for the day his seed will rule these tribes, as payment for what they did. R. Moshe Alshich states that one hundred *kesitah* is the same as twenty silver pieces. How amazing that Yaakov bought a field at Shechem (33:19), which became Yosef's burial place, for a hundred *kesitah*, the same price for which Yosef was sold as a slave - twenty silver pieces! Note that when Yaakov said to Yosef (48:22), "And I have given you one 'shechem' (portion) over your brothers," which is simply understood to mean that he became two tribes, it may also hint at a deeper meaning: I have given you [the city of] Shechem where you (your descendants)are destined to be [The] *one* (i.e., attain the monarchy) over your brothers (at that place)! How amazing are all these hidden ideas dispersed through the Torah, and who knows how many others there are that we have not even discovered, known only to our blessed Creator.

How marvelous is the fact that when Yosef asked the man whom he met while looking for his brothers at Shechem, saying, "Tell me where they are pasturing (ohgr)," the word is written without the "o" vowel. This can be read as "evil." The Baal HaTurim states that this hints at the evil of the days of Yeravam who was crowned at Shechem. He found them at Dosan, where later, Yehudah spoke in Yosef's favor [to sell him, not to kill him]. Amazingly, from the coronation of David until the end of his descendants' rule, the span is 454 years (David ruled forty years and Shlomo four more up to the building of the First Temple, which stood 410 years). This is the gematria of it!

I will add a point. Since Yehudah spoke up for Binyamin (guaranteeing his safety to Yaakov), and later offered to take his place as a slave to Yosef, he merited that Binyamin remained with Yehudah throughout all the years of the kingdom of Yehudah/Binyamin [although they came from two competing mothers!]. Furthermore, since Yehudah, at Chevron, stated to Yaakov that he would be the guarantor for Binyamin, he merited that his seed, David, ruled as king in Chevron. In chapter 20 and 21 I will clarify further evidence that the Torah foresaw Binyamin's attachment to Yehudah.

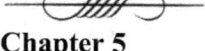
Chapter 5

Analyzing the footsteps of Avraham and Yitzchak at Mt. Moriah will demonstrate that the Torah foresaw that Mt. Moriah (Yerushalayim) will be between Yehudah's and Binyamin's territory; that Yerushalayim will be the site of the eternal Jewish kingdom; as well as of the Holy Temple, the sacrifices, and the Great Sanhedrin. Many other details are covered in this chapter.

Come, let us ascend the mountain of G-d's house and His glorious Shechinah, and you will see His glory and hear the voice of an angel call twice from the heavens. At the akedah, the angel announces, "I swear by My existence, says G-d, that because you did this thing..., I will bless you (a double use of "bless") and increase (double use of "increase") your seed like the stars of heaven and the sand...at the sea's border, and your seed shall conquer the gate of his enemies...." It is amazing that the angel is only repeating promises made earlier to Avraham in the Torah. More surprising is that the promise here is made only because Avraham "did this thing," yet these promises were already made before the akedah took place! The double-verb form for "bless" and "increase" hints at more than what is recorded in the text. Of course I do not speak to those who feel that repetition in the Torah is insignificant. But those who truly understand Torah and wish to know the significance of these repetitions will understand the truth [as we will explain it.]

Here too the location is the key, and once we focus on Mt. Moriah we will understand how perfect are all the things that occurred there. We know that this mountain is in Yerushalayim, {as clearly spelled out in *Divrei HaYamim II*, (Ch.3),} which was located (as discussed earlier) at the border of Yehudah's and Binyamin's territory. More specifically, as clarified in Rashi (*Yehoshua*, Ch.15), it was primarily in Binyamin's area, but a strip from Yehudah's territory stretched out into Yerushalayim, making it a city of two tribes. We can now understand why, in this very location, the blessing of increase of Avraham's seed was repeated.

For consider the amazing facts about the tribes of Yehudah and Binyamin in terms of their population. In *Chumash BeMidbar* (ch. 1 and ch. 26), Yehudah is the largest tribe by far, numbering well over seventy thousand. Several of the others do not even attain half that number. So too, in *Divrei HaYamim I* (ch. 21), Yehudah represents about one-third of the entire Jewish people! In later times, during the reign of Aviyah Ben Rechavam (*Divrei HaYamim II* ch. 13), Yehudah musters an army of four hundred thousand against Yeravam's army of eight hundred thousand, comprised of ten tribes together. As for Binyamin, we must remember that in the great civil war, near the end of the Book of *Shoftim* (ch. 21), they were diminished to six hundred men. Yet, we find an astounding statistic not too many decades later in *Divrei HaYamim II*, ch. 14, during the reign of Asa Ben Aviyah. Binyamin supplied two hundred and eighty thousand soldiers for his army, while Yehudah supplied three hundred thousand! The increase of Binyamin's tribe is thus quite staggering and miraculous. Surely, the special blessing Avraham received at the border of their territories must be the source and reason for these unique statistics. In fact, the double verb used for "I will increase" that was mentioned earlier is surely a hint for these two tribes specifically. Thus, when the angel said "because you did this thing...," it meant that as Avraham's reward, two of his tribes would increase in a unique and (in Binyamin's case) supernatural way, the very tribes who will reside at this territory in later centuries! G-d brought Avraham to this particular mountain for this very purpose. Furthermore, these two tribes had an additional advantage over the others. While the latter went into exile by the conquest of Ashur, Yehudah and Binyamin continued to live in their territory with the Holy Temple still fully functioning for many years. Thus, the double verb used in "I will bless you..." (ברך אברך) may be understood at referring to two aspects of blessing: significant population increase, and a longer life in Eretz Yisrael.

Note that the Jewish people are compared by G-d to three objects: stars, sand, and dust. As the *Kli Yakar* explains, each has a special meaning and application. In periods of peace and success, they are like the stars, implying greatness, as Rashi comments in *Chumash Devarim* (1:10). When they face enemies who rise up against them in war like mighty waves, they are compared to the sand, which withstands the force of the waves and beats them back. In bad times, they are like the dust that is trampled upon. Although these descriptions surely indicate a great number, these additional aspects are very logical, for otherwise three different comparisons would be unnecessary. I will demonstrate in chapter 80 that wherever these comparisons were used, the appropriate one applied to that time and situation.

Therefore, in the present case, Mt. Moriah (the Holy Temple) served as the great spiritual center of the people, and the location of the kings of Yehudah/Binyamin beginning with David and his descendants. Many kings and nations attempted to conquer it and fought battles over it, in which we were successful for centuries. How appropriate, therefore, that in the blessing to Avraham, both stars and sand are utilized. At least five times in Tanach, Yerushalayim was under siege (*Kings I*, ch. 14 – *Kings II*, ch. 14 – *Kings II*, ch. 27 – *Divrei HaYamim II*, ch. 21 – *Divrei HaYamim II*, ch. 24), but remained in Yehudah's control until the destruction of the temple. Indeed, when Ashur rose against Yerushalayim, the navi Yeshayahu proclaimed his mighty vision (*Melachim II*, 19:32-34), "Thus says G-d to the King of Ashur: 'He will not come upon this city, nor shoot an arrow there, ... and I will protect this city....'" [Spoken on the day before the army of Ashur was stricken by the angel and died overnight in their sleep, near Yerushalayim].

Thus, the promise of being like the sand protected this place throughout the centuries, just as in the future this verse will serve as a wall of fire around it. How striking that this is the only place that received the blessing of "sand" in the many promises that G-d gave to our forefathers in *Chumash Bereishis*, for the holy city of Yerushalayim required special blessings to resist all the attacks against it. So too, the blessing of great increase surely helped at the time of the terrible plague upon the people (*Shmuel II,* ch. 24). When the angel came to Yerushalayim to continue the destruction, G-d stopped him at the spot where the Holy Temple was later built, and where the promise of increase had been given! At that time, it was in the possession of Aravna, a *Yevusi*, descended from Avimelech King of the Plishtim. We may suggest that since Avraham had once made a covenant with Avimelech never to attack him, and since this promise was never broken even to the extent that Aravnah was paid a full sum for his field by David, G-d made the marvelous promise to Avraham at the Aquedah with the powerful opening phrase of "I swear by My existence" as a reward for our keeping the oath made to Avimelech throughout our history (which G-d foresaw since He stands above time). (3)

Note how perfect is the fact that at this site, G-d used the expression (v. 17) "your seed shall inherit the gate of his enemies," in contrast to the usual "I will give this land (or "all these lands") to your seed." The term gate is so appropriate for Yerushalayim, which is the great gate to the world and to Eretz Yisrael. How often we find "the gate of Yerushalayim" in Tanach. "Gate" is also used for a place of judgment, and Yerushalayim was the seat of the Great Sanhedrin. Just as one builds a house and then erects the gate, we conquered the land and finally gained the site for the gate to the land, namely, Yerushalayim and the mountain for the temple.

Here, too, G-d promised (v. 18) "all the nations of the earth will bless themselves by your seed," i.e., the Jewish people will be the model for gentiles to bless their children. This took place in the days of King Shlomo in Yerushalayim, as recorded in *Melachim I*, (10:24-25), "And all the earth (people of other lands) would seek the face of Shlomo, to hear his wisdom... and bringing him gifts of silver and gold...every year."

Indeed, all the blessings of G-d in this chapter were manifest in fullest form in the days of Shlomo.

The very fact that G-d chose this mountain for Avraham to be tested with Yitzchak, and to finally bring a sacrifice on that altar, surely points to the eventual choice of that site for the Holy Temple and the sacrifices brought there. Even the blind can see this obvious connection. When Avraham "raised his eyes", after the angel halted the slaughter of Yitzchak, "and he saw, and behold, a ram, another, held in a brambles-bush by its horns," -- the term "another" is very strange. However, understand it this way. Avraham lifted his eyes *into the distant future*, and beheld a vision of another and still another ram held *tight* (בסבך) to this event by the foundation ("keren") that Avraham had now established by this test of his faith. I.e., Because of his great act of absolute faith, Avraham laid the foundation for many other rams (sacrifices) that would be offered here, by the merit of this event. Of course this does not rule out the simple meaning of the verses, but only adds a deeper dimension to the phrases used here.

Note further, that while Avraham built (at least) four altars, (and Yitzchak and Yaakov added to this number), this is the only one named (v.14) "G-d will see." As Shlomo expressed in his prayer (*Melachim I*, ch. 8:29-30), "that *Your eyes be open* to this house day and night, to hear the prayer of Your servant... and your people Israel...and You will hear and forgive." This place is like the window through which G-d will see the deeds of His people, hear their prayers, and send them His blessings and His forgiveness for their trespasses forever. Thus, Avraham's title for this location is the perfect one.

The Torah states (*Shemos* 25:8), "They shall make Me a sanctuary and I will dwell amongst them." So too, Moshe says to Binyamin (*Devarim* 33:12), "and He *dwells* between his shoulders." These verses indicate that G-d, in His glory and essence, shall reside in the Holy Temple, as we find when Shlomo consecrated the temple (*Melachim I*, 8:11), "And the kohanim could not stand and serve...for the glory of G-d filled the house of G-d." Yet, Shlomo also states (*ibid.* 8:27), "For can G-d indeed reside on earth – even the heavens cannot contain You, surely this house that I built!" Hence, the other verses must be understood as saying that G-d's watchful eye is so potent in that place *as if* He literally resides there. Thus, when Avraham adds (*Bereishis*, 22:14), "...as it is said {today} 'on the mountain where G-d is seen.' he surely alludes to the feeling of the presence of G-d through His *Shechinah*. So too, the name "Mt. *Moriah* is perfectly chosen. Its root, y-r-h (ירה), means teaching. It became the seat of the Great Sanhedrin. Onkelos equates this name with myrrh, a component of the incense brought in the temple, while Ramban interprets his words as referring to the root ירא -

(fear) – to indicate the place where G-d would be worshiped. All of these readings are appropriate for this holy site!

Hence, all the actions, words, and hints that occurred when Avraham brought Yitzchak to this site match perfectly with the future events that unfolded on this mountain. It is clear that the Torah foresaw all that would eventually take place here, just as we will demonstrate regarding all the journeys and actions of our forefathers, which were precursors of later events at those locations.

In summary, we have seen in this chapter that the words of the angel to Avraham (and his response) eventually came to fruition in later centuries: 1) Mt. Moriah would be the boundary between Yehudah and Binyamin; 2) these two tribes would have an exceptional blessing of great increase beyond all the others; 3) Yerushalayim would be the site of the eternal kingdom; 4) many kings would seek in vain to capture it; 5) the site would remain for a long time in the hands of the Yevusi, descendants of Avimelech King of the Plishtim, because of Avraham's oath not to attack them; 6) the Great Sanhedrin would meet there; 7) all nations would use Shlomo as a model for their own blessings; 8) this would be the site of the temple and the sacrifices; 9) G-d would especially focus His eyes upon this place; 10) people would say that at this place the presence of G-d is felt more powerfully than any other location on earth. This entire chapter is like a mighty staff to pound the heads of any who would question the Divine nature of the Torah as given to us by G-d.

Chapter 6

Following the footsteps of Avraham and Malki-Tzedek at the city of Shalem confirms the previous evidence that Avraham foresaw Yerushalayim as the site of worship to G-d, and that it would be the place for giving maaser (tithes). This chapter also examines some items about Avraham's visit to Egypt.

See again how the places where our forefathers tread are a prophecy for their children, from the verse (*Bereishis* 14:18) "And Malki-Tzedek King of Shalem brought out bread and wine, and he was a priest to the most high G-d. And he blessed him and said, 'Blessed is Avraham to the most high G-d, possessor of heaven and earth. And blessed is the most high G-d Who has delivered your enemies into your hand; and he gave him tithes from all."

We know that Shalem is Yerushalayim, as in the verse (*Tehillim* 76:3), "His tabernacle was in Shalem and His dwelling-place in Zion." Consider that of all the dozens of towns in Eretz Canaan, this priest of G-d chose Yerushalayim as his home, the site for priestly functioning almost nine centuries later. Even the very name Malki-Tzedek rings with the verse about Yerushalayim (*Yeshayahu* 1:21), "Tzedek (righteousness) lodged there..."

The bread and wine that he brought forth surely symbolizes the libations and the "show-bread" of the temple. There, the kohanim blessed the people just as Malki-Tzedek did with Avraham. And just as Avraham gave this priest tithes, the Jewish people brought theirs to the temple to present to the kohanim. It is obvious that Avraham foresaw the future status of the kohanim at this place, and became the first to offer *maaser* there.

We see that after Avraham ceased his pursuit of the vanquished kings at Dan (because he became weakened when he saw that centuries later his children would establish a golden calf there, as Rashi writes), he returned to Shalem, for he knew the great sanctity of that site, although it remained hidden for the Jewish people for centuries until revealed through David. It is clear that the Torah recorded the event of Malki-Tzedek to show us a glimpse of the future service of kohanim at this place. Avraham's *maaser* to Malki-Tzedek shows us that he had a vision of the future grandeur of the temple and the kohanim.

All that we have written is to demonstrate that the events occurring with our forefathers are precursors for their children, and situated at chosen locations. It is therefore worthwhile to note some interesting points about Avraham's sojourn to Egypt, even if it brings us outside the boundaries of Eretz Yisrael. Here too we find connections to the future. 1) Avraham went down there only for temporary habitation to set the precedent that his descendants would also be there only for a time. 2) Thus, for both journeys, the Torah emphasizes the term for temporary residence - *lagur sham*. 3) Avraham went because of a famine, just as his children did. 4) G-d brought a plague upon Pharaoh, similar to the Ten Plagues in later history. 5) Pharaoh gave Avraham gifts of cattle, donkeys, servants, camels, etc., a sign that his children would leave Egypt laden with great wealth. Indeed, Moshe told Pharaoh (*Shemos* 10:25), "You too will hand us sacrifices...and we will "make" them for our G-d." 6) G-d prevented Pharaoh from contact with Sarah as a symbol that the Egyptian overlords will have no power over the Jewish women in Egypt, as the midrash tells us, for which reason G-d stamped his name upon all their families with a v and a h at the beginning and ending of their names. 7) Just as Pharaoh called Avraham to tell him to leave, Pharaoh summoned Moshe to speed the people out of Egypt. 8) Pharaoh sent a delegation of Egyptians to accompany Avraham from the land, just as an *erev-rav* of Egyptians joined the people during the exodus. 9) Just as Avraham left with everything that he had, his descendants left with all their possessions intact. 10) Avraham came up to the south of Eretz Yisroel, just as *bnei Yisrael* first came by the negev and Yehudah received his territory in the south as spelled out in the Book of Yehoshua. From all of the above, we can understand that Avraham's adventure in Egypt was only meant as a prelude to his descendants' later life in Egypt, and so too many other events in the life of our forefathers.

Chapter 7

We will bend an ear to hear the words of the angel to Hagar at the well on the road to Shur and follow the footsteps of Avraham and Yitzchak between Kadesh and Shur – and demonstrate that the angel sent to Hagar by G-d's command saw that Shur will be the border between Eretz Yisrael and the land of Yishmael as well as between Yisrael and Amalek. Other details will also show that locations are paramount in these events.

Let us now proceed to the well on the road to Shur, where we will hear the angels, G-d's messengers, speak to Hagar. We read (*Bereishis* 16:7), "And an angel found her at a well in the desert, at the well on the road to Shur." The angel said (v.10), " I will greatly increase your seed that they will be uncountable for multitude." His final words were (v. 12) "and before all his brothers he shall dwell." It is simple to understand why the angel met her specifically on that road. Eventually the territory of Yishmael extended up to Shur (25:18), so she was met at that border to receive that promise, exactly up to the place where Yishmael's expansion and increase reached. Indeed, the repetition of "the well" may hint at the other meaning of *haayin* (i.e., the eye) as if to say that the angel looked and saw the perfect place to confront her with a blessing that will reach to that border. Once again, the location adds extra dimensions to the events that unfold there. Is it not amazing?

Further on, in ch.81, I explain at length, that Shur stood between Eretz Yisrael and Yishmael. For Onkelos consistently renders " Shur" as *Chagra*, and Shur is clearly near *Gerar* (*Bereishis* 20:1), which was part of Plishtim territory. The land of the Plishtim is actually part of Eretz Yisrael. To dispel any doubts about this statement, note that when Yitzchak sojourned in *Gerar*, G-d said to him (*Bereishis* 26:3), "Stay in this land... for to you and your seed I will give all these lands...." Since Shur is close to *Gerar,* it is evident that Shur is proximate to Eretz Yisrael, and thus a border to the land of Yishmael, which stretches further southward. After the drowning of the Egyptians, Moshe led the people into the desert of Shur (*Shemos* 15:22), showing that Shur is far south, near Egypt. All these geographic indicators mesh well and logically.

It is also clear that the Pelishtim territory stood between Egypt and Yisrael. We see that when Yitzchak sought to go down to Egypt during a drought, G-d stopped him as he passed through Plishtim territory. Be-eir Sheva was in Pelishtim territory in the south of Eretz Yisrael, but obviously a bit north of Shur. Thus, the "desert of Be-eir Sheva" is very close to, probably touching, Yishmael's territory. It was in that desert that the angel told Hagar (*Bereishis* 21:17) that "G-d has heard the voice of the boy [Yishmael] where he is."

The area in which he would prosper in later history is surely the best place for such a message.

R. Eliezer Ashkenazi writes in his *Maasei HaShem* that the description of Yishmael (*Bereishis* 16:12) that "he will be a wild-ass of a man," indicates that he would live a nomadic life, spread about in tents, rather than in towns or cities. Thus, the phrase "where he is" may be a hint that, just as at that moment he was lying in the desert, so will his descendants live in open areas around and about Shur.

We should also note that this territory between *Chavilah* and *Shur* later became populated by Amalek. This is proven in Tanach where we find (*Shmuel I*, 15:6) "And Shaul smote Amalek from *Chavilah to Shur* which is before Egypt." Radak [R. David Kimchi] suggests that perhaps Amalek conquered the land from the Yishmaelim. I think his second suggestion is better, namely, that the two peoples intermarried (just as the Torah relates how Eisav married a daughter of Yishmael). It is also possible that Amalek built towns in that territory, while Yishmaelim lived between these towns in tents, like nomads. Whatever idea is best, the fact is that Amalek, just like the Arabs, was situated south of Shur which touched Eretz Yisrael. I will return to this with further proofs in ch. 81.

When the nearly-dead Yishmael was saved by the angel (ch.16), Hagar named that well *Be-eir LaChai Ro-ee*. She was on the road to Shur at the time. Later we find Yitzchak lived there (24:62) "in the land of the negev (south)." Hence we may presume that this is the area where Yaakov and Eisav were born. Hence, their birth occurs in the area where eventually the border between the territories of Yaakov and Amalek (Eisav's vicious descendant) would exist. We may suggest that when they fought in the womb of Rivkah, it was to prevent any incursions by one to the other's territory, and perhaps even to attempt to conquer the land of the other. When Rivkah received the message that these twins will "separate from your womb," it could mean simply that one would go south and Yaakov would go north, from the area where Rivkah was at that time.

In summary, the area of Shur becomes a focal point dividing the territory of Yisrael from that of Yishmael, and later of Amalek, and events occurring there have ramifications to the future status of that location.

Chapter 8

Let us examine the footsteps of Yitzchak to Be-eir Sheva and prove that the Torah foresaw that this place would be the boundary of Eretz Yisrael.

Here, dear brother, is an area that you might not look at, but it is a precious gem to light your way and recognize the Divine nature of the Torah. In *Bereishis* (26:24), G-d tells Yitzchak, "I am with you and I will bless you and increase your seed for the sake of my servant Avraham." This seems entirely superfluous for G-d made this promise earlier, in this chapter (vs.3-4)! But we have already shown that whenever a blessing is given, it is crucial for that location to hear it. Here too, it is given at Be-eir Sheva as the preceding verse specifically states (v. 23). We find many times in the Torah the expression "from Dan to Be-eir Sheva," indicating that it is the original southern boundary of Yisrael. Thus, the promise in this verse guarantees that up to this boundary the Jewish people will multiply uniquely. When G-d promised (*Shemos* 23:30), "I will drive them out little by little, until you increase and inherit the land," this indicates that at first the land will be much larger than necessary for the influx of the people. But G-d set the boundaries with the knowledge that in time they would need that much territory for the great increase of population. Indeed this may be the intent of Bilaam's words (*BeMidbar* 23:10), "Who counted the dust of Yaakov and numbered the reproduction of Israel." I.e., Only our holy Creator could have precisely calculated the land that Yaakov would occupy based on His vision and knowledge of the eventual *increase* of His people. Thus, when Yitzchak arrived to Be-eir Sheva, G-d repeated the promise of great increase to indicate that this would occur up to this boundary, the very location of Yitzchak's birth. The city itself would witness the fruition of this promise in later centuries and affirm G-d's blessing.

In fact, we must consider that to the south of Be-eir Sheva was Egypt. The actual miraculous increase of the Jewish people began in Egypt, as stated clearly in the beginning of *Sefer Shemos*. Hence, Be-eir Sheva was strategically located to receive this blessing, for it took place both to the south of it, and north of it up to that point. While some offer differing analyses as to the precise location of Be-eir Sheva, all agree that it was in the south of Eretz Yisrael and north of Egypt. It was surely the best location for G-d to repeat his promise to Yitzchak about the great increase that would occur with His people.   In Parashas Haazinu (32:8) Moshe describes how G-d separated peoples (after the generation of Babel) and established the boundaries of nations "for the number of bnei Yisrael." This probably means that when He gave Canaan its territory, he foresaw how much territory Yisrael would need and gave it to Canaan in preparation for the time that Yisrael would conquer Canaan! Thus, the preceding verse states (v.7) "understand the years of each generation," i.e., understand how G-d manipulates nations and boundaries to prepare the territory that His people would someday require, based on their eventual population. As verse 9 continues, "For G-d's portion is His people, Yaakov is the lot (חבל) of His inheritance." "Chevel" is a term used in Tanach for taking measures — a further hint at the ideas we are recording here (i.e., Yaakov is the ultimate measure of how He apportions land to various peoples, in preparation for the future). How marvelous and amazing are these facts that clearly establish the Divine authorship of our holy Torah, for only G-d could foresee and prepare for His children the land they would inherit many centuries later. I will designate a major chapter later to analyze the great and miraculous increase of the Jewish people, promised to Avraham when he was one hundred years old and the father of one primary son, Yitzchak!

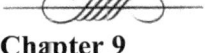

Chapter 9

We will examine Yitzchak's blessing to his sons in Be-eir Sheva. This chapter will look through the windows of the Torah and show that it foresaw the rebellion of Edom against Yehudah in the days of Yehoram Ben Yehoshafat, and already saw eight Jewish kings (Shaul, Ish-Boshes, David, Shlomo, Rechavam, Aviam, Asa, and Yehoshafat). It also saw how David would punish Moav with "measurements" of who will die and who will live, as well as how David would destroy the fortified walls of Ammon.

It is amazing and obvious that the Torah saw the eight great Jewish kings beginning with Shaul, who would rule over Edom in later history. Otherwise, why would it bother to review the eight kings who ruled over Edom "before a king ruled over *bnei Yisrael?*" Surely, this was a hint that once the Jewish kings arose, there would be eight who would dominate Edom, until Edom would break that yoke in the days of Yehoram, when finally (*Melachim II*

8:20) "they crowned themselves a king." Until then, beginning with Shaul and concluding with Yehoshafat, (*Melachim I,* 22:48) "there was no king in Edom." (4) It is apparent that the Torah listed the eight kings of Edom only to strengthen our faith in G-d. When the reader observes that Yaakov and Eisav were twins and Eisav came first, his instinctive reaction is to feel that he will be the head and Yaakov will hang on to his heels, i.e., a secondary nation. Then, he reads that indeed Eisav established himself long before Yaakov, and had already eight kings. Then he ponders the phrase (*Bereishis 36:31*) "before there ruled a king over *bnei Yisrael*" and recognizes the hint that there will be kings over Yaakov's descendants too. He then finds that, centuries later, Yaakov's eight kings control and dominate Edom, in keeping with Yitzchak's blessing to Yaakov (*Bereishis* 27:29), "Be lord over your brothers, and the sons of your mother will bow to you." At this point, only the mentally blind cannot see that listing the eight kings of Edom was only meant to point at later history when eight Jewish kings would rule over Edom, king for king, and confirm that Yaakov is truly lord over his brother.

I strongly believe that this secret is actually hidden in the words of the Torah, when Yitzchak gave his secondary blessing to Eisav (*Bereishis* 27:40), "And you will live by your sword and serve your brother; and it will come to pass והיה that when you rule, you will remove his yoke from your neck." The phrase "when (כאשר) you rule" should be understood on a deeper plane. The term *kaasher* also means "just as," [as in the phrase (*VaYikra* 24:19), "*Just as* he did, so shall be done to him."] In this verse, Yitzchak prophetically informs Eisav when the rule of

Yaakov will be broken, saying, in effect, "And it shall be" – i.e., and your service to him shall be – "just as you ruled" in the world with eight kings, so too shall you serve his eight kings, after which - "you will remove his yoke from your neck.". I truly believe that this new interpretation was a gift from heaven for me to conceive a true and deep interpretation of this verse. Thus, in this verse, Yitzchak had a vision of Jewish history over eight centuries later, when Eisav would break the yoke of Yaakov. And the Torah indicated this by supplying the seemingly irrelevant listing of Eisav's kings.

Note how appropriate this place – Be-eir Sheva – was for Yitzchak to bless Yaakov (and Eisav). This was the southern-most area of Eretz Yisrael that our forefathers lived in. It was the final springboard from which Jewish kings launched their battles with Edom, which is situated, as is Amalek, south of this city. They are the "sons of your mother" who, as Yitzchak said, would bow to Yaakov. The best location for such a blessing!

Actually, the Torah also prepared us for future events involving the Plishtim, Ammon, and Moav. The Plishtim will be discussed in chapters 19 and 37. I will discuss Ammon and Moav now. We find the prophecy of Bilaam (*BeMidbar* 24:17), "A star shall step forth from Yaakov and a sceptre shall rise from Yisrael; and shall smite the corners of Moav and break down all the sons of Sheis." The *meforshim* say that this is a prophecy about King David. Several of the great commentators (e.g., noted by Ibn Ezra and accepted by Chizkuni) claim that "Sheis" (שת) is actually the buttock (*Yeshayahu* 20:4), and thus a crude reference to Moav's paternal half-brother Ammon who was born from the incest of Lot and his daughter. It is fascinating to focus on the strange expression "the corners of Moav." For when David smote Moav (*Shmuel II* 8:2), the verse describes how he "measured them" with rope and killed two of three, leaving a third of them alive as servants. We can visualize that as he "cast them to the ground," for each group of three, he left the middle one alive. Thus, he smote the corners! As for Ammon, they were all "broken down." The violent destruction of Ammon is graphically described in Tanach (*Shmuel II* 12:31).

Thus, Bilaam had a vision of David's vengeance upon both Moav and Ammon many centuries before it occurred, as Bilaam himself first stated (*BeMidbar* 24:17), "I see him but *not now*; I behold him but *not imminent*. The Torah thus foresaw the future history of Edom, Moav, and Ammon, in their battles and confrontations with the Jewish people, centuries before these events unfolded.

Chapter 10

Let us examine the blessing that Rivkah received from her family in Aram Naharayim [as she left to marry Yitzchak] and demonstrate that the Torah foresaw David's conquest of Aram. It also saw that Damascus would be the capitol of Aram, and would be conquered by David.

The Torah records (*Bereishis* 24:60) the blessing given to Rivkah by her family as she left to marry Yitzchak, "They blessed Rivkah and said to her, 'Our sister, become multitudes of thousands, and may your seed possess the gates of its enemies.'" The *meforshim* [Abarbanel and others) state that [although given by Lavan's family] this blessing is from Heaven, for the living G-d placed these words in their mouths. It is almost identical to the one given by G-d to Avraham at the akedah (21:17). In my opinion there is no need to bother to defend this idea. Once the Torah recorded these words, it becomes a blessing of the Torah, just as Bilaam's pronouncements become holy Torah blessings. Furthermore, once we see these words come to fruition in history, it is clear beyond any doubt that the Torah confirmed them as valid. This brings us to the question: Since Avraham already received this promise, why indeed bother to tell us that Lavan and his family repeated it? What could they add to Avraham's blessing?

Once again, the location is the key. They were in Aram Naharayim, as mentioned in the story (24:10).This territory was conquered by David as recorded in *Shmuel II* (ch. 8). Chazal call this area Syria, which is treated in certain halachos as part of Eretz Yisrael, and in others as beyond it. The details are covered in the gemara (*Gittin* 8a/b). Thus, G-d put these words in their mouths at this spot, so that this promise should take place *there*, expanding, as it were, the blessing given to Avraham, where this territory was not yet implied. This is similar to what we wrote about G-d's blessing to Yitzchak at Be-eir Sheva to establish that his great increase would reach that area. So too, the expansion of Yisrael's territory would reach the place where the blessing was pronounced. The reason it was placed in unholy mouths is surely because this territory had limited sanctity compared to the heartland of Eretz Yisrael. Furthermore, it was later reconquered from the Jewish people, as we will discuss further on in connection with the tribe of Dan (see ch. 80).

It is especially relevant that the expression "gate of his enemies" was used. "Gate" frequently implies the place of judgment throughout the Torah and Tanach. The text states specifically that David conquered Damesek (*Shmuel II* 8:5-6), which was the capital of Aram (*Yeshayahu* 7:8), and surely the seat of their courts of justice. Thus, this expression implies total conquest, including the capital city of Aram.

Marvels of Our Blessed G-d's Torah

Once again, a blessing is given at a location which later witnesses the fruition of that promise. In other territories, like Germany, Greece, or Media, you will not find or hear any voice in Tanach pronouncing such blessings in those places. The Torah consistently announces blessings in the locations where they will take place centuries later. This confirms again that G-d alone wrote our holy Torah.

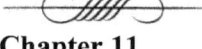

Chapter 11

We observe the footsteps of Yaakov to Machanayim, and prove that he saw that Machanayim would be the boundary of the half-tribe of Menashe, that this spot would be the beginning of Jewish possessions on the east side of the Jordan River.

We find (*Bereishis* 32:2-3), "And Yaakov went on his way and angels of G-d met him. And Yaakov said..., 'This is G-d's camp,' and he called the name of that place Machanayim." Rashi explains that angels of Eretz Yisrael came forward to accompany him into the holy land. The plural form of the term Machanayim implies two groups of angels: those of outside the land who must leave him, and the welcoming group to escort him further. Ramban finds this analysis very perplexing. After all, he writes, Yaakov was still far from Yisrael, and sent messengers to Eisav from afar. He crossed the Yabok crossing, the boundary of Ammon, southeast of Yisrael, and still had to cross Ammon, Moav, and Edom, eventually arriving at Shechem, his entry point to Eretz Yisrael. R. Eliyahu *Mizrachi* complains that Ramban should not have written that Rashi feels that Shechem was Yaakov's entry point to Yisrael, and writes at length on this point. However, this is a minor technicality! Ramban's major point was that

Yaakov was very far from Yisrael when the angels came to accompany him to the land, and this objection was not answered.

However, since all that Rashi wrote is found in the midrashim, and since we are firmly convinced that they make no errors, it behooves us to do geographic investigations and eventually confirm their words. When Yaakov called his youngest son Binyamin, Rashi interpreted this name as "son of the south," for he alone was born in Canaan, which, for one arriving from Aram Naharayim, is in the south. Ramban objects strongly, saying that Aram is east of Yisrael, not north, as we find when Yaakov headed there (*Bereishis* 29:1), "And he went to the land of the people of the east." Crossing the Jordan, he approached Eisav's territory for his confrontation with him, and Edom was southward, and afterward he headed north, so why would Binyamin be a "son of the south"? However, *Mizrachi* and many others write that Aram is northeast of Eretz Yisrael, and that Yaakov returned directly from Aram to Yisrael, traveling southward. This is elementary in many sources, e.g., the Rambam (*Laws of Terumos* 1:9) who writes that Aram Naharayim is at the Euphrates River up to Bavel, and it is well-known that Bavel is north of Yisrael [as in *Yirmiyahu* 1:14].

Nevertheless, the basic problem lingers. Yaakov was far from Yisrael at Machanayim, and the Rashi comment remains very puzzling. *Mizrachi* argues that perhaps the *Yabok* crossing stretched from east to west and crossed over past the Jordan into Canaan. Thus, Yaakov may have crossed the Jordan and later come to Yabok. Thus, he could have encountered the angels as he entered Yisrael. In my opinion, this is a far-fetched suggestion, since we never find the Yabok Crossing in Yisrael in the Tanach. Furthermore, we find (*Yehoshua* 13:30) that Machanayim is situated on the east side of the Jordan, making this suggestion untenable. This is confirmed again in *Shmuel II* (2:29 – 17:24 – 19:23). [There are other geographic difficulties with the *Mizrachi*'s analysis.]

It appears that, first of all, we must acknowledge that Aram Naharayim is northeast of Yisrael. However, before crossing the Jordan moving eastward, Yaakov turned southward into Ammon's territory, crossed the Yabok, and [after confronting Eisav] headed back northward, and then crossed the Jordan into Yisrael. The ancient *Kaftor VaFerach* has a similar view. Thus, the question about Machanayim being in or very close to Yisrael is still not answered. Let us proceed. As Yaakov headed southward to meet with Eisav (for Edom is south of Yisrael), he was informed that Eisav is coming (northward) towards him. After that meeting, Yaakov reversed direction and headed northward, stopping for some time at Sukos (which is in Gad's territory east of Canaan), and then crossing into Eretz Yisrael.

One might ask: Since Yaakov fought the angel after crossing Yabok and later called that area Peniel, this would place Peniel east of the Jordan, while a description in *Melachim* I (12:25) seems to place this town near Shechem. However, in *Shoftim* (8:6-8), it appears to be east of the Jordan. The best solution to this matter is to presume there are two towns by this name, and, in fact, using two variations in the texts: Peniel and Penuel, as in

Bereishis (32:30-31). Now we will solve the Machanayim problem raised by Rashi's comment:

As discussed in the ancient *Kaftor VaFerach*, the territories of Gad, Reuven and Menashe east of the Jordan attained the sanctity of Eretz Yisrael. Otherwise: 1) the decision of these tribes to remain there is totally baffling; 2) Why did David wait so long to allow Avshalom back from Geshur, of the territory of Sichon King of the Emori, to Yerushalayim? 3) Why did the righteous Barzilai the Giladi turn down the invitation of David to live out his life in Yerushalayim, preferring to be buried east of the Jordan? Obviously that territory also had the sanctity of Yisrael.(5) So too wrote Rashi at the beginning of Chumash *Devarim*, that Moshe did not wish to rebuke the people "before they enter part of the land," so he waited until he had conquered the territory of Sichon and Og.

Thus, our question can be answered. As Yaakov returned from Aram Naharayim, traveling eastward, he first entered Menashe's territory. Then, moving southward towards Edom, he passed through Gad's portion, and finally through Reuven's, the furthest south. The angels accompanied him from Machanayim, situated in Menashe's territory, as he moved southward for his encounter with Eisav, in anticipation of his eventual entry into the heartland of Eretz Yisrael. Thus, they actually met with him as he first entered the area that would attain sanctity in Moshe's time.

Even if anyone might question the sanctity of that land, there is no problem. The fact that it was destined to be an area populated by tribes of Israel is enough reason for angels to be permitted to come forward there to greet Yaakov, as he headed home. As long as it became the land of the Jews, and not of the gentiles, it is significant enough to merit that angels could come there to welcome our forefather to Eretz Yisrael.

It is now quite clear and obvious. Yaakov had a long journey to return to Eretz Yisrael. Only when he reached Machanayim, in the north area of Menashe's territory, the beginning of the eventual land of bnei Yisrael, did the angels come forward to greet him. Surely, not only we, but also Yaakov himself, had to realize that this indicated that this town would someday be Jewish territory as part of Eretz Yisrael. This would explain his statement which the Torah had to include (32:2), "And Yaakov said... 'a G-dly camp is this." What significance does this statement have? I would suggest that we remember that the Jewish people are called "G-d's camp," for they are His "army" and He is their king who chose them of all nations as His special treasure.

Therefore, when Yaakov saw them at this spot, he understood that this place is the beginning territory of the camp of Israel, and we can read the expression as "a godly camp (the Jewish nation) is at this place," for sometimes the term *zeh* (this) implies "at this location", as when Yosef says to his father (*Bereishis* 49:8), "They are my sons whom G-d gave to me *in this* (i.e., in this land)." Thus, when we read in the Torah that at this specific place, Yaakov's entry into future Jewish territory, angels met him and he called the place Machanayim, we can hear the voice of G-d, looking to the future, as He directs us to recognize the significance of this spot in history when it will mark the start of Menashe's territory.

We already noted that on his return to Yisrael, Yaakov ventured down to the Yabok. This river is the boundary to the land of Ammon, and continuing westward, one passes through Moav and then Edom. We may suggest that Yaakov saw that in the end of time, these three territories would be ours, but not soon.. He therefore fought the spiritual representative of Eisav in the hope of claiming all that territory for his children as soon as battles rage between them and Israel. The angel prevented him from attaining a real victory, just as in our history, this conquest still awaits the future. This may be understood from the fact that Yaakov left that wrestling-match limping. Once we recognize the historic implications of that night's wrestling, we can better understand the Zohar about that event. He writes that in the phrase "the children of Israel do not eat את the thigh-vein" [although "ess" in usually used before writing the object of a verb], in this verse these two letters stand for "tishah B'Av) [תשעה באב]. The *Bael Haflaah* writes that each vein in our bodies is somehow connected to a particular day of the year, and that this forbidden vein is associated with Tish'a B'Av. This is the day on which the Satan has special powers. His name – שטן – is 364 in gematria, but on that one other day of the year (Tish'a B'Av), he is powerful. Surely, Yaakov's limp symbolizes the time that his descendants will be driven from the land into exile, after the destruction on Tish'a B'Av. The Zohar explains the entire event of Yaakov's wrestling as directed towards the future exile of the Jewish people.

Soon after (ch. 35), G-d appears to Yaakov and says,

"Your name is Yaakov. Your name should not be called Yaakov any longer, but rather Yisrael shall be your name; and He called his name Yisrael." Many have noted the strange verbiage in this verse. There is also the well-known question of why we continue using the name Yaakov, while it is forbidden to use the earlier name of Avraham ("Avram").

Perhaps we may say: The opening phrase states that your name has been only "Yaakov" until now. The day will come in the future that it will no longer be Yaakov at all, but *only* Yisrael. "And He called *ess* his name Yisrael." The term *ess* also means "with", and here it implies that "with his name of Yaakov," he was called an additional name.

Hence until that future time, both names are used. So too, when the angel gave that name earlier, he also had only the distant future in mind at the time when "Yaakov" would be dropped. Soon after, the Torah describes the rising of the sun. This could symbolize the great dawn of that very day in the future.

Chapter 12

We follow the footsteps of Yaakov to Sukkos and show that he saw visions that the land of Gil-ad would be chosen by his descendants as an ideal place for cattle-raising.

We read (*Bereishis* 33:17) that Yaakov journeyed to Sukkos, built himself a house, made *Sukos* (huts) for his cattle, and this is why he called the place Sukos. This is an astonishing verse, with many puzzles. Why did he build a house here, of all the places he passed through without doing so? At this time, he was on his way home anyway! Why are the Sukkos for his cattle important? Why would he call the location "Sukos" just because he built huts for his cattle? Why did the Torah bother with this little account at all, especially after we have noted many times that each recorded incident has ramifications for the future of the Jewish people in that area.?

However, once again later history offers answers. This is the area where his offspring built enclosures for their cattle. Sukkos is in the land of Sichon, later occupied by Gad, the center area taken by the three tribes (Reuven, Gad, and Menashe). Yaakov built a house as a sign of his descendants' permanent possession of this land. This strengthened their ownership of the land, necessitated by the fact that they left their wives and children alone for the many years they joined their brethren in conquering Canaan for the other tribes. This was the perfect area for such demonstration, not only because it is the center area of the three territories, but because Gad was in a position of greater danger from surrounding gentile nations. As Rashi clarifies in *Devarim* (33:20), Gad's land spread farther to the east and bordered lands of aggressive neighbors, requiring a special blessing of Moshe that he be mighty as a lioness. In fact, Gad was the primary tribe that swayed Reuven to join together in the approach to Moshe that is documented in Chumash *BeMidbar* (ch.32), which is why Gad is mentioned constantly *before* Reuven, the elder!

Building huts for his cattle symbolizes that Yaakov knew that their primary reason for choosing this land was because their main interest in their cattle outweighed the great merit of living in the holiest area of Canaan. By naming the town Sukkos, he showed his displeasure with their choice, even as a loving father he demonstrated their ownership of the territory by also building a house. The construction of these huts gave protection to their huts for their cattle during the years of Gad's and Reuven's troops helping to conquer Canaan across the Jordan.

It is interesting to note that there is also a town called Sukkos on the west side of the Jordan, as indicated in *Melachim II* (7:46). However, the sources of *Yehoshua* (13:27) and *Shoftim* (ch. 8) make it crystal clear that Sukkos is on the east side of the river, and it is the one which we speak of in this chapter.

In summary, the amazing, seemingly trivial, tale of Yaakov spending his valuable time to build huts and a house in the very area where later this took on great significance, demonstrates that he foresaw later history at this location, and in writing this Torah for us, G-d showed us once again that all of Jewish history is reflected in His Divine words even as the dawn of Jewish history is being recorded.

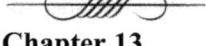

Chapter 13

Investigating the footsteps of Yaakov as he approaches Efras (Beis Lechem) shows that the Torah foresaw here the tragedy of the concubine in Giv-ah – that she would be from Beis Lechem – that near Beis Lechem would be the boundary of Binyamin – and that David would acquire the kingdom from Shaul - and some other details as well.

We read (*Bereishis* 35:16-18), "And they journeyed from Beis-El, and a distance remained to arrive to Efras, and Rachel gave birth in hard labor....And, as she died, she called him 'Ben-Oni,' but his father called him Binyamin." Why did the Torah record the name she gave, when it was never again used anyway? Since we know that the Torah never records insignificant items, it is certain that this name too must have importance in history! Rashi writes (*BeMidbar* 26:24), "We find five families of Binyamin missing, part of Rachel's prophecy (calling him 'son of my sorrow') is accomplished here, and with the concubine at Giv-ah, it was fully accomplished; this I found in the writing of R. Moshe the Preacher." Thus, it was not in vain to record her chosen name and vision, for the Torah reveals here a sorrowful detail of later history, when almost all of Binyamin were killed.

Now examine the powerful signs behind the words of R. Moshe. Rachel died and was buried near Beis-Lechem (Efras), as stated there (35:19). From this town came the concubine (*Shoftim* 19:1-2) whose murder caused the near annihilation of Binyamin. The abominable acts of the men of Giv-ah, of the tribe of Binyamin, took place when she and her husband left Beis-Lechem late in the day and were invited in for the night by a resident of Giv-ah, obviously not far away from Beis-Lechem. Thus, the name given by Rachel, "son of my sorrow," is a vision of the terrible tragedy that took place there centuries later. Perhaps by the merit of Rachel the tribe of Binyamin was saved to leave six hundred men alive to perpetuate that tribe. [According to Chazal], King Shaul was one of those survivors. How amazing that the prophet Shmuel tells Shaul (*Shmuel I*, 10:2) that he will meet two men "near the grave of Rachel in Binyamin's territory."

Thus, Rachel's death at this spot and the term *Ben-Oni*, serve as markers for events that unfolded there in later history, and once again the Torah's history intertwines past and future together. In fact, it is a marvelous thing to note that of all the areas that Yaakov passed through on his way home, Rachel's death and burial take place in the territory that later becomes that of her son Binyamin, whose territory ends where Beis-Lechem begins the area of Yehudah. Looking into the future and knowing the eventual boundaries of each tribe, G-d arranged for Rachel to be buried in her son's territory. I believe it reasonable to suggest that her burial was very close to Giv-ah, which was adjacent to Ramah, as proven from the verse in *Shoftim* (19:13). This burial place was, of course, also fairly close to Beis-Lechem, as the text in Bereishis says. Ramban, who lived in Eretz Yisrael in his later years, was puzzled by the expression in *Yirmiyahu* (31:14) which implies that Rachel's weeping voice for her children arose from the town of Ramah.[6] He notes that, although there are two towns by this name in the land, neither is at the location of her burial site which he visited, (one is a two days journey away, and the closer one is about four *parsa* away,) and Ramban confirms the grave's proximity to Beis-Lechem. If we may presume that Rachel lies buried four *parsa* from Ramah in the direction of Giv-ah, it is quite possible that she is very close to Giv-ah, or even in Giv-ah itself. Thus, she may be buried where her descendants committed the atrocity that almost annihilated her younger son's tribe! (7)

Rachel's burial near Beis-Lechem, in my opinion, indicates another significant idea, i.e., that a man from Beis-Lechem, David Ben Yishai, will take the kingdom from Binyamin's descendant, Shaul Ben Kish. Therefore, Rachel could not reach Beis-Lechem for burial in Yehudah's territory. Of course, you could ask how can we derive a second purpose for this burial site, since we already derived important ideas about it above. However, it could be indicated by the fact that the Torah (*Bereishis* 35:19) identified the site by a second name – "Efras." Why was this necessary, since Beis-Lechem is a well-known place? I believe that this hints at David of whom we read (*Shmuel I*, 17:12), "And David was the son of this *Efrasi* from Beis-Lechem...." Rachel was buried *on the road to* Beis-Lechem -Efras, for G-d wanted her to lie in the territory of her own son, not in the location of the man destined to take his kingdom away.

Thus, once again, the Torah, in this chapter, prepared us for significant events that would occur centuries later in this location.

Chapter 14

Here we will examine Yaakov's purchase of the field at Shechem from Chamor, and show that he foresaw that Yosef would be buried there (about 280 years later). He also foresaw: the boundary of Yosef's descendants, the indications that Shechem would be in Ephrayim's land, not Menashe's, and that this area would be closer to the Holy Temple than Menashe's territory.

It is clear that Yaakov knew that Yosef would lie in Shechem. We read (*Bereishis* 33:18-19), "And Yaakov came ... to Shechem... and pitched his tent before the city. And he bought a parcel of the field... from the sons of Chamor for one hundred *kesitah* (type of coin)." This is astonishing! Yaakov and his family were on their way to return home to his aged father, Yitzchak, as G-d had told him to do. Even at this field, he only pitched a (temporary) tent. Why make a purchase of real estate?

However, this very spot is precisely where Yosef was buried, as specifically stated in exact detail in *Yehoshua* (24:32). Obviously, Yaakov prepared for that moment which took place centuries later. In fact, the holy R.

Moshe Alshich states that the twenty silver pieces received by the brothers for selling Yosef is equivalent to one hundred *kesitah*! As an atonement for their base act, an equal amount was spent to acquire a burial site for him. One could wonder why Yaakov had to make such a purchase since all the land of Canaan was promised to him anyway, and eventually conquered. There are three reasonable answers:

1) He wanted his sons *to know* that he wished Yosef should be buried there, and he said so specifically as we will show soon, and that is why they did so.

2) He preferred to pay for the holy site of Yosef's burial, just as David paid Aravna for his granary, although it was offered to him as a gratuity. Yosef's grave has sanctity similar to the Cave of Machpelah, and Yaakov wished to establish it as fully paid for, for perpetuity.

3) (Perhaps the most important), he wished this site to be separate from the division of the land for all the tribes in later history. No tribe could later claim that it was taken from them improperly (even if it were to be located in their territory). As purchaser, Yaakov could give it to whomever he wished. This is emphasized in *Yehoshua* (op.cit.), in describing Yosef's burial: "And it was an inheritance of the children of Yosef." I.e., it was inherited directly from Yaakov since he purchased it.

Yaakov made his wishes clear to his son, Yosef, when he told him (*Bereishis* 48:22), "I have given you Shechem, one [share] above your brothers." Since "shechem" also means a portion, it is commonly translated as "one portion above your brothers." Even so, this is a perfect case of a double-meaning. Later history bears out the obvious intention that Yosef got this field for his burial in

Shechem. Abarbanel also follows this approach. By postulating that Yaakov gave Yosef this area in advance of the conquest of Canaan by his descendants, we may find indications of this idea in Yaakov's blessing to Yosef (*Bereishis* 49:26), " The blessings of your father are mighty beyond the blessings of my progenitors to the utmost bound [or boundary] of the everlasting hills." The boundaries of Eretz Yisrael, as spelled out in the Torah (*Bereishis* 15:18-21), could only take effect by later acts of conquest. But Shechem was given by Yaakov, as its purchaser, to Yosef, from that moment. Thus, Yaakov says, that his blessings are greater. His fathers' blessings speak of future boundaries, the mountains of Eretz Yisrael. But Yaakov gives him Shechem " עד תאות גבעות עולם" as of that moment – "prior to marking off the mountains of the world" – i.e., prior to the other brothers' receipt of their territories – his blessings "shall be (now) upon the head of Yosef" - for he is immediately named the possessor of Shechem. The final phrase, "and for the crown (or *skull*) of the Nazarite among his brethren," could be an allusion to the burial spot for Yosef's bones in Shechem. Therefore Yaakov emphasized that he gives Shechem "to you," a personal reference, beyond what the tribe will have in the future. The reference to his being a Nazarite may be a clue as to why Yosef is getting special treatment. A Nazarite is one who separates himself from Jewish society with special stringencies. Since he was separated from his brothers by their abominable treatment of him, he gains a separate area for himself beyond the usual distribution of land amongst the tribes. In view of the fact that Yosef was indeed buried in Shechem, and it is part of Ephrayim's territory, there can be no doubt that Yaakov foresaw this future result in his vision to Yosef, including the fact that Shechem itself would be part of his son's territory.

We can even show that he knew it to be Ephrayim's inheritance. Consider the following: In Bereishis (ch. 48), after a detailed description of Yaakov placing his hands in a crossed fashion to honor Ephrayim and his explanation to Yosef that Ephrayim will be greater, he pronounces the blessing that "G-d should make you like Ephrayim and Menashe." Why did that verse continue with stating the very obvious "and he placed Ephrayim before Menashe"? It makes perfect sense to argue that this adds a new element, i.e., that he placed *the territory* of Ephrayim *before* Menashe, in terms of their distance from the Holy Temple. Moving northward, Binyamin's land touched the temple, followed by Ephrayim and then Menashe. Ephrayim merited being closer to the holy center of Jewish life in Eretz Yisrael.

Thus, all the events in Chumash Bereishis, from the "strange" act of Yaakov stopping on his journey home to buy a field, through all the acts that he did with Ephrayim and Menashe, and his statements to Yosef, point in one direction – that Yaakov had clear visions of all the events in future history regarding Shechem, Yosef's burial site there, and the surrounding territory as well. G-d's divine will revealed these secrets to him – and to us – in His Divine Torah.

Chapter 15

We will examine Yaakov's footsteps to Beis-Eil, and the death of Devorah there, and ponder the title "Alon Bachus" which Yaakov gave to this place. This chapter will probe an ancient parable and find that the Torah saw how Yeravam would erect his gold calf at Beis-Eil, that he would descend from Yosef, and the expulsion of the ten tribes would be caused by him – and some further powerful points.

We find an amazing account (*Bereishis* 35:8) of Devorah's death which raises several cogent questions.

1) Why is the death of Devorah, Rivka's nurse, given more prominence than that of Rivka, or of our other matriarchs? (Except for Rachel, Yaakov's other three wives are also unaccounted for in death, like Rivka!)

2) Why must we learn of the site where she died, and the precise location of her grave?

3) Why is her name given only at her death, but omitted when she was first introduced in the Torah as "her nurse" (24:99)?

4) Why this great weeping over a gentile nurse, about whom we know nothing at all, to even naming the oak under which she was buried as "the oak of weeping" (*alon bachus*)? If we make a mathematical account, we quickly

find that she was extremely old [at least 120 years old], so why such weeping anyway? It is clear that there is something significant hidden in this account for us to uncover, for our holy Torah wastes no words.

I will discuss in ch.100 the famous tale of Yechezkel who awakened the dead by G-d's command. In the Talmud's discussion (*Sanhedrin* 92b) of this amazing event, R. Yehudah states that "in truth it was a parable." However, I will prove that he did not mean that this occurrence did not actually happen, but rather, that its entire purpose was to serve the people as a parable. The Jewish people were at that time so down and disheartened that they felt the end of their nation was at hand. By reviving the dead, Yechezkel demonstrated that by G-d's will, even dead bodies can rise from the earth, and certainly a living nation, even if the future looks so bleak. In the same way, the death of Devorah took place in fact, but the purpose of recording this event in detail was to provide us with a parable for the future, for events that Yaakov foresaw.

Eretz Yisrael is frequently referred to is Tanach as "flowing with milk and honey." G-d's gift to us of this land is pictured by Moshe as follows: (*Devarim* 32:13), "He made him to ride on high places...and He made him to suck honey out of a rock...." Thus, the sustenance the people got from the land is called by the term *y-n-k*, which means to nurse. This blessing, we were warned time and time again, would cease if we abandoned G-d and His Torah, and eventually we were exiled for doing so. How did our terrible spiritual decline begin? The Tanach blames Yeravam many times, for establishing his golden calf in Beis-Eil, and another later in Dan. The blame for the exile of the ten tribes is specifically placed upon Yeravam (*Melachim II*, 17:22-23) and the idolatry he introduced, which led to Jewish weeping for many centuries. Hence, we may say that just as Devorah the beloved nurse of Rivka died at Beis-Eil, so too Eretz Yisrael, that nursed the Jewish people with beautiful produce for centuries, "died" through the abominable acts that took place at Beis-Eil. Yaakov's vision of this tragic future, not merely her death, caused him to name her burial place "Oak of Weeping." The Torah also gave clues about the second idol that Yeravam established at Dan, as we will show in chapters 17 and 50.

How perfect that the Torah recorded Devorah's name here, and omitted it when she was mentioned once before. For Eretz Yisrael is like a bee, which gives honey but can sting as well. It is a land which flows with milk and honey, yet has the power to expel people who behave abominably. The Torah warns (*VaYikra* 18:28), "The land should not vomit you out when you defile it...." Thus, here the Torah symbolically states that at Beis-Eil, the source location for the terrible abominations of the ten tribes, death came to the nursing power of the land, and the cessation of its honey, represented by the nurse Devorah. The Emori, a major group of the seven Canaanite nations, is actually referred to as a bee (*Devarim* 1:44). Ashur, the nation that drove the ten tribes into exile, is also called a bee (*Yeshayahu* 7:18)! Thus, the bee that gives honey dies and is replaced by the bee that stings. The specific mention of her name here, and Yaakov's naming of the oak under which she was buried, surely means that Yaakov foresaw the terrible decline of his descendants at this location, and wept over this disastrous future. Only because the Torah wanted us to see and understand these messages for the future, it recorded in detail the death of an otherwise minor figure in the Torah narrative, and added her name when it became relevant to the situation.

In the following verses, Yaakov receives G-d's blessing and is named "Yisrael." After promising Yaakov that great nations and kings will emerge from him, and that he will have the land promised to his fathers, the verse adds (35:13) "And G-d went up from him, at the place that He spoke with him." M*eforshim* wonder about the need for this verse, and the awkward second phrase. However, since Yaakov was in Beis-Eil at the time, and the idol built there later in history was the primary cause for G-d to abandon His people, the statement that G-d left that spot hints at His later abandonment due to Yeravam's idol. Thus, the emphasis on "at the place that He spoke with him." Elsewhere, i.e., where Yehudah and Binyamin dwelled, G-d did not "go up," and they remained for a long time after the ten tribes were exiled. Perhaps that is why this was the perfect time for G-d to affirm the name of Yisrael, for this is the term used later in Tanach for the ten tribes. Thus, when G-d "went up from him" represents G-d leaving these tribes to their sad fate at the hands of Ashur.

Similarly, when Avraham is informed that he will have a second son, Yitzchak, who will carry on the covenant, we find (*Bereishis* 17:22) that after concluding His message, "And He finished talking with him, and G-d went up from Avraham." This too probably means that G-d removed His glorious presence from there, either because of Avraham's laughing, or/and because Avraham asked that G-d bless Yishmael too, as Abarbanel states.

With this background we may now examine this entire subject and find some new and interesting points, by examining Ch. 35 from v.1 to v.15. There are three units here. V.1 through v.7 describes Yaakov returning to Beis-Eil, where he builds an altar to express his thanks to G-d [obviously for his safe return] at the spot where he had his great dream of the ladder. V.8 is the story of Devorah's death and burial. V.9 through 15 details a vision from G-d at that site promising wonderful news for the future of his descendants. Yaakov erects a monument there. Despite the fact that he had renamed this area (Luz) a long time before as "Beis-eil", in this section (v. 7 and 15) he seems to do so again *twice*! It is strange that the incident of Devorah is inserted in middle of two sections that fit together perfectly. However, now we may logically explain:

When he built the altar to thank G-d (v.7), he called the place "Eil Beis-Eil", for Eil is one of G-d's names of mercy, as Chazal state many times. This is why it is one of the terms in the Thirteen Attributes of Mercy.

However, now Devorah dies, and Yaakov understands the sad symbol of this event for which reason he calls the oak "the oak of weeping" as detailed above. Soon after, he receives a vision from G-d, who goes up from him, etc., which we explained is a symbol of G-d's reaction to the future abomination of Yeravam at that site. Even that vision contained some stings within the honey. For when G-d said (v. 11) "a company of nations will be from you, and kings will go forth from your loins," Chazal explain the nations are Ephrayim and Menashe. Two of their kings (Yeravam of Ephrayim and Yeihu of Menashe, were leading promoters of the idolatry at Beis-Eil. The clue that Yaakov understood this message is that he now (v.15) renamed the place "E– lohim Beis-Eil". This name of G-d represents strict judgment, for Yaakov now senses the force of judgment that will permeate this location, and prays for his children at this monument.

We must carry this analysis further. In Yaakov's original dream of the ladder, the angels were "ascending and descending," although logically this is in reverse order for heavenly angels. This was a sad image. Originally, this place was a holy site, and remained so for a long time, symbolized by ascent. But when Yeravam made it a center for idolatry, it "descended" to low depths. (In the next chapter we will analyze the dream carefully.) Nevertheless, upon awakening, he prayed that this site would become the "house of G-d," and Chazal claim that G-d had rolled up the land beneath him so that he was, in effect, sleeping on Mt. Moriah that night! Now, years later, he returns there and builds his altar, just before Devorah dies. The expression that (v. 8) "she was buried beneath Beis-Eil" is exceptionally unusual and awkward. Perhaps the term for beneath (*tachas*) is used here in its other meaning of "because" (as in *Devarim* 22:29, and 28:47) and hints at the end of the honey of that land giving its sweet products to *bnei Yisrael* because of the abominations of that place by Yeravam.(8)

By assuming that Yaakov recognized the truth about the eventual decline of Beis-Eil, we can answer an astonishing verse near the end of Chumash *Bereishis*. Yaakov, on his death bed, says to Yosef (48:3), "G-d... appeared to me in *Luz* in the land of Canaan...." After naming that town Beis-Eil more than one time, why would he now revert to the rejected name? However, if he knew about the future, he may have decided that "Beis-Eil" was no longer appropriate. In fact, Rada'k states that the root of Luz means depart, or being removed, as in (*Mishlei* 4:21) " Let them not depart (*yaleezu)* from your eyes." Thus, the town that departed from G-d by establishing an idol and removing itself from the fold may appropriately be called Luz.

Reviewing all of the above information and amazing clues of the text should convince every reader that only G-d Himself could have written this text for us, and He alone connected our early history with hints of what He foresaw would occur at that location. We must therefore observe all His commandments and statutes as presented in His holy Torah.

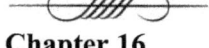
Chapter 16

We will re-examine the first journey of Yaakov from Be-eir Sheva to Beis-Eil and reinforce our evidence that the Torah foresaw the future events of Yeravam's time, and also the entire future wandering of the Jewish people to Ashur, Bavel, and Edom, and their return to the land with the arrival of Mashiach.

We return to the ladder-dream in Beis-Eil. We have previously explained the significance of G-d's going up from him "in the place that He spoke with him," to indicate G-d's desire to depart from the site of the golden calf of Yeravam. Also, because of this idolatry, the Jewish people will also "go up" from the land into exile. The message he received that night had some disturbing features too. Quote: (28:14-15) "And your seed will be like the dust of the earth and you will burst forth to the west and the east, and the north and the south, and all the families of the earth will be blessed in you and your seed / And I will be with you and will watch over you... and return you to this land for I will not abandon you until I have done what I have spoken to you (or "about you")." Of course, the simple meaning of bursting forth in all directions is that his seed will multiply greatly. However, it also indicates that they will be spread all over the earth in exile from their homeland. Since it is crystal clear that here, as in so many other places, "Yaakov" means the Jewish people, G-d immediately promises His protection during the long exile to guarantee the eternity of the Jewish people until their return. Returning from all corners of the earth obviously implies the arrival of Mashiach. Similarly, the following section is a review of the description of R. Eliezer Ashkenazi in his *Maasei HaShem*:

G-d is informing him what will occur to his seed at the end of days after being spread all over the world, as is also written (*Yirmiyahu* 46:27), "Have no fear my servant Yaakov... for I will save you from afar, and your seed from the land of their captivity... etc." There too, the prophet wrote immediately before, "And their King David whom I will raise up for them." Now, based on this background, I will carefully examine all the elements of this chapter to the full extent of my ability.

It is certainly clear that "Yaakov" represents, in this chapter, the people of Israel of future generations. Several phrases (e.g., "wherever you go," "I will return you to this land," etc.,) could not have meant Yaakov personally. He only went to Aram and later returned, so why "wherever"? This was the first time G-d spoke to Yaakov, so "what I have spoken to you" must be understood, as Rashi writes, spoken "about you," a reference to the promise made to Avraham that Canaan would belong to his seed. In that case it was not carried out with Yaakov himself, for he lived his last years in Egypt and returned only for burial. Hence, the purpose of this dream was to present a vision of the future of the Jewish people until Mashiach's arrival.

We have earlier clarified all the future events that the Torah foresaw at this historic place. We must now proceed to find all the other future events that are hinted at in this chapter.

Note that here, and only in one other place (*Bereishis* 13:15), is the increase of descendants called "the dust of the earth,." rather than "the stars" or "the sand." Each symbol has its special meaning, and each is used in the most appropriate place. In our chapter, where future exile is revealed, "dust" represents being trampled upon by enemies, and is therefore accompanied by the description of being sent to all the corners of the earth. In the earlier comparable description, the Torah adds that it symbolizes the impossibility of counting them, here even that addition is omitted. Obviously, the message is that the Jewish people will be dispersed and trampled by enemies, until "I will return you to the land..." when Mashiach comes. (See further discussion in chs. 79 and 80.)

In this vision, the order for the four directions was west, east, north, and south. This is different from the order earlier in ch.13, which begins with north, and (*Devarim* 3:27) another that begins with west. I will explain each of these elsewhere, but here I must explain the order that is given. It is quite correct. Our first journey out of Eretz Yisrael was to Egypt, which is to the west. We returned to our homeland eastward. Much later we were exiled to Ashur and Bavel, northward, as mentioned clearly (*Yirmiyahu* 1:14). Returning southward to Eretz Yisrael we were driven further southward into the exile of Edom, which is south of Yisrael. Hence, these directions foresee the wanderings of the Jewish people from their beginnings to their final exile. At this point, G-d expresses His promise not to abandon us until we are returned finally to our homeland. So too, when *Yeshayahu* speaks (43:6) of the final redemption, the last area from which Jews return is the south.

In view of the negative connotation of "breaking out" all over the world, one might question the very positive tone of the concluding phrase in that verse, "And all the families of the earth will be blessed in you."

However, as noted by Rabbeinu Avraham son of the *Rosh* in his *Tur Al HaTorah,* several commentators have interpreted the verb "blessed" by its other meaning: "to graft (two trees together)," a usage found often in the Talmud and in modern Hebrew (*mavrich*). Thus, the verse states that your descendants will spread across the world, where many other peoples will graft themselves to the Jewish people by conversion to Judaism [or, alas, by intermarriage *rachmana litzlan*]. Indeed, R. Elazar states (*Pesachim* 87b), "G-d only exiled Israel in order that converts should be added to them."

Here is the total picture. Yaakov went out from Be-eir Sheva (the southern border of Eretz Yisrael, a symbol of the Jewish people beginning their venture into golus). He arrives at Beis-Eil, the site where later idolatry will cause the exile. Here was the ideal location for G-d to appear to him and outline the full course of Jewish history, as we have described in the section above. The culmination of this dream is that we will eventually return to our homeland in the final redemption, for G-d will not abandon us. You will see the full development of all these aspects in the coming chapters. In ch. 49, I will show that the Torah foresaw the discovery of the Torah scroll in the days of King Yoshiyahu, and that the destruction of the temple would 0take place in the reign of his descendants. In ch. 50 we will show that Yaakov saw the exile of the ten tribes and prayed for them. In ch.18, you will see that the Torah foresaw both exiles, what day they will occur, and that the longer exile would be that of Edom. In ch. 68 you will see that many details of both exiles were foreknown, including the knowledge that these exiles would not be in the same era. In ch. 70 I will show that the seventy years of exile were foreseen as well as other interesting details. Continuing to chs.71 and 72, the Torah knew various details of the second temple, and of the miracle of Chanukah. In ch. 73 we will show that the predictions for the end of time in the Book of *Daniel* were foreseen, and in ch. 74, also some details about the third temple, with further elaboration in ch. 87. In effect, every major event in Jewish history was foreseen in the chumash by the Divine author of the Torah.

On his way down to Egypt, Yaakov had a vision in Be-eir Sheva (46:4), in which G-d said, " I will go down with you to Egypt and I will surely bring you up (in a double verb: *aalcha gam alo*). Why repeat the verb? The ending phrase, "And Yosef will place his hand upon your eyes, "is somewhat mystic, and does not seem to fit this verse. Commentators discuss this verse. I will give my interpretation, based on certain premises:
1) As explained earlier, "Yaakov" often is used for the Jewish people.
2) When an exile is discussed, statements can be made to include other, later exiles.

3) The Jewish people had three redemptions: from Egypt, Bavel and the ultimate one from Edom.

4) With the final redemption, there will be resurrection, and our forefathers will see G-d's promises fulfilled, although they did not see the first two redemptions.

5) Often when G-d speaks, he mentions Himself in third person (e.g., *Bereishis* 18:19).

6) It is well-known that "on" (*al*) often means "near" or "next to."

7) "His hand" can symbolize "his strength."

We may now give this interpretation: In Yaakov's vision, HaShem says that He will go down with him "and I will bring you up" (from Egypt), "also up" (implying another return from an exile —this is the return from Bavel. "Also" hints that it will not be as complete as the first return from Egypt, for it was limited in scope – but is will *also* be considered a return). "And Yosef will place his hand upon your eyes" may now be entirely reinterpreted. "And He (G-d) will *continue* to place His *power near* your eyes (for you will rise up to witness this final redemption with the arrival of Mashiach). I believe that this is the simple meaning of this verse. How marvelously the Torah hides sublime ideas in phrases that have double meanings. The choice site for such a vision was Be-eir Sheva, the southern boundary of Eretz Yisrael, to imply that from here Jews will be driven out in two exiles, but will eventually return to reclaim their homeland.

. You should know that there were two cities named Beis-Eil. When Avraham first entered Eretz Yisrael, he pitched his tent between Ai and Beis-Eil. This city was in the territory of Binyamin (*Yehoshua* 18:22) on a plane near the Jordan River. The city of Luz, renamed Beis-Eil by Yaakov, was further north in Ephrayim's area (*Yehoshua* 16:2), at the border that separated Ephrayim from Binyamin. It is in the mountain area, which is why the verb "going up" is often used for those heading to Beis-Eil. Chazal say that the northern Beis-Eil, due to the golden calf, was given another appropriate name in Tanach: Beis-Aven (Home of Evil). There is a midrash (*Bereishis Rabbah* 39:15) that seems to place Yeravam's idol in Binyamin's Beis-Eil, for it notes the change of name to Beis-Aven. But other midrashim clearly place it at the site of Yaakov's dream at Luz, in Ephrayim's territory. This is certainly correct and obvious, for Yeravam ruled in the Kingdom of Yisrael, with no control over Binyamin's land. He was himself of the tribe of Ephrayim. Perhaps, the conflicting midrash was entirely focused on the *name "Beis-Eil,"* but actually had the other city in mind.

This may sound farfetched, but there is another example of such thinking. In the first great war in Chumash (*Bereishis* 14:7), the army of Kedorlaomer comes to "*Ein Mishpat* which is *Kadesh.*" Rashi quotes a midrash that it was called Ein Mishpat (Well of Judgment), for Kadesh is where Moshe and Aaron were judged in the incident of the rock and denied entry to Eretz Yisrael. The Ramban is astounded. This Kadesh is identified in that text as being near Paran, and is not the far distant Kadesh of the desert of Zin, where the judgment was made. Ramban then adds, "Perhaps this midrash only dwelled on the name alone, and meant that 'Kadesh' is a term that (elsewhere) became a site for judgment." We must use this type of reasoning to answer our conflicting midrash, for it does not match the geographic facts otherwise.

Chapter 17

We will examine Avraham's journey to Dan and some other places, and its placement here is for its connection to the events of Beis-Eil as the reader will see. We will prove that the Torah already saw the idol of Micha at Dan, and Yeravam's calf at Dan. It knew that Dan would be the northeast end of Jewish land, and foresaw all the areas that would be added to Jewish lands. It also knew of all the Jewish exiles.

Look my friends at the city of Dan (and Chovah) and there, too, you will find that the Torah foresaw events of the future centuries.

When Avraham pursued the kings who captured Lot, his nephew (14:14-15), he raced to Dan. He attacked the enemy at night, and pursued them to Chovah, which is "left" of Damascus. Rashi records the midrash that there is no such town anywhere in Tanach. Actually, Chovah is another name for Dan, deriving from "obligation", for the golden calf erected there by Yeravam placed a heavy obligation upon the Jewish people. This must be true. We find many times, the Torah used names that were familiar at the time the Torah was given for places that had primitive names, so that the reader would know what city the Torah was discussing. E.g., (*Bereishis* 14:3), "All these [armies] gathered to *Emek haSidim,* which is (i.e., it later became) the Salt Sea." This way, we know where the battle took place, for the earlier name was long forgotten when the Torah was given. There is no logical reason for the torah to record "Chovah," since this name is never found again, unless it wishes to tell us the special connotation that Chazal found. If it is really Dan, we understand the clue about its sad spiritual downfall. (9) The recording of two names for one location should not trouble us. We similarly find Avraham (12:6) arriving "to the place of Shechem, to the plain of Moreh." Here too, the two names identify the same location. (10)

There is a proof that here the Torah used names of the future. For Dan itself only acquired this name after Yehoshua's time (*Shoftim* 18:29), by dropping the earlier name of *Layish*. Thus, it is clear that both Dan and Chovah are recorded long in advance of their origin, and may therefore truly be one city, referred to by a name that recalls its spiritual descent to idolatry. It would also be very farfetched to suggest that there were two cities named Dan. We find that the Torah identifies cities with similar names to make clear of which it speaks. E.g., it mentions *"Beis Lechem Yehudah"* because there was a second Beis-Lechem. In Tanach there is never a label attached to Dan, indicating that there was only one such city. It is clear that the Torah added the title Chovah only to let us know that it was aware of the eventual tragic events that would take place in Dan during the reign of Yeravam.

In fact, Dan is mentioned again in the Torah, still before it gained that name. G-d showed Moshe the entire land of Yisrael (*Devarim* 34:1) "... and Gilead up to Dan." At that time it was still called Layish. We might add that the expression "up to Dan" is both in terms of geography and time. Geographically, it is the northern border of Yisrael. As a time indicator, "up to Dan' could imply that the vast borders of the land that G-d was showing to Moshe would be in their full power and glory up to the period of Dan. Thereafter, the idolatry of that city brought it into steady decline, culminating in the golus. In ch. 50, we will find other clues that the Torah foresaw the golden calf in Dan.

The use of two names in proximity for one location (Dan / Chovah) should not be disturbing. This city experienced two abominations in later history. It was the site for establishing the idol of Michah (*Shoftim* ch. 18), at which time the name of Dan was given. The greater sin of Yeravam, leading to the exile, was making it the northern center for idolatry, the ultimate "obligation" of the people. The two names match perfectly these two situations. By using both names here, the Torah indicates that Avraham had visions of both historical periods, causing his weakness.

In Avraham's campaign, the expression that he "divided [his forces] upon them at night," (14:15) may serve as a clue to the two historical situations. For between them in time, occurred the division of the Jewish people into two kingdoms. Hence, this division led from the lesser shame of Michah's idol to the terrible disgrace of Yeravam's deeds. Yeravam only arose to kingship because of this division, hence it too may be seen as a "nighttime" division, leading to the night of *golus*. In ch. 52 I will show further proof that the Torah foresaw Michah's idol in Dan, and the Kohen (who was a Levite) who served as the priest there.

In Rabbeinu Yaakov's *Baal haTurim* on Torah, he states that G-d's directive to Avraham (*Bereishis* 13:17) to walk all over the land of Canaan was, in effect, a method for him to take possession (*chazakah*) of the land. We find him traveling east and west, and down to Be-eir Sheva. It is very logical to say that in the great war, his pursuit up to Dan was the act of taking possession of the north part of the land, for Dan is seen as the northern border. Had he not weakened, he might have gone further north and expanded Jewish territory.

In fact, we may perceive just what his goal was. For we find (*Yechezkel* 47:17) that Damascus will eventually be part of Jewish territory. This must have been Avraham's objective, to possess Damascus for his descendants, if not for his sudden debility. (11)

It may also be worth noting that G-d's directive for Avraham to traverse the land comes right after Lot departed from him. Since the lands allotted to Lot are Moav and Ammon, which we were told in the Torah not to attack, this phrase serves as a hint to the conditions G-d made about our extent of conquest. I.e., now that Lot was gone to stake out his lands, Avraham should traverse the balance of the land for his posterity.

Having found all these marvelous clues in this chapter, it is also clear that the expression "left of Damascus" was itself a hint of Avraham's ultimate goal in his pursuit, and a way of telling us that it will someday be part of Jewish territory. Rashi also notes this future status of Damascus in *Shir HaShirim* (7:5).

Historically, it was already established as a metropolis in Avraham's time, as indicated by referring to his trusted servant as "Eliezer of Damascus" (15:2). After David conquered it from Aram, it changed hands several times, finally falling to Ashur. In the future, it will be part of Eretz Yisrael, as hinted by referring to it in Avraham's military campaign. In all other references to Dan in Tanach, We do not find the additional "left of Damascus," for it is relevant only here. (12)

I was puzzled for a long time about the need to describe in detail the war between the four kings and their five adversaries, with the names of the places conquered, etc. The Torah is not a simple history book! What do we gain from all these descriptions? At first I concluded that only Eliyahu HaNavi can explain this to us. However, I finally realized that all the places named in their campaign are part of Jewish land; some in our past history, and some for the future. Thus, after the four kings took these places in war, Avraham conquered them, becoming the owner of these sites for his descendants. Let us examine these locations carefully.

In that first great war (*Bereishis* ch.14), the victorious kings smote the inhabitants of *Ashteros Karnayim,* the *Zuzim* of *Hum,* and the *Eimim* of *Shaveh Kiryasayim.* Ahstaros belonged to Og, king of Bashan (*Devarim* 1:4), later part of the land of Menashe (*Yehoshua* 13:31). The Zuzim are apparently the tribe that lived in Zuzin, a city that is one-half day's northward journey to Ashtaros. Kiryasayim was given by Yehoshua to Reuven's tribe (13:19), although the Eimim reached as far as Moav's territory (*Devarim* 2:9-11). In the Ramban's account in the first chapter of *Devarim,* he includes the land of Ammon as hosting these tribes. These lands were promised to

Avraham in the covenant "between the pieces", named there as Keini, Kenizi, and Kadmoni. Of course, Bashan was conquered by bnei Yisrael in Moshe's time.

The kings then vanquished the Chori at Mt. Sei-ir, and then came to Ein Mishpat "which is Kadesh" (14:7), subduing the "field of the Amaleki," and the Emori at Chatzatzon Tamar. Commentators struggle to identify Kadesh, uncertain whether it is Kadesh Barnea or another Kadesh at the Tzin Desert. Kadesh Barnea is identified as part of our land (*BeMidbar* 34:4), and the other Kadesh is at the border of Edom (*BeMidbar* 20:14), whose territory is destined to be ours in the final redemption. Rashi states that Chatzatzon Tamar is Ein Gedi, part of our land in Yehudah's portion. The final battle took place at Emek haSidim, which became the Dead Sea. Hence every site mentioned in this war of the kings already was, or will be, part of the expanded land of Israel. Thus our eyes are drawn to recognize all these sites for future reference.

I found a fascinating interpretation of the *Tur on Torah* about this chapter of history. He equates the four kings with the four kingdoms that will rise in the world to subjugate the Jewish people until they are all vanquished and forced to return all the plundered wealth. Shinar (Amrafel's people) is Bavel, and Elasar is Media (perhaps Elasar was a city in Media or Persia). Eilam (Kedorlaomer's kingdom) is Greece, and the last king is ruler of "Goyim," a hint of Edom, which brought many tribes and nations under its reign. Thus, even these kingdoms represent clues to future events in our history, so that every place enumerated in this chapter has relevance to later Jewish history.

At this point, we have shown numerous examples of how all the travels and events of our forefathers related to future occurrences that took place in the same places. In chapter 21 we will demonstrate the great significance of Yaakov's presence at Migdal Eider. Unfortunately, I have not been able to find the deeper meaning of the place called Peniel/Penuel (*Bereishis* 32:30-31), which Yaakov passed on the morning after his battle with the angel. Perhaps it is a reference to a future event (e.g., the final redemption) yet to occur. In fact, Yaakov states there that he saw G-d "face to face," which rings of the expression in the navi (*Yeshayahu* 52:8), "for eye to eye they will see when G-d returns Zion." So too, the phrase that "the sun arose for him" may hint of the light of the redemption - perhaps then the real significance of Penuel will be understood.

Chapter 18

Analyzing the dispatch of the spies from Kadesh Barnea and Aharon's ascent to Mt. Hor near Edom's border to derive that the Torah foresaw the golus to Edom, and to strengthen our faith in the redemption. There is proof that the Torah saw both temple demolitions, the precise calendar day too, and that the golus of Edom would be our longest.

We are ready to see the full glory and splendor of G-d's Torah as we examine this topic. When the spies returned with their evil report, the people cried all of that night (*BeMidbar* 14:1). We can prove Chazal's statement that this occurred on the ninth of Av from the text itself. On the twentieth of Iyar, the cloud of glory lifted and the journey from Mt. Sinai began (*BeMidbar* 10:11). They traveled for three days (10:33).

The sad tale of the people's grumbling for better food and G-d's miraculous supply of quail took up a full month, bringing us to the twenty-second of Sivan. Then Miriam was punished for her speaking and the people waited seven days for her leprosy to subside, thus the twenty-ninth of Sivan. The spies were sent forth and returned in forty days, on the eighth of Av. Thus, the night of weeping was the ninth of Av. The fact that this was the date of the destruction of the first temple points clearly to the hand of G-d, who turned that night into (as Chazal refer to it) "a night of weeping for generations." Indeed, Rabbeinu Bechayei states that the first temple destruction took place at night, based on *Yirmiyahu* (39:4). I believe that G-d directly alluded to this event when he said to Moshe (*BeMidbar* 14:11-12), "How long will this people provoke me..../ I will smite them with a plague and 'drive them out' and make of you a greater nation...." Even if the reference to a plague can mean their death in the desert, the expression to "drive them out" clearly appears to be a reference to a time when they are settled in their land. When, in response to Moshe's prayers, G-d says, "I have forgiven as you say," He surely meant only that He would not wipe them out then and there, but not that He withdrew His punishment of a future temple destruction. This is why the Torah doesn't state that G-d "relented" as it usually does in such cases of threatened punishments. David certainly understood this verse as referring to golus, for in describing this scene he writes (*Tehillim* 106:26-27), "And G-d pledged to cast them down in the desert...../ and to spread them out amongst the nations." He could only have derived this idea from the word *orishenu* (I will drive them out). Since this eventually occurred, G-d's statement that He forgave them could not have meant a total pardon, leaving the punishment of golus in its place. How perfect is the remark of Rav Pinchas HaLevi Horowitz in his *Panim Yafos*, that where the Torah states (*BeMidbar* 32:10), "And G-d was furious on that day," it means that He was angry at the day itself, the ninth of Av, and fixed it as a day of continuous mourning on the Jewish calendar.

However, we must note that not only the day was already determined in the Torah centuries before, but the place is also significant. Our long *golus* is, of course, the present one which is known as the *golus* of Edom. All our prophets spoke of this exile, but also promised that we will be triumphant in the end, as the prophet Ovadiah promised (*Ovadiah* v.21), that the Mt. Eisav (Edom) will be judged, and the kingdom will be restored to G-d. We see that the spies were sent forth from Kadesh Barnea, a southern border of Eretz Yisrael. Examining the geography of the southern area of Eretz Yisrael in *Parashas Mas-ei*, and noting Rashi's comments there, it is clear that Kadesh Barnea is slightly north of the territory of Edom, and as also indicated at the beginning of *Chumash Devarim* (1:2), "Eleven days (journey) from Chorev, by way of Mr. Sei-ir (Edom) to Kadesh Barnea." Thus, the site from which the spies went forth, and brought about our long exile, is in proximity to the enemy who has held us in *golus* for so many centuries. (13) The place and the time (the ninth of Av) come together to point to a finger of G-d at events that take place about nine centuries later! These are the marvels of G-d's ways and His Torah. It is noteworthy that upon being sent forth, the Torah only states (*BeMidbar* 13:3) that they went "from the Paran desert," but upon returning it adds (v.26) "to the Paran desert, *to Kadesh*." For now, we are about to be introduced to the terrible event that will lead to the exile of Edom, and the Torah points to the precise location to show its proximity to Edom's territory.

In G-d's first reaction to the people's rebellion the day after their night of weeping, He said to Moshe (14:11), " עד

אנה (How long) will this people provoke Me, and how long will they not believe in Me?...." Abarbanel points out that the term "ana" is a geographic one and the correct term should have been *ad masai*. However, the term used would actually translate as *"how far."* But, according to our analysis, it is quite correct. G-d is saying that He has already determined that they will be eventually exiled to *golus* Edom, which is close by. *How far* do they want to be driven out, if they continue in this terrible way – to the ends of the world?

Note also, that when Aharon ascended Mt. Hor to die there, for him alone the Torah spells out the day and month of his demise (*BeMidbar* 33:38), the first day of Av. There is deep meaning here. For the priesthood is firmly linked to the holy temple in a powerful bond. The Torah foreshadows the connection of Av to the "death" (until Mashiach) of the priesthood in the month of Av. Just as when Yaakov foretold the future of his sons in *Chumash Bereishis,* the individual name connoted the tribe, so too, "Aharon" connotes the priesthood. Furthermore, the Talmud *Yerushalmi (Taanis)* states that the first temple was destroyed on the first day of Av! Elsewhere, I have argued convincingly that the *Talmud Bavli* does not disagree with this statement. Hence, it is quite clear that the exceptional mention of the precise day and month of Aharon's passing was recorded to indicate that in the future this day will mark the demise of the active priesthood (until the building of the third temple) through the destruction of the temple. His passing near the border of Edom pointed to the source of this exile, demonstrating the finger of G-d in every event in the Torah.

A careful examination of the Torah's descriptions of Aharon's death produces further astonishing facts. The first time the impending death of Aharon is mentioned (*BeMidbar* 20), the text reads (v.22): "And they journeyed from Kadesh and bnei Yisrael... came to Mt. Hor." (v....23) "And G-d said to Moshe and Aharon at Mt. Hor *on the border* על גבול *of the land of Edom,* saying: (v.24) "Aharon shall be gathered to his people, for he will not enter the land...". Several verses later (v.28), Aharon dies on the mountain. Recounting this event later (ch. 33), the Torah states (vs.37-38), "...they encamped at Mt. Hor at *the edge* בקצה of the land of Edom. And Aharon... ascended Mt. Hor... and he died there in the fortieth year of the exodus... on the fifth month on the first day." There are several questions that can be raised here:

1) Why at 20:22 does the Torah state only that they arrived to Mt. Hor, and in the next verse it reveals that Mt. Hor was at the border of Edom?

2) Why is Mt. Hor described as "on the border" of Edom, and later (ch. 33) as "at the edge"?

3) Why is the death of Aharon told twice in the same Chumash?

I see here that the Torah reveals the exile of Edom, and the repetition of his death hints at the two destructions, for it symbolizes the suspension of the priesthood. The account in ch.33 hints at the first *churban*, which was not carried out by Edom. Therefore, when the Torah tells that it is near Edom's territory, it uses "at the edge" simply as a geographic fact, for this description does not imply extreme closeness as much as "at the border." It does give the date (first day of Av) for that *churban* took place on that day, as indicated above.. The description in ch. 20

alludes to the second *churban* (we know that there is no strict chronological order in Torah). Since the death of Aharon implies the suspension of the priesthood carried out by Edom, here the Torah adds "at the border of Edom" to connect that site to the exile, in the mind of the reader of the Torah.

We can see that all these clues and descriptions show that the Torah already foresaw the day and month of the destructions of both temples, and who the primary enemy would be. Here is another powerful "fingerprint" of the divine author of our holy Torah. The reader should be aware that all our great Rabbanim of the ages in the Talmud and the midrashim always mentioned the Romans by the title of "Edom." This continued with the scholars of the Middle Ages, like Ibn Ezra, Rambam, Ramban, Radak, Abarbanel, etc.

Radak (R. David Kimchi) was convinced (at the conclusion of his commentary on *Yoel*) that most of the Romans were genealogically Edomites. On this basis I wrote that the present long *golus* is the exile of Edom. (13)

Chapter 19

We examine the story of Yehudah in Bereishis (ch. 38) to understand: Why did Yehudah go down to Adulam? Why was Yehudah in Keziv when his wife gave birth to Sheilah? We will show that the Torah foresaw that Adulam would be at the border of Yehudah's territory; that David would conquer the land of the Plishtim, and that Keziv would be outside Eretz Yisrael.

We know that Yehudah was the greatest of the tribes from whom came forth King David to form the great chain of our kings [until Mashiach]. Yehudah was also the first to take his territory in the conquest of the land. G-d was concerned with him and dedicated a special chapter to detail the beginnings of Yehudah's tribe.

The first verse informs us that he left his brothers and befriended Chirah in Adulam. He chose this location over hundreds of choices. This town later was part of his territory (*Yehoshua* 15:35), and stood at the border (see Rashi there). Thus, Yehudah established his family, the start of his kingdom, in his own land. His separation from his brothers indicates that they (excluding Binyamin) would indeed separate from him and found the kingdom of the Ten Tribes. Both Chevron (where G-d told Avraham that kings would descend from him) and

Adulam (where Yehudah began the chain of his descendants) are appropriately situated in his own domain.

Tamar, the mother of Peretz (ancestor of David) by Yehudah, is the mother of the kingdom. The strange way she became pregnant from Yehudah, on a roadside, is clear testimony that this was a manipulation of G-d. Yehudah met her just before arriving to Timnah, which was later part of the land controlled by the Plishtim (*Shoftim* 14:1). After all the conquests of bnei Yisrael during and after Yehoshua's time, the Plishtim territory was conquered by David. How perfect that David's ancestor was born near Timnah, for from him came the man who would conquer that territory for the Jewish people.

I once read a parable (I think it was based on a tale about Julius Caesar) about a pregnant woman who was moving about her home. Suddenly she gave birth and the child came out on the floor, on a mosaic image of a lion. The wise men told her that it was an omen that he would become a great powerful warrior, and so it eventually happened. So too, Tamar became pregnant with Peretz near Timnah, and his descendant conquered Timnah and the other towns under Plishtim dominion centuries later. Here is another demonstration of the divinity of G-d's Torah. In chapter 37 we will explore this topic further.

Let us proceed and show once again that the places where events occur to our ancestors become significant in later history. When Yehudah's wife gave birth to his third son, Sheilah (38:5), Yehudah was away in Keziv. How much has been written by commentators who wondered about this seemingly insignificant detail!

However, the mishnah (*Sheviis* ch. 6:1) indicates clearly that Keziv is beyond the border of Eretz Yisrael, and the Rambam (*Laws of terumah* 1:8) follows this opinion. Thus, this town never acquired the sanctity of Eretz Yisrael. By informing us that the father of this child stood outside the holy land during his birth, the Torah is telling us, in effect, not to expect him to become the ancestor of our kings. Then, on a roadside near Timnah, in Yehudah's territory, Tamar gives birth to twins in a very strange turn of events. We sense that something unique is occurring. Zerach's arm appears, and is withdrawn by Peretz breaking out ahead of him. What a perfect image to presage the true ancestor of the chosen king of Israel, who will break out in many directions like a mighty lion, to conquer the lands destined for the Jewish people. We see, as we examine this chapter, that after Yehudah's first two sons die for their sins, Sheilah and Zerach are eliminated from contention to become the ancestors of our kings, leaving Peretz, born is such a spectacular manner, to claim the throne. Obviously, the primary purpose of this entire chapter was to prepare us for the eventual rise of David as the king of the Jewish people forever.

In this chapter, G-d was already pointing a finger at Peretz to show us: 1) that he would be the progenitor of Mashiach; 2) that Adulam would be part of Eretz Yisrael; 3) that David would conquer the land held by the Plishtim; 4) that Keziv would be beyond Eretz Yisrael.

Let us also note that the first step of creating the kingdom of David began in an act of *yibum* (Yehudah with Tamar) and later a second such act (Boaz with Roos). While these were not the precise method of *yibum* as defined in the Torah, they closely follow that pattern based on the pre-Torah custom of a relative marrying the childless widow. Many of the births were unusual. David traces back to Roos, a Moabite convert, and to the mother of Moav, born out of incest with her father Lot. David's grandson, King Rechavam is born to Naamah, a convert from Ammon, and Ammon was born out of the incest of Lot's other daughter. Peretz is born from Tamar, fathered by Yehudah, who did not know who she was at the time. All these women were widows, since even Lot's daughters had already been betrothed to men who died in the destruction of Sedom.

Yet from all these strange circumstances Mashiach came forth! It appears clear that G-d looked forward to the distant future, seeing that the kingdom of David will cease for a long period, and that Yerushalayim will itself be like a widow [as it is so called in the first verse of *Megillas Eichah*]. Eventually, the final great act of *yibum* will be accomplished when the Mashiach will redeem Yerushalayim and the holy temple, for Yehudah's family is experienced in this type of activity. May it occur soon. Note that in the laws of redeeming property, the Torah writes that it may be done by "his uncle or the son of his uncle," written in the Hebrew as דדו או בן דוד, and the *Baal HaTurim* notes that these letters spell out David and Ben-David.

Chapter 20

Examining the prophecy of Yaakov to Yehudah (Bereishis 49:10), "Until Shiloh comes" — to prove that the Torah foresaw what would occur at Shiloh and in Shechem. – It saw Achiyah HaShiloni, who would crown Yeravam – and that Binyamin would join forces with Yehudah – that the boundary of Binyamin would reach to Shiloh – and that the seat of the Sanhedrin would be on both sides of Binyamin's boundary.

The volume *Zera Avraham* (in *Megillas Eichah)* records the following comment on the verse in Bereishis (49:10) "The staff shall not depart from Yehudah": "I found the following analysis in the name of the Rashba'm: The division of the kingdom into Yeravam's (Yisrael) and Rechavam's (Yehudah) occurred at Shechem (*Melachim I* 12:1). We find (*Shoftim* 21:19) that Shiloh was so close to Shechem that Rashi writes that the coronation of kings took place at Shiloh. Thus, in effect, Shiloh and Shechem are almost synonymous. Hence, Yaakov's vision was that the staff will remain in Yehudah's hands until the nation will gather at Shiloh and divide the kingdom into two, followed by "and unto him will be the obedience of the peoples," i.e., that nevertheless the primary kingdom will remain Yehudah's. I also found that others explain that the term "Shiloh" in this verse was a reference to Achiyah HaShiloni (from Shiloh) who informed Yeravam, in the name of G-d, that he was chosen as king of the ten tribes. This too fits very well in the text of this verse."

There is another way to understand the reference to Shiloh. Binyamin remained with Yehudah to form their kingdom. Yehudah's land was from the south up to north Yerushalayim. Binyamin stretched from that border up to (but not including) Shiloh, at which point Ephrayim's territory begins. We may now explain the text about Shiloh in a new way. The term for "staff" – *sheivet* – also means "tribe." Hence, there is one tribe (Binyamin) that will not depart from Yehudah, but will remain attached to him, until "one comes to Shiloh," where his province ends. Thus, Yaakov prophesies that there will be a time when Yehudah's kingdom will encompass territory only as far as Shiloh (a vision of the division of David's kingdom).

Going a step further with this verse, we read, "The tribe shall not depart from Yehudah, and the scepter from between his feet, until one comes to Shiloh." The "scepter" is understood by all commentators to refer to the Sanhedrin, for the literal meaning of *mechokek* is "law-giver." We find in the Talmud (*Zevachim* 118b) the statement that the *Shechinah* appeared in only four places in Eretz Yisrael, and all of them were in Binyamin's portion: Shiloh, Nov, Givon, and the holy temple in Yerushalayim. The gemara challenges this by showing that Shiloh was in Yosef's (Ephrayim) territory. The answer given is that Shiloh was at the border, with the

Shechinah in Binyamin's area and the Sanhedrin in Yosef's (during a period when it met there). So too, in the temple in Yerushalayim, the *Shechinah* hovered over Binyamin's section, while the Sanhedrin met in Yehudah's. Thus, the short phrase "the 'law-giver' from between his feet acquires an interesting meaning. We may imagine Binyamin's "feet" straddling over his entire territory from south to north, and the phrase states that the law-givers will be situated at both ends of his land up to his borders.

We may confidently argue that all these interpretations are correct, since this is what actually occurred in Jewish history. Explanations of the Torah are like sparks that fly from an anvil, so all are correct [as Chazal say "there are seventy facets to (everything in) the Torah"].

In summary, this one verse indicated that the Torah was looking ahead, through the vision of Yaakov, to coronations that would take place at Shiloh/Shechem – to Achiyah HaShiloni's part in declaring Yeravam as king of Yisrael – to Binyamin's attachment to Yehudah – to the borders of Binyamin's territory both south and north – to the seat of the Sanhedrin at both ends of Binyamin's province. Truly a divine document!

Chapter 21

Here we will bend an ear to hear what it was that "Yaakov heard" in the verse (35:22) about Reuven and Bilhah, and the significance of Migdal Eider. We will show that the Torah knew that Migdal Eider would be close to the eternal city of Yisrael, i.e., Yerushalayim, the seat of the kingdom. Although we showed this in an earlier chapter, here there are further proofs, and as we know, (Koheles 4:9) "two are better than one." Other matters will also be explained.

As Yaakov was returning home after his many years in Padan Aram, we read (35:21-22), "And Yisrael journeyed and he pitched his tent beyond Migdal Eider. It came to pass, as he dwelt in that land, that Reuven went and lay with Bilhah, his father's concubine; and Yisrael heard; and the sons of Yaakov were twelve."

Any logical person must be astounded at this description. What purpose is there in mentioning Migdal Eider, if this place remains totally unknown to the reader, as the holy Alshich asks?

However, I searched and found that this site is close to

Yerushalayim. The mishnah (*Shekalim* 7:4) rules that any animal found anywhere from Yerushalayim up to Migdal Eider, or a similar distance in any other direction, is presumed to belong to the temple. As Rashi explains that in such a short distance it may be a sanctified sacrificial animal that wandered away from the temple area. It is an inescapable conclusion that the Torah was hinting that Yaakov, who was "beyond" Migdal Eider, had arrived at Yerushalayim. Just as in his original journey to Aram he passed Yerushalayim, now on his return he passed there once again. Additionally, Rachel had just died near Bethlehem, which is close to Yerushalayim. The Targum Yonasan also realized this fact, and in this verse identified Migdal Eider as "the place from which the king Mashiach will reveal himself in the end of days," a concept directly based on a verse in Tanach (*Michah* 4:8).

Throughout the chumashim, Yerushalayim is never mentioned by name, but only hinted at by various clues. At the akedah, it was a mountain in the land of Moriah, which Avraham named "G-d will see." Moshe always referred to it as "the place that G-d will choose." The Rambam in his Guide to the Perplexed and other writers have given various reasons for this fact [the most common: that in dividing the land amongst the tribes, there should be no jealousy or controversy over who would receive that coveted area.]. In our verses, Yaakov "dwelt" there, and the Hebrew term is שכן, equal in gematria to שלב, a name use for Yerushalayim.

Once we acknowledge that Yaakov was at Yerushalayim, we can clarify several mysteries in this chapter: 1) Why mention that he dwelt there, after already

stating that he pitched his tent?
2) Why state that Yaakov heard, without adding that this had some kind of ramifications?
3) Why within that verse, use both names of Yisrael and Yaakov?

Before explaining all these items, we must introduce some ideas that point the way to recognizing that these verses announce the choice of Yerushalayim as the site for the throne of the kings of bnei Yisrael.
A) It is established that Yerushalayim is the eternal city of the Jewish kingdom now and forever.
B) Reuven was the logical choice to be king, as the firstborn. He lost this right for his actions with Bilhah (however we interpret that event is presently unimportant). This is precisely what Yaakov addressed to him (49:3-4) as he spoke to his sons at the end of his life.
C) The primary use of the name Yisrael (vs. Yaakov) is to indicate greatness and leadership, as the angel explained to Yaakov when he stated that he should be known as Yisrael. The *Or HaChayim*, at the beginning of *Parashas VaYechi* demonstrates that the name Yaakov is used for events that reflect sorrow and anguish. Therefore, the statement here that *Yaakov* had twelve sons points to the sad action of Reuven with Bilhah
But he does not explain the use of Yisrael at the beginning of that verse! I will do so with G-d's help.

When Yaakov arrived at that holy spot, and the tragedy of Reuven occurred, he realized then that Reuven cannot possibly be king. This is the deeper meaning of "Yisrael heard," i.e. he *understood*. The name Yisrael is used here, for it was a matter that involved the future of his descendants and their kingdom.. This is why the verse emphasized that Yisrael "dwelt in that land" for that sanctified location was crucial to understand why Reuven lost his right to the kingdom. (Recall the earlier discussion in chapter 5.)

The concluding statement that Yaakov had twelve sons appears to hint that, if not for the ugly deed of Reuven, there might have been more sons born to Yaakov, who now separated from his wives and ceased thinking of adding to his offspring. This is probably the meaning of his words to Reuven (49:4), "you defiled he who rose upon my bed," i.e., you defiled me, your father, who rose upon his bed for the mitzvah of procreation, but now the bed itself was defiled, and there would be no further tribes from Yaakov.(14) We must recall that only a short while before, G-d had said to Yaakov (35:11) that "a company of nations will be from you." Yaakov may have hoped that this meant more sons. Only now, he realized that this was not so, and later told Yosef that his two sons will become two tribes. As this indeed came to pass, we may be certain that this was G-d's intention. Thus, if not for the incident of Reuven, there may well have been another tribe descending from Yaakov. The verse therefore concludes that Yaakov had (only) twelve sons. It then proceeds to list them. Yet, the statement about the number of twelve is attached to the verse about Reuven's ugly deed, but with a space separating the two phrases. The Torah shows that the Reuven's action is connected to the number of twelve, which might otherwise have expanded to thirteen or more. At the same time, the phrase about the number continues on with the list of names. It therefore can be seen as pointing both backward and forward.

The Hebrew phrase for "he pitched his tent" spells "his tent" as אהלה, usually meaning "her tent." In two earlier such spellings in this chumash (9:21 and 12:8), Chazal explained this female form in special ways. Here, the midrash is silent. We may offer a fine explanation. Having been told just before by G-d (35:11), "Increase and multiply; a nation and a company of nations will be from you," Yaakov concluded that, now that he was at the holy site of Yerushalayim, where the future kingdom of Israel will be situated, he would merit having another son born in the holy land. So he pitched *her tent*, i.e., he wished to have a child from Bilhah. When Reuven interfered with his wishes in an ugly way, he realized that this was not to be, just as he realized that Reuven was now disqualified to be the tribe that will produce kings.

The way that we have uncovered the deeper meaning of so many terms in this chapter shows once again the mastery of expression that only G-d Himself could use in giving us His holy Torah.

Chapter 22

In this chapter we will find the hidden references that demonstrate the Torah's vision that the conquest of Eretz Yisrael culminating in the building of the first temple would take 440 years, and that 410 years later the temple would be destroyed.

In *Chumash Shemos* (6:2-3) G-d mentions His appearances to our forefathers and states that He established ....His covenant "to give them Eretz Canaan, the land of their pilgrimages *that they dwelled in.*" The final phrase appears totally extraneous for it adds nothing to the concept. (We might also ask about "to give them...," since in fact they never themselves actually received Canaan. Later we will see how Chazal reacted to this question.) However, we can show that that final phrase is very meaningful and hints at great matters of the future.

G-d promised the land of the seven Canaanite nations to His people, but it was His intention that this conquest would stretch over several centuries until the advent of Shlomo's kingdom and the building of the first temple. Yehoshua's primary conquest was for five of the tribes, and during the period of the judges continuing to Shlomo's time, small conquests continued until it was completed This is clearly stated in Tanach (*Melachim I*

9:20-21), "All the remaining people of the Emori, the Chiti, the Prizzi, the Chivi, and the Yevusi..../ Their children who remained in the land...whom bnei Yisrael were unable to destroy – Shlomo imposed upon them a tribute of bondservants....." Clearly, these people were now subjugated by Shlomo, but not before, and had to accept upon themselves the seven Noahide commandments. They numbered a little over 150,000 (*Divrei HaYamim II* 2:16), and were put to work on building the *Beis haMikdash* in Yerushalayim. Since this was done in the early years of Shlomo's reign, their subjugation occurred near the start of his reign.

Now note how many of the Torah's promises come to fruition at one time period. The destruction, and subjugation of the remnants, of the Canaanite tribes – the expansion of the borders of the land, from (*Melachim I* 5:1) "the river at the land of the Plishtim to the border of Egypt," exactly the terms used in G-d's promise in *Chumash Shemos* (23:31) – preceded by the phrase (23:30) "until you increase...," and accomplished in Shlomo's rule, as described there (*Melachim I* 4:20), "...many like the sand by the sea in multitude...." – (*Shemos* 25:8) "they shall build me a sanctuary and I will reside in their midst," – all these come together at the start of Shlomo's reign. R. Abraham Ibn Ezra also noted that the great increase of the people would coincide with the final conquest of the Canaanite tribes.

Actually it was clearly indicated in the Torah itself, that the elimination of those tribes and the building of the Beis HaMikdash would occur at the same time. Moshe states (*Devarim* 12:10), "You will cross the Jordan...and [when]

He gives you rest from all your enemies so that you will dwell in security / It shall come to pass, [to] the place that G-d will choose to cause His name to dwell there you will bring all that I command you, your sacrifices...." The term "security" (בטח) is indeed used to describe the serenity in Shlomo's days in *Melachim I* (5:5), "And Yehudah and Yisrael dwelt in security (*lavetach*) each man under his vine...and his fig tree...all the days of Shlomo."

We know that the first temple stood 410 years until its destruction, as mentioned many times in the Talmud, an account which I clarified and proved elsewhere. Now observe the amazing fact that this number is the number of years our forefathers lived in Eretz Yisrael, cumulatively. The account in *Bereishis* shows that Avraham settled in Yisrael at age seventy five (12:4), lived there for *one hundred years*, and died at age one hundred and seventy five (25:7). (As Chazal state, Avraham's trip down to Egypt lasted only about two months). Yitzchak never left the land, and died at the age of *one hundred eighty* (35:28). Yaakov lives his final seventeen years in Egypt, dying at the age of one hundred forty seven. Subtracting those last years, we can count his life in Eretz Yisrael as *one hundred and thirty*. Since his years at the home of Lavan were viewed as temporary, for he always planned on returning home, it is very reasonable to subtract them from this account. Thus, 100+180+130 = 410. While many of these years found two, or even all three, forefathers in the land simultaneously, this is no detraction, for each is worthy by himself to count his years separately, for by the righteousness and merit of each we earned entitlement to live in our land in later generations. This method of accumulating years of our forefathers is actually used in the *Talmud Yerushalmi* (*Berachos* ch.1).

As for the fourteen years that Yaakov spent at Yeshivas Shem V'Eiver as Chazal tell us, this yeshivah was surely in Eretz Yisrael, for our tradition says that Malki-Tzedek is Shem, who ruled at the ancient site of Yerushalayim.

If the reader objects and wishes to subtract the twenty-two years that Yaakov spent away from home building his family, we could point out that this matches the twenty-years of King Menashe's sinful reign in which he brought idolatry into the holy temple itself, and was the final cause of its destruction (see *Sanhedrin* 103a). Additionally, it may be argued that the 410 years in Eretz Yisrael that the temple stood may indeed be reckoned as 388! The first step in the destruction actually began with the exile of King Yehoachaz (with his significant entourage) to Egypt. After that, in the reigns of Yehoyakim (11 years) and Tzidkiyahu (11 years), conditions kept building towards the destruction. (The three months of King Yehoyachin's rule are insignificant.) These twenty two years of building turmoil match the twenty-two years of Yaakov's difficult years in Aram. The Rava'd, in his Seider HaKabbalah also speaks of twenty-one years of the beginning of the exile until the *churban*. Since there is some overlapping, the difference of one year is not meaningful. It is therefore clear that the years of the first temple match well with the years that our forefathers spent in the holy land, giving their children merit year for year. Note also that Yaakov's stay at Sukos during his return to Canaan is immaterial, since it is part of Gad's territory east of the Jordan (*Yehoshua* 13:27) and therefore part of our land. In the volume *Parashas Derachim* (by the author of the *Mishneh LeMelech*, R. Yehudah Rozanes), in his eighth *drashah*, he strongly defends the thesis that the territory of Sichon and Og is considered part of the land of the seven

Canaanite nations.

In fact it is logical that the years our forefathers spent in the holy land should afford equal time to their descendants particularly during the period of the holy temple. The *avos* made their physical bodies into an abode for the *Shechinah*, as we find in Chumash *Shemos* (25:8), "Let them make for Me a sanctuary, and I will dwell in *their midst*." [Chazal interpret this to mean that we should make ourselves into a sanctuary for G-d to dwell within us.] The very fact that the first temple served for the same number of years that the *avos* were in the land shows that this was a measure for measure reward granted to their descendants, especially since they won the land primarily through the great merit of their *avos*, as the Torah states so many times. Thus, their residence in the land is another of their "actions" which cast ramifications for their children centuries later. We exclude the period of the second temple during which 1) we were under the rule of the Romans most of the time, and 2) so many Jews did not return from their exile.

This explains why the Torah informed us that Avraham was 75 years old when he moved to Eretz Yisrael, so that we could then compute the number of 410 for the *avos* as was done above. G-d wanted us to see how He measures the years and grants His rewards with appropriate precision. While Chazal state that Avraham made his first visit to the land at age 70, all agree that his real permanent move to Eretz Yisrael was at age 75, as the Torah states clearly (12:4).

With this background, we may offer a response to a historical puzzle. It appears odd that it took 430 years to complete the conquest of all the Canaanite people to begin the count of 410 years for the existence of the temple. Why did G-d declare to Moshe that this conquest would take so long while the Jewish people would gradually increase in number? Could He not have allowed us to increase speedily as He did in Egypt and greatly reduce the time for the conquest of the land? However, having foreseen that the temple would have a span of only 410 years to match the years of our *avos*, He wanted in His loving way to grant us additional centuries in the holy land. Thus, our increase proceeded naturally and the conquest of the Canaanites stretched out for four centuries, allowing us to be in the land for over eight centuries before the temple was destroyed. This also explains why He did not instruct any of the judges to build the temple sooner, which would have started the count of 410 years so much earlier.

We now understand in a new dimension the message G-d gave to Yitzchak (26:2-4), "Do not go down to Egypt..../ Sojourn in this land... for I will give to you and to your seed all of these lands, and I will perform the oath that I swore to your father Avraham. And I will multiply your seed like the stars of heaven and I will give all these lands to your seed, and all the nations of the earth will be blessed in your seed." There are many questions to ponder here. Even granting all the promises in these verses, why do they require that Yitzchak not go down even temporarily to Egypt? Why add "to you and...," since Yitzchak was never given all these territories? Why insert the oath to Avraham, since G-d is now making promises to Yitzchak? Why insert a promise about multiplying his seed, and then repeating the promise to give these lands to them? Why first state "to you and your seed," but omit "to you" in the repetition? Let us suggest some answers:

Our first possession of the land was given solely by the merit of our *avos* [and calculated by the years they spent there]. This is stated by Moshe (*Devarim* 9:5), "Not through your righteousness... are you coming to possess their land, but for the wickedness of these nations...and that *He may perform the pledge that G-d swore to your fathers*, to Avraham, to Yitzchak, and to Yaakov." Thus, G-d gave them the land (legally by His decree, even if they did not physically possess it) so that they could transfer it to their children. This is the deeper meaning of G-d's command to Yitzchak to remain in Yisrael, so as to transfer it to his descendants without subtracting time for any stay in Egypt. Similarly, this is what He meant when He said to Avraham and Yaakov, "I will give it to you" (i.e., legally, to transfer to your children). However, lest we suggest that the 410 years would begin from the moment the tribes stepped into the holy land, G-d added, " I will perform the oath that I swore to Avraham," i.e., the entire oath that included the full boundaries of the land and the names of the nations that will be driven out, and "I will multiply your seed like the stars of heaven,"(which will take several centuries, as explained above). Only then, after 440 years, will come the fruition of "I will give to your seed all these lands," and King Solomon will build the temple, increasing the settlement of Eretz Yisrael for another 410 years. With this analysis we have answered all of the five questions raised above.

This is surely Moshe's intention when he states at the beginning of Chumash *Devarim* (1:7-8), "Turn about and... go to the mountain of the Emorites... and by the sea side to the land of the Canaani and the Lebanon unto the great river the Euphrates River. See, I have set the land before you; come and possess the land that G-d swore to your fathers... to give to them and their children after them." Note that the full boundaries are spelled out first. After they are attained, the verse speaks of possessing the land sworn to the fathers, for now the count of 410 years begins. The names of Avraham, Yitzchak, and Yaakov are enumerated for the number of 410 is determined by their years in Eretz Yisrael, as explained.

The last verse of the second chapter of the Shma (*Devarim*, 11:21) states, "So that your days and the days of your children shall be multiplied upon the land that G-d swore to *your fathers to give them*, , as the days of heaven upon the earth." Following the verses of that chapter that call upon His people to carefully observe the mitzvos, study the Torah, etc., this verse states that "your days" (which have been fixed at 410 years beginning from the erection of the temple) may be increased to many more, if we do as we are commanded. Since the 410 years are given to (by the merit of) *them*, the way to add to them is in the hands of their children. The potential addition of days would be unlimited, like the days of the heaven upon earth, i.e., forever. (The statement in *Sanhedrin (*90b) that the phrase "to give to them" implied the concept of *techias hameisim*[i.e., that the *avos* would be resurrected and physically take possession of the land] does not conflict with all we have written about this expression, for it is an additional interpretation based on the repetition of this phrase so many times in the Torah (*Shemos* 6:4 – *Devarim* 1:8 – *Devarim* 11:9, 11:21).

See, now, how perfect is the expression quoted much earlier (*Shemos* 6:4), "the land of their pilgrimages *that they dwelt in.*" This added phrase points directly to the 410 years that the *avos* lived in Eretz Yisrael, equal to the time the first temple stood. Therefore the previous verse (6:3) listed all their names, rather than the cumulative word ("the fathers") used many other times in the Torah, for the count of years will include separately all their individual years of habitation, as noted earlier. The phrase that follows their names (v.8), "And I will give it to you as a heritage/inheritance..." shows that the land is seen as inherited from our *avos,* as explained above in this chapter.

From all the evidence presented here, it should be crystal clear that the Torah foresaw the period of 410 years during which the first temple would stand, for G-d stands above time, and shows us that the Torah is His word, so that we should honor it and observe all the commandments. In chapters 65, 66, and 68, we will elaborate further on these topics and demonstrate that the sum of 440 and 410 (850) years, from the entry to the land until the destruction of the temple, was also foreseen in the Torah.

Once G-d promised a period of 410 years as minimum for the period of the first temple, this figure could not be diminished even if the people were sinful. It was guaranteed to our *Avos*! We must understand that when the Torah warned (*Devarim* 11:17) that if we are undeserving we will be *"driven out speedily from the good land,"* it meant immediately after the 410 minimum number of guaranteed years. In fact the Talmud (*Gittin* 88b) states that "speedily" in G-d's eyes means within no more than 852 years.

We must, however, answer the objection that some might raise, that the simple reading of being driven out speedily could mean as soon as we abandoned the Torah, even in a short time period. This is untenable. Moshe himself foresaw the future, stating (*Devarim* 31:29), "For I know that after my death you will corrupt yourselves and turn from the path that I commanded you...." As I will show later, it took only 30 years for the people to begin practicing idolatry in Eretz Yisrael. He had also stated that they would be driven out speedily. How could he then have stated also that the Canaanites would be expelled gradually and the people would increase slowly. This could surely not mean within thirty years! The only satisfactory explanation is that "speedily" means after the centuries foreseen by G-d, as the Talmud explained perfectly.

The reader might still object by perhaps claiming that we know that G-d can reverse an evil decree, hence "speedily" is literal, but G-d recanted and was patient for centuries. This is also a foolish suggestion. G-d reverses an evil decree in two situations:
1) A sincere repentance is undertaken [as with Nineveh, in the days of the prophet Yonah].
2) As the decree is made, G-d leaves open the ready option of withdrawing it, as when He states to Moshe (*Shemos* 32:10), "And now, leave Me alone... and I will consume them......." It would be absurd for G-d to state that He would speedily destroy them if they turned to idolatry, and then to reverse the decree even when they did not desist from their wicked ways, for He stands above time and foresees the future. In fact, even Moshe, speaking of their turning to idolatry, stated (*Devarim* 31:29) that evil results would occur to them "*in the end of*

days." Clearly, this expression contradicts the term "speedily"! We must agree with Chazal that they are one and the same, for "speedily" indeed means, to G-d, a period of no more than 852 years!

We have demonstrated in this chapter that G-d set a definite date for the occupancy of the Jewish people until the *churban*, and for Him "speedily" is not what it is for us. Clearly, the number of 410 years was derived from the tenancy of our *avos* in the land for 410 years. Note an amazing fact. The number 410 has a third application. The turn to idolatry did not begin until two years after Yehoshua's death, when all the elders of his period passed away. Yehoshua lived twenty-eight years in Eretz Yisrael. Thus, of the 440 years of residence that culminated with the building of the temple, 410 years were the years of decline to idolatry. (In fact, the *Baal HaTurim* found a novel hint about this figure in Moshe's words (*Devarim* 31:27), "While I am still alive with you, you have rebelled against G-d, certainly after my death." "Certainly" is the translation of *"af kee,"* written in Hebrew as אף כי. Since *kee* equals 30 in gematria, he translates, hermeneutically, "even thirty years after my death!") Thus, the 410-year period of the gradual expulsion of the Canaanite people simultaneous with the spiritual decline of the people, equals the years that the temple stood.

We find this fact expressed centuries before in the Torah (*Devarim* 8:19-20). It states, "And...if you forget your G-d, and go after other gods...I warn you that you will be destroyed. *Like the nations* that G-d will destroy before you, *so will you be destroyed* [repeated!] as a result of not listening to the voice of your G-d." The hidden message is that just like the nations" will be eliminated over a 410-

year period, so too, will you be driven out of the land after only 410 years of establishing the Holy Temple and beginning a period of serenity and prosperity under Shlomo. This is the reason for repeating, and the emphasis of, "*so* will you be destroyed", i.e., equal even to the number 410. This idea of equivalence may also be read into the text elsewhere, e.g., (*VaYikra* 18:28 – and *BeMidbar* 33:56).

It is evident that the Torah had foreseen the first thirty years in Eretz Yisrael, after which would begin the 410 years of idol worship, in conjunction with the gradual expulsion of the Canaanite nations, followed by the 410 years of the temple era, earned for us by our *avos*, as explained earlier. The warning that we would be expelled quickly (after 850 years) was based on G-d's time calendar, much different than ours. These facts all demonstrate that the author of the Torah could only be the Creator Himself, and none other..

Part II: In His Hands Are the Investigations of the Earth

Chapter 23

Dear reader, these things that I write here are actually almost elementary, and with little analysis you can understand them as fundamental. But the difference between not examining them and after examining them is like the difference that occurred with the Jewish nation at Mt. Carmel, before vs. after Eliyahu brought down that heavenly fire to consume his sacrifice. Before that miracle, the people's hearts were confused, but moments later they were shouting "Havaya He is G-d." So too, throughout the Torah there are great flames of truth hidden in the text, but once revealed all can see that awesome fire. Perhaps your mind was invaded with foolish thoughts and incorrect ideas about the Torah, but once you read these analyses you will see so clearly that the spirit of G-d fills every page of our holy Torah. You will find yourself calling out "Havaya is G-d." Please read these chapters carefully with concentration, for I have drawn these waters from the fountain of deep thought to uncover the living waters and countless secrets hidden therein.

Our major goal in the coming chapters is to uncover deeper meanings in the Torah to reveal great allusions to events that would occur in (primarily) the books of

Yehoshua, Shoftim, Shmuel, Melachim, and Divrei HaYamim, centuries after we received the Torah. You might ask, perhaps there are other/better meanings to be read into these verses, and they are the true meanings. Let me respond with a parable:

Pharaoh had his dreams of seven cows and seven stalks, etc., which his interpreters explained as referring to daughters who would be born and die. Let us imagine that Yosef never appeared to offer his interpretation. All Egypt would have waited to see if the king's people were correct or not. However, once Yosef explained the dream and it occurred exactly as he said, no fool would have stated that they should wait to see if he would have seven daughters! So too, once the butler and baker experienced what Yosef predicted for them, nobody would have offered any other interpretation, for the facts spoke for themselves. Similarly, when we offer readings into the Torah's verses or expressions, and find significance in extra words, unusual or repeated phrases, etc., and discover logical explanations for them which actually took place in Tanach years or centuries later, there is no logic to ignore them and look for other interpretations. They bear the stamp of truth. If you will proceed with this concept in mind, you will indeed find amazing and countless prophecies hidden in the Torah awaiting you.

Chapter 24

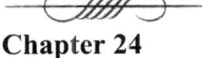

Here we will show that the Torah foresaw that the Girgashi nation will leave the land without a fight (as indeed happened), and that the Chivi (the Givonim) would make peace with us, while the Yevusi would be the last to be conquered. Also, that only five of the Canaanite peoples would have land that is "flowing with milk and honey." The Torah also offers clues that Yehoshua: a) would not conquer territories for five of the tribes; b) would battle 31 kings, fighting ten wars; c) would lead the people for twenty-eight years; and d) that his battles would extend for a total of seven years.

There is evidence in the text that the Girgashi would never battle the Jewish people. The Torah lists Girgashi as one of the seven Canaanite nations (*Devarim* 7:1) to be eliminated from the land. However they are omitted in lists of only six nations in many places (*Shemos* 3:8 – 3:17 – 33:2 – 34:11 – *Devarim* 20:17).

As Rashi notes, it is clear that the Girgashi fled to avoid battle. Surely this is why in the listing which did include them, the Torah spoke of "uprooting them" [ונשל], a term which could also imply without a battle. In all the lists, the Chivi and the Yevusi are always last, while the other four change positions. This is the clue that they will indeed be the last to be conquered. For part of the Chivi was identified as the "Givonim" (*Yehoshua* 11:19), who tricked Yehoshua into making peace with them. David finally conquered the Yevusi as described later (*Divrei HaYamim I* ch.16). (15) The commentators also explain that only three of the seven were driven out by swarms of hornets, and this is why the text only mentions (*Shemos* 23:28) the Chivi, Canaani, and Chiti as victims of the hornets. (These Chivi were, of course, not the Givonim, but the other members of this nation. The Ramban writes that only five of these nations had land that was truly "flowing with milk and honey," and therefore only those five are mentioned (*Shemos* 13:5) when the Torah promises that we will come to this blessed land, omitting the Prizi and Girgashi. (16)

The expression "flowing with milk and honey" is found sixteen times in the Chumashim, hinting at the area of 16 square parsa that the *Baal HaTurim* testifies about, claiming that is the dimension of the area that is uniquely blessed. He also notes several other interesting mathematical facts:

1) When Moshe strove to convince his father-in-law to join him and enter Eretz Yisrael, he used the term "good" five times in various grammatical forms (*BeMidbar* 11:29-32). In time Yisro's descendants received the city of Yericho. The five terms for goodness add up in gematria to 236, which is also equal to ביריחו.

2) Also, while G-d spoke to Moshe (*Devarim* 11:24) about "every place [המקום] where the soles of your feet shall tread will be yours," in the repetition of this precise promise to Yehoshua (*Yehoshua* 1:3), the word "place" is written מקום, with the *hei* omitted. Since this letter equals five, it hints that Yehoshua will fail to distribute territory to five of the twelve tribes..

3) When G-d promises Yitzchak (*Bereishis* 26:3) that He

Marvels of Our Blessed G-d's Torah

will give his children "all these lands," the term for "these" is the unusual האל. Using the gematria of the final two letters, this could be rendered as "the 31," representing the thirty-one kings that Yehoshua conquered. 4) Moshe's appeal that G-d should find a proper replacement for him (*BeMidbar* 27:16-17) was expressed in twenty-eight words. Yehoshua was appointed, and led the people for twenty-eight years. 5) In *Shemos* 13:5 and 13:11, Moshe speaks of G-d bringing us to the land that He swore to give us. In the first reference "He will bring you" is written יביאך, but in the second repeated phrase it is written יבאך, with a *yud* missing. This hints (since *yud* is equal to ten) that in our first arrival Yehoshua will fight ten wars, but in our final arrival with the mashiach, there will be no wars.(17) Perhaps this is an additional reason that G-d added a *yud* to Yehoshua's name!

By noting all these distinctions and differences, spelling variations and gematrios, in the Torah itself, confirmed in later history, we have surely found clear evidence that only G-d Himself had to be the author of our holy Torah.

Chapter 25

We will explore the Torah to find a reference to Yehoshua stopping the sun and moon. Also, clues to the kings who will descend from Yosef, (and the reason Yehoshua is called naar (a boy) in the Torah.)

We know that Yehoshua caused the sun and moon to halt (*Yehoshua* 10:12). Afterward, the verse states, "Behold it is written in the Book of Yashar." The commentators agree that this is a term for the Torah and they look for a clue for this great event. Rashi says it lies in the verse (*Bereishis* 48:19), "And his [Ephrayim's] seed will be a multitude of nations." As Rashi writes, "When? On the day that the sun stopped for Yehoshua, the entire world filled with the name of Yehoshua." Some others have found it in Chumash Shemos (34:10) when G-d says to Moshe, "Before all your people I will do marvels that were not created in all the earth or in any nation..." These verses, however, do not refer directly to the sun or the moon, and are rather vague.

I believe that the hint is in the dream of Yosef (*Bereishis* 37:9), "Behold, the sun and the moon and eleven stars bow to me." Rachel had already died, so some commentators claim the moon represented Bilhah. Ramban rejects this idea, convinced that she had died before their descent to Egypt, and feels that the moon is the family in general. It seems a bit difficult to presume that the moon itself symbolizes an entire family. (It also seems farfetched to use the argument of Chazal in various places: "Every dream has some meaningless material," for this dream was a powerful vision from G-d. I suggest that this dream [in addition to the obvious meaning] represents Yehoshua, descended from Yosef, becoming master over the sun and moon, which bow to him on the day of his great victory, and do his bidding. They were created for the sake of man, and the righteous rule over them by the power of their speech. Bowing down represents subjugation to another's will. Thus, Yosef foresees the sun and the moon bowing to the will of his descendant. (However, the stars symbolize a vision of the more immediate future of all eleven sons bowing to Yosef in Egypt.) I found that in the *Midrash Talpiyos*, the *Kli Yakar* is quoted as coming to the same analysis.

Interestingly, Ephrayim is called (*Bereishis* 48:19), "the smaller brother," who will become greater than Menashe, and his descendant Yehoshua stopped both the "great" and "small" lights (*Bereishis* 1:16). I also am convinced that Yosef's first dream, in which he pictured his sheaf as "rising, and also standing upright," symbolized his eventual rise to kingship in Jewish history, for otherwise the added "standing upright' would be extraneous. Eventually, eleven kings arose over the kingdom of Yisrael in history. Also, Mashiach Ben Yosef may be part of this vision.

[The discussion about Yehoshua being called a *naar* (boy)

is exceptionally mystic and kabbalistic. It proposes that the angel who led Yehoshua in battles, and the one who confronted him at Yericho, are also called *naar,* based on the writings of HaRav Moshe Alshich in his volume *Maros Hatzov-os.* This entire paragraph, page 105, is unfortunately beyond me. If I rendered it literally, I doubt if more than one in a thousand readers could make sense out of it.]

Chapter 26

Here we will show how the Torah, G-d alone, built entire edifices of Jewish law for the generations living in Eretz Yisrael years later. Moshe also recorded laws that were only applicable centuries later, after the conquest of the entire land, reflecting G-d-given prophecies for later centuries.

How clearly we can see that Moshe is true and the Torah is true. For most of the mitzvos given to us in the desert by Moshe depend on our arrival into the land – e.g., building the temple, bringing sacrifices, the *shemittah* years and the *yovel,* and all agricultural laws. Would any human author write an entire volume of laws and detailed statutes for a country which he only hoped to possess some day in the future? Only in a book dictated by G-d to Moshe do we find the fundamental foundations for a society of law and order, of morality and ethics, presented before the wicked inhabitants of that land were spewed out to make way for a holy nation. This book was given to a people who had sinned grievously, and were condemned to forty years in the desert, already presuming that they would conquer the land, settle it, and require ethical and spiritual laws to guide their society. No human author, no matter how wise, would have presented such a detailed volume without a divine source. We must note, of course, that all these laws became practical and were put into practice in the later years exactly as described in the Torah. Since the Torah is G-d-given, this is not astonishing at all.

Actually, the entry into the land and its conquest was entirely a supernatural phenomenon. As the Torah states (*Devarim* 9:1-3), "Hear o Israel, you are crossing over...to possess nations greater and mightier than you; great cities and fortified up to the heavens. A people great and tall, sons of the *anakim*... and you know and you have heard [say] "Who can stand before the sons of *Anak?*" Know this day that your G-d crosses over before you, a consuming flame, ... He will destroy them...and you will drive them out and destroy them quickly as G-d has said to you." I find the description of the volume *Torah Min HaShamayim* very precious, and will quote from it, with my parenthetic comments added: The flow of these verses is clear to all who understand well. They call upon the people to understand that these are the words of G-d (for "hear" has the meaning of understanding, as in "Hear O Israel, Havayah our G-d, Havayah is one"), you are crossing the Jordan (I think that this also calls for special understanding, for it will be by amazing miracles so that you will see this crossing as a sign that you will succeed in the conquest.) Indeed, just preceding the crossing of the river, Yehoshua proclaimed (*Yehoshua* 3:10), "With this [miraculous crossing] you will know that the living G-d is with you and He will drive out the Canaani and the Chivi, etc.") In three ways nature was bypassed: 1) "You will possess nations greater and mightier than you (both in number and in power) – 2) "to conquer great cities, fortified up to the heavens (I believe that the expression "to the heavens" implies that they are unconquerable by natural means, as we find in the conquest of Yericho, which was accomplished by supernatural forces (*Yehoshua* ch.6) – 3) A people great and tall, the sons of the *anakim* (I think that the term "*ram*" (tall) implies beyond human conception, heights that engender total fearlessness of any power).

"You know" (refers to Yehoshua and Calev) and "you have heard" (all others who did not see the giants) "who can stand before the sons of *Anak*?" "Know this day" – i.e., I am telling you on this day, long before it happens, that your G-d will cross before you, (a) consuming flame, (I believe that the best way to explain this phrase is that G-d consumes any flame, not that He is viewed as a flame that consumes. I.e., even if the enemy seems to be powerful like a mighty flame, G-d will "eat" them.) *He* will annihilate and vanquish them before you (not by your sword), and you will destroy them quickly as He spoke to you. (Here, Moshe is able to forecast mighty actions, even the destruction of the sons of the *anak*, that will occur well after his passing. Clearly these promises were guaranteed by G-d, and therefore these conquests of great fortified cities occurred as promised. This is a further demonstration of the absolute truth of the Torah, the word of G-d, whose words cannot be overturned.

I believe we may also find a similar foreknowledge of our future abandonment of G-d in Chumash *Devarim*, (ch. 30). Moshe declares that we have a choice of life or death (v.15). In v. 16, he presents the positive choice of loving G-d and observing all the mitzvos with the reward of our being blessed in the land with long life and large families, etc. Here, the positive choice and the reward are found in one verse. Not so with the negative situation. V. 17 describes our abandonment of G-d and worship of other gods. V. 18 begins with a seemingly extraneous phrase, "I tell you today," and depicts our destruction and expulsion from the land. Why could this not have been placed in one verse?

I believe that v.18 is not the conclusion that follows v. 17. The consequences of not following G-d are left to our imagination and logic. This is similar to G-d's pronouncement in *Bereishis* (4:15), "Therefore, whoever kills Kayin," and does not spell out the consequences, but proceeds to set the time for the punishment that Kayin will receive (as Rashi explains there.) Having pictured both choices, v.18 then offers a vision of what will eventually occur. "I tell you today" (that I see in the future) that you will indeed make the wrong choice and will be driven out of the land that you are crossing over to inherit. Thus, here too, the Torah foresees the eventual spiritual decline of the people some centuries later, a fact that only G-d in heaven can foresee and warn us about.(18)

Here are some further details. When G-d stated that we would drive out the seven nations a little at a time (*Shemos* 23:30) until we have increased and taken over all the land from the Sea of Reeds to... "the river" [Jordan], history shows that this took 480 years. As noted before, Yehoshua only settled five tribes, and many territories remained unconquered (*Yehoshua* 13:1-6).The conquest continued throughout the period of the judges (Shoftim) and of King David until we find (*Melachim I* 20-21) that Shlomo subjugated the last remnants into servitude, at the time he completed the building of the Beis HaMikdash. The text informs us (*ibid,* 6:1) that it was built 480 after the exodus. This can be compared to a king who informs a beloved servant that he intends to give him 10,000 silver ingots over a period of time. Over a period of ten years, he continues giving him silver until the sum is completed as promised. Now, this servant understands that it was the king's intention to take ten years until his promise was fulfilled. So too, we understand that when G-d said we would acquire the land "a little at a time," he meant over a 480-year span. This included the promise of our great increase, as we find indeed that we had multiplied (*ibid,* 4:20) "like the sand at the seashore." Shlomo ruled the entire expanse of Eretz Yisrael from the borders of Egypt. Hence the Torah's promises were fulfilled almost five centuries later. Only G-d could have recorded such promises, for only He can fulfill them to the letter. So too, all the laws of the Kohanim and numerous other mitzvos were given centuries before they were actually practiced. No human being could have conceived and recorded all these matters long before they actually occurred, for a human writer could hardly be certain that all these mighty nations would actually fall into our hands. How can any skeptic believe that this Torah was not given to us by the Creator who stands above time and foresees both our ascent and our downfall in the future clearly?

We will detail in later chapters how the Torah marked off the boundaries of the land generally, and specifically for various tribes and even for individuals, exactly how it eventually occurred. This would have been an absolute impossibility for any person to even attempt, let alone to do it correctly.

Chapter 27

This chapter will offer extensive reviews of the military campaigns of Yehoshua, and how many details were already revealed in the Torah in advance. One word in chumash ("quickly") in the verse (Devarim 9:3) "You will drive them out and destroy them quickly," is a key term to explain many aspects of this subject. The Torah's foreknowledge includes: 1)the conquest of Yericho and Aay; 2) the victory over many of the Canaanite nations soon after that period; 3) the manner of that victory, that they will come forward to confront our army, rather than our attacking individual cities separately, and also the mass confusion that will overtake them; 4) that their kings will fall into our hands; 5) that these kings will be hiding out in caves afraid to exit even when our army will be elsewhere in battle; 6) the incident of Achan taking from the doomed objects ("cherem"); 7)the list of objects that he took; 8) the acceptance of the Givonim to join our people; 9) the two gatherings of Canaanite nations quickly after the Givonim event; 10) which led to our army conquering large cities; 11) that the conquest would continue gradually until the era of Shlomo when our land would stretch from the Sea of Reeds to the east end of

Eretz Yisrael.

There is an apparent contradiction in the Torah. In the paragraph above, we are promised to complete the conquest "quickly". However, elsewhere (*Shemos* 23 30 and *Devarim* 7:22), we are informed that it must take place gradually ("*you cannot destroy them quickly*"), lest wild animals overrun the land. I have not seen any commentators explaining this puzzle. However, if we carefully note how the conquest proceeded we can explain these verses very well. There were two stages in the period of conquest. The first was the speedy subjugation of five nations led by Yehoshua, and the second stage was *the completion* of the conquest of all seven after his death, which proceeded slowly for four centuries.

In fact, Yehoshua's campaigns are described (*Yehoshua* 10: 42) as a conquest that took place "at one time." This stage was called "quickly." Where the Torah speaks of gradual conquest, it adds the full boundaries of the land. As explained earlier, this was accomplished in Shlomo's time, after centuries of battles, following Yehoshua's demise. As the verse reads (*Shoftim* 2:23), "G-d left these nations without driving them out quickly, and did not deliver them into Yehoshua's hand."

Now, in order to see all the hidden elements that lie in the expression "you will destroy them *quickly,*" we must examine at length this topic to find marvels of the Torah never revealed before. You will be filled with awe before the Author of the Torah as you find revealed secrets hidden in the texts.

A) The Battle Campaign at Aay

We read (*Yehoshua* ch.8) about the battle for Aay in exceptionally full detail. [They had lost their first battle with Aay because Achan had taken from the forbidden spoils of Yericho. Now, after his execution, G-d promised them a great victory.] He sent 30,000 soldiers at night to lie in ambush west of Aay, between Beis-el and Aay. In the morning, Yehoshua led the people north of Aay, where a steep valley separated them from the city. Then, he sent five thousand men to be in front of the large army lying in ambush, placing them between Beis-el and Aay. All the men of Aay came out in attack in the morning, presuming they would route the small battalion of five thousand as they had done in the first battle. The Jewish army retreated with the men of Aay in pursuit. Once they were drawn away from town, on a signal from Yehoshua (an uplifted spear) the 30,000 men arose from their hiding place, and entered the city unopposed, destroying and burning it down entirely. When the men of Aay looked back at their burning city, they realized too late that they were caught in a squeeze from both sides, and they were wiped out to the last man.

Close examination of the text shows that there are many problems in this account:
a) In describing his strategy, Yehoshua stated "we will flee before them" *two times*. Why?
b) After setting up all units, we find that the next morning "he counted the people." Why at that moment?
c) In verses 10-11, the people took positions, after Yehoshua and the elders went forward. Shouldn't they move as one unit?
d) Why was it important to state, in v.11, that there was valley separating them from the town?
e) In v. 12, Yehoshua sends five thousand troops to lie in

wait west of Aay. Is this a second group preparing an ambush?

f) In v.13, *the people* place two groups of soldiers north and west of Aay. Wasn't this what Yehoshua had done? If not, is this *a third group* to lie in ambush? I have found this question raised by others, but no satisfactory response was given.

g) V. 13 inserts, "And Yehoshua went that night into the midst of the valley." But v. 9 stated that he lodged that night among the people! The people were north of Aay, not in any valley! The entire insertion of v. 13 seems irrelevant anyway.

h) V. 14 describes the enemy charging forth to attack "*before the plain*." Why is this description necessary?

I) In v. 15 Yehoshua's army ("all Israel") pretended to be beaten and retreated. In the previous verse they are simply called "Israel." Why are they now referred to as "*all Israel*"?

j) Finally - Why was this lengthy description needed of every step in the campaign? It could have been abridged significantly, primarily highlighting the concept of the ambush. However, since the holy Scriptures do not waste words, we must now analyze this section by noting the marvelous analysis of the holy [R. Moshe] Alshich:

Yehoshua's goal was to entice the enemy to send forth every able-bodied man from the city. Knowing that they were mighty warriors and clever in warfare, he feared that they would be wise enough to suspect a large group hiding in ambush. Thus, they would only send forth half their forces against the retreating Jews to protect themselves from a second force. Therefore he devised a clever plan:

It is quite certain that the two sides had determined, by

use of messengers, when the battle would begin, as is usually done in war situations. This explains the expression in v. 14, that the enemy came out against Israel "at the appointed time." Yehoshua understood that the enemy would be on the alert for a large force waiting in ambush to enter the city after the army had come forth from there. Therefore, in preparation for the war, he sent a first force of 30,000 soldiers to lie in ambush two nights before the battle. V. 3 clearly speaks of early preparation for battle ("Yehoshua rose up...to go up against Aay"), sending the 30,000 soldiers "at night." V. 9 affirms that they were in place by the first night, while Yehoshua "lodged that night among the people." The next morning, he counted his forces (so that the enemy, watching the activity from the distance, would assume that this was his entire force, being counted before entering into battle.) He then approached the city with the elders in accompaniment, and the rest of the people, and they encamped north of the city, with a valley separating them from the city. Understanding that the enemy was surely watching every move, he sent forth a force of five thousand soldiers in the early morning to take positions on the west side of the city, in front of the hiding force of 30,000. This second ambush-group acted as if they were trying to hide from the enemy, although they understood that they were being observed. The people spread out north of the city, and sent a third group to the northwest corner of the city, acting as another ambush force, but not attempting to hide their actions. The king analyzed Yehoshua's strategy just as Yehoshua hoped he would.. He thought that Yehoshua had divided his forces into two to entice the king to send forth all his forces to attack the two groups, so that his hidden force of five thousand could enter the city unopposed. The enemy would presume that he was unaware of being watched, and that the force of five thousand was his secret and unseen ambush group. Yehoshua (v. 13) went into the valley that night, i.e., *the second night,* hoping that the enemy observed this act as well. It would suggest to them that his followers were afraid to accompany him that close to the city. This would suggest to them that the Jewish people were very frightened of the approaching battle. However, the Jewish forces would find this encouraging, for it showed that their leader was entirely devoid of fear. V. 14 begins with "When the king of Aay saw [this]," i.e., that the five thousand soldiers were lying in ambush incorrectly thinking that they were not detected, (the) men of the city went forth on the third morning to battle (but a large force remained in the city to resist the five thousand), unaware of the force of 30,000 hiding behind them. Only the 30,000 force is described as being "behind the city" (v.14), unlike the smaller group of five thousand, to indicate that the larger force was behind the smaller one, undetected by the enemy until it was too late for them. When Yehoshua and *all* his people fled (i.e. the *five thousand soldiers joined them* in fleeing as planned, convincing the enemy that they were in total retreat). v.16 emphasizes that "*all the people* in the city" now joined the pursuit, and "no man remained in Aay... who did not chase them, and the city remained open...." At this point, the 30,000 arose from hiding, rushed into town, and quickly set it afire The enemy realized the trick, and was now caught between two forces. Losing heart and in total confusion, they were wiped out. This analysis has answered all the questions raised above. Further on, I will explain why G-d wished this battle to be fought in natural ways, unlike the conquest of Yericho. I was pleased to note, when I had available the commentary of the Malbim for a few moments, that he has a similar analysis, although he differs in one or two points. I remain with my opinion about this mighty and brilliant campaign.

[Note: This was a bit complicated, and can be better understood by reading the chapter in the original text carefully. The author adds additional conjectures, which I found less relevant, a bit confusing to follow, and beyond the actual textual analysis, so I have omitted them.]

B) Understanding the Deception of the Givonim

You must know, my brother, that these natural strategies that Yehoshua used were indicated to him by G-d. He had said "Place an ambush behind the city." Why did HaShem not give him a supernatural victory as He did at Yericho? Surely this was due to the sin that Achan had committed nearby, so that G-d did not wish to allow them a miraculous victory at that place. Nevertheless, although the campaign was carried out within natural law, some marvelous results emerged from this battle at Aay. For it served as an introduction to the deception carried out by the Givonim and to the great war afterward with the kings of the Emori. The war at Aay helped to accomplish and confirm a promise made in the Torah, as we will now explain:

Moshe tells the people (*Devarim* 6:10-12), "When G-d will have brought you to the land which He swore to your forefathers... great cities that you did not build. And homes filled with all good things... vineyards and olive trees that you did not plant....Beware lest you forget your G-d who took you out from the land of Egypt, from the house of bondage."

Rav Shmuel wrote in his volume "*Torah Min HaShamayim*" (ch.17), [synopsis], that one who reads these promises with a clear mind and open eyes can absolutely confirm that only G-d alone could have recorded such pledges. For in the heat of battle and conquest, the Jewish army, for some strategic reason, or, more likely, the enemy realizing that their defeat was imminent, might very well burn down and destroy all their homes and supplies. Yet the Torah promises that they would take over all these things intact and ready for use. In fact, Chazal actually claim that in the first days after the exodus, before Amalek attacked, the Canaanites and the Emori cut down their fruit trees and destroyed their homes so as to deny these benefits to the advancing Jewish people, of whom they were deathly afraid. However, as the forty years in the desert progressed, they lost that fear, rebuilt their homes, and planted new trees. How could any human author promise that now, as they prepared for the conquest, the enemy would not carry out the same acts of destruction as they did decades before? However, G-d made His promise and it was carried out marvelously. As we find (*Yehoshua* ch.11), the only city that was burnt down was Chatzor [which had incited many kings to come forth to battle the Jewish army], while the other cities, with their vineyards and fields, remained intact and ready for use, as mentioned later in the volume (ch.24:13).

I reflected on R. Shmuel's analysis to find the reason for the inaction of the enemy, since it is usual practice to destroy supplies before an advancing powerful army [and we do know from the first chapter of *Yehoshua* that they were all in great dread of the Jewish people]. First, I must explain how it came about that the Givonim concluded that it was best to make peace with Yehoshua. The following is the amazing analysis of the holy [Rabbeinu Moshe] Alshich, in his volume called *Mar-os Hatzov-os*.

We read (*Yehoshua* 9:1-4):When all the kings ... in the hills and in the valleys... the Hittites, the Emorites, the Canaanites (etc.) heard....The gathered together to battle ...Israel with one accord. And the inhabitants of Givon heard what Yehoshua did to Yericho and Aay. They *also* acted slyly... and took old sacks for their donkeys, etc..... Now the Rav quotes from an early source (*Mahari'v)* that we can understand how clever the entire campaign against Aay was. Actually, just as Yericho was captured by great miracles, G-d could have done the same with Aay. Because ambushes and sophisticated strategies were used, the surrounding tribes logically concluded that the Jewish army would be battling under natural law, without G-d's direct intervention. This is why they organized all their peoples together, presuming that in massive numbers they could defeat Yehoshua. Thus, instead of requiring thirty-one campaigns, we conquered all these kingdoms in several days of battles, some with individual cities and some with organized armies of many kings, as detailed through ch.12. Before these battles began, the people of Givon, which was a large city with mighty warriors (10:2), heard about the battles with Yericho and Aay, but they were much wiser. They understood the clever strategy of Yehoshua, and knew that the Jewish army would be invincible. This is why the verse states (9:4) "They *also* acted slyly," an otherwise strange expression. They conceived their sly deception and saved their lives, accepting the condition of becoming servants to the Jewish people rather than dying in battle.

I believe that we can now understand the emphasis in the verse which says that the people of Givon heard of both campaigns, of Yericho *and* Aay. Since the first campaign was so awesomely miraculous, they understood that the second "natural" campaign was only designed to fool the other kingdoms into presuming that all battles would be by natural law. This trick would indeed give them the audacity to prepare for war, and nobody would think of simply surrendering. But the clever Givonim gave the appearance of having come from a distant land, as they claimed, where they had only heard of the miraculous exodus from the Egypt and the two wars against Sichon and Og. Of course they did not mention the battle of Yericho, since the Aay campaign followed immediately, and this would raise suspicions. Nevertheless, the trick of Yehoshua's Aay campaign was ultimately the trigger for the Givonim to conceive their own deception. It succeeded because b'nei Yisrael did not consult with G-d [through the Urim v'Tumim]. It appears that G-d was satisfied with this arrangement for reasons we will soon discuss.

C) The Consequences of the Peace Agreement with the Givonim

The agreement with the Givonim led to two results, based on the fact that the other Canaanite nations observed everything. One: that five kings united together to war with Yehoshua (as I shall soon explain in the next section). Second: that this directly caused all the other kingdoms not to follow their example, as we read (*Yehoshua* 11:19), "There was no city that made peace with... Israel...except Givon... all [others] they took in battle. For it was G-d's [will] to harden their hearts for war with Israel so as to destroy them utterly...."

Let us consider what would have been the law had they all come forward and asked for a peace covenant. In the Yerushalmi Talmud (*Sheviis ch.6*), also quoted by Tosafos (*Gittin* 46a), R. Shmuel Bar Nachman states: "Yehoshua sent three proclamations to the Canaanites before he entered the land: Whoever wishes to leave, leave; to make peace, do so; to make war, do it. The Girgashi left and went to Africa; the Givonim made peace; the thirty-one kings made war and were defeated." The verse cited previously that no other city made peace itself indicates that this had been an acceptable option. We must now reconcile this with the language of the Torah which appears, at first glance, to deny the possibility of making peace with the Canaanite people.

We are instructed (*Devarim* ch.20) that upon approaching a city for battle, we should offer them the option of surrender. If they refuse, when G-d delivers them into our hands, we kill only the mature males, and keep the children and women as part of the spoils. This applies (v.15) to distant cities beyond our borders. However, regarding the seven Canaanite nations (v.16-17), we must entirely wipe out every living soul, so that (v. 18) we might never learn to imitate their abominable practices. These verses appear to be a glaring contradiction to the text in *Yehoshua*, which implied that these people could have made peace with us!

I believe that the following argument solves the problem: The first verse in this section that allowed for peace, referred to all situations, *including the seven nations*, as indicated in *Yehoshua*. When v. 12 began discussing the possibility of war because of the refusal to sue for peace, the Torah described (vs.13-14) leaving women and children alive. Then, v.15 stated that this applies to distant cities beyond our borders. When v. 16 discussed the rules for the seven nations, it *continued on the premise of a refusal to make peace*! It explained that with these nations, we do not allow any captives to live. The final verse (18) added that in cases where peace is made, we must remain alert to prevent these people from influencing our way of life, e.g., they must accept the seven Noahide laws and end all idol worship, etc. Thus, the law of the Torah is reconciled with the book of *Yehoshua*. Furthermore, in support of this argument, consider the following: If we were actually forbidden to make peace with any Canaanite king, the oath we took to keep the peace with the Givonim would be null and void, for an oath against a mitzvah of the Torah is not binding at all!

The Canaanites saw that after all the efforts of deception that the Givonim went through, many of the people grumbled about the oath and wanted to kill them anyway (9:18), and that, finally, although this was avoided, they became the lowliest of servants to the Jewish people. This strengthened the resolve of the seven nations not to surrender. They convinced themselves that the messages from Yehoshua about making peace were false, and they organized for battle. This was G-d's ultimate wish in order to rid the land of these abominable and immoral people. (19)

One might ask, why did the Givonim go through all that trouble when they could have simply come forward to sue for peace? The *meforshim* [i.e., those who agree that the peace option for the Canaanites was a valid one] offer many answers to this question. I believe that the following one is the most sensible: The Givonim knew the conditions under which they could remain in Eretz Yisrael: a) to accept servitude to the Jewish people; b) to take upon themselves the seven Noahide commandments; an undesirable condition for people who had never practiced such things before; and c) to destroy all their idols, with the gold, silver, etc. trimmings in which these idols were decorated in their temples and in their homes. They hoped that by being believed that they were from a distant land, and after being accepted by an oath, while they would have to serve the Jewish people, they could continue their own practices and idolatry, just like cities conquered beyond Jewish borders.(19) They presumed that Yehoshua would honor his word, even if he discovered their ruse, and they would thus be able to keep their idols with all the expensive trimmings.

When the people (and Yehoshua as well, apparently - see 9:6) answered them at their first encounter (when they requested to make a peace covenant), "Perhaps you live amongst us, and how can we make a covenant," they meant that the conditions for peace are different for Canaanites vs. distant cities, so they must know exactly their place of origin. The Givonim feigned ignorance of this distinction and simply answered, "We are your servants," i.e., what difference does it make as long as we are willing to be your servants? At this point, Yehoshua demanded to know the location of their homeland. It was, after all, possible that even coming from a distant place, it was still within the boundaries of the seven kingdoms, whose territories stretched far and wide. They now added, "from a *v e r y distant* land," compared to the previous "a distant land." The additional mention of having heard of the exodus of the Jews, but not about Yericho and Aay, finally led Yehoshua to accept their story, and to make an unconditional peace treaty with them. Actually, once their deception was discovered, Yehoshua could have ordered their execution as a tribe of the seven kingdoms who obviously did not want to be held to the harder conditions of the Canaanites, and thus the oath was null and void. Nevertheless, they upheld the oath, but demoted them to the lowest level of servitude. Meanwhile, this entire event served to convince the other kingdoms not to pursue peace, but to go to war, as G-d really wished.

D) Further Consequences of the Treaty with the Givonim

The second result of the Givonim episode was that the Canaanim decided to organize a large army, not one king at a time. A great dread overcame the kingdoms, since Givon was known as a mighty city, yet they had meekly surrendered to Yehoshua and accepted servitude. Furthermore, they were now part of the Jewish population and would probably join them in any future battles. No lone king could withstand such an army, and the only option was to organize a huge force of many kingdoms together. The text (*Yehoshua* 10:1-2) clearly emphasizes the conquest and destruction of Aay and the peace treaty with Givon for good reason. Since Aay was destroyed in natural battle without the miracles associated with Yericho's fall, it indicated that the Jewish army was a mighty one. The execution of all Aay's inhabitants convinced them that the offer of peace was dishonest. Then, the meek surrender of Givon who are described here as "and they were amongst them" means that they were now like a part of the Jewish people. It also proved, furthermore, that Jewish forces were mighty enough to frighten a powerful city into surrender. Therefore, Adoni Tzedek king of Jerusalem, sent for the four other kings (of Chevron, Yarmus, Lachish, and Eglon) to form a huge force.

Had the campaign against Aay not occurred, these kings would have had only the precedent of Yericho to focus upon, and they would have been deathly afraid of the power of the mighty G-d who vanquished that city with miracles. The Aay affair indicated that now G-d had stepped aside, and they might succeed in war.

[Their first target was Givon, since they considered them traitors to their cause. The chapter then details the result of this confrontation and the battles that followed. The Givonim desperately sent to Yehoshua that they were in mortal danger. With G-d's encouragement, he came with his army, attacked at night, and had a huge and total victory. In this battle, G-d directly intervened, hurling great stones from heaven upon the enemy.]

E) The War against the Five Kings Provided Bnei Yisrael with Great Cities, Homes, and Provisions

We can understand that had the Canaanite nations fled the country in fear, they would have taken all their flocks and possessions with them, after burning down their cities to ashes. This would have nullified G-d's promise of finding mighty cities full of wonderful possessions and commodities. On the other hand, this nullification would have occurred had these kingdoms sued for peace, and thus remained in their homes and cities. However, based on the conquest of Aay, and the peace treaty of Givon and its consequences, as detailed above, these Canaanites decided to go to war. Following the conquests of so many cities and kingdoms, bnei Yisrael were able to overpower the remaining inhabitants and take over whole cities, intact with all their goods. Yehoshua instructed his forces (10:19), "Pursue your enemies... do not allow them to come to their cities...," for he understood that if they reached their homes, they would immediately burn down the homes and rush their families out in great haste.

We can now appreciate the broader picture, and how it led to the accomplishment of all that G-d had promised His people. The first set-back at Aay had encouraged that city to proceed with battle and empty the city of soldiers. Their defeat by strategy rather than by miracles, resulting in the total annihilation of all their people, led the Givonim to seek peace by their deception. These two facts were the direct cause of the other Canaanite kings to go forward into a major confrontation with Israel. Their speedy defeat granted the victors all that G-d had promised them in the Torah: great cities full of good supplies and mighty walls. How marvelous are the deeds of our Creator, who fulfills His pledges to us!

This clarifies a seemingly extraneous word in Moshe's vision for Yosef (*Devarim* 33:17). After showering him with great blessings of abundance, Moshe compares him to a unicorn with mighty horns, "with which he will gore enemies *together* to the ends of the earth; and they are the tens of thousands of Ephrayim....". This is surely an allusion to the campaign of his beloved Ephrayim (Yehoshua) who succeeded against a united army of many kingdoms, by vanquishing them *together*.

F) The Torah Foresaw Many Aspects of Yehoshua's

Battle Campaigns

We will now demonstrate that the Torah previewed for us all the details of the conquest of Eretz Yisrael. Moshe states (*Devarim* 7:22-2), "And your G-d will cast out [ונשל] these nations before you little by little; you cannot destroy them [כלותם] quickly lest the beasts of the field will increase upon you. And your G-d shall deliver them to you, etc....The graven images of their gods you shall burn in fire, etc." Here we are told that the first conquests will not be speedy. Thus, the capture of Yericho took place separately, and then Aay was conquered [after a defeat there], as the Alshich HaKadosh describes. Thus, there is nothing extraneous in the Torah. It had already recorded (*Shemos* 23:29-31), "I shall not drive them out before you in one year; lest the land become desolate and the beast of the field increase against you. Little by little I will drive them out... until you increase and inherit the land. I will set your boundary from the Sea of Reeds to the Sea of the Pelishtim and from the desert to the river...." We must ask, why did the Torah have to repeat this promise in *Devarim*? However, In *Shemos* the entire conquest from Yehoshua until Shlomo was being described, culminating in our control of the entire land, while in *Devarim* only the beginning campaigns against Yericho and Aay were involved. This is why it did not add anything about our population increase and conquest of the entire land.

However, we must understand why Moshe mentioned avoiding the possible increase of wild animals, for even after conquering Yericho and Aay, and even some other cities, there was no such fear. The entry of wild beasts can only be feared when vast areas are conquered and people do not inhabit them! Additionally, why did Moshe change from the root נשל to the word כלותם, rather than "you cannot cast them out quickly?"

Clearly, the statement about not destroying them quickly stands separated from the previous verse. This is the flow of the text: You will cast them out little by little - refers to Yericho and Aay. Then the text adds that you cannot destroy all seven nations quickly in a huge war, for this would bring wild animals into many locations. Yet, after the Aay campaign, there was a major battle with the five kings and a few other cities. This had been foreseen in the phrase (*Devarim* 9:3), "You shall drive them out and destroy them *quickly*...." It was for the period after this campaign that Moshe indicated that the conquest would proceed in gradual stages, until completed by the era of Shlomo. Thus, three stages were described. The phrase "little by little" representing the conquest of Yericho and of Aay - the "speedy" destruction in Shemos referring to the great campaign that immediately followed - and the limitation of being unable to complete the *entire conquest* with speed (*Devarim* ch.7) or in one year (*Shemos* ch. 9), in order to eliminate the land filling with beasts.

The description in *Devarim* (above) has deep meanings. Having removed the possibility of a speedy complete conquest (7:22), the next verse states that G-d will hand over the enemy *"before you,"* rather than "in your hands." Since, after the Aay campaign, the five kings with their armies approached the Jewish army in united fashion, coming before us to battle. The next phrase states that G-d will confuse them mightily, using the Hebrew term מהומה (confusion). This is the precise term we find in *Yehoshua* (10:10) describing the battle. Our next phrase (v.24) adds that "He will place their kings in your hand," a fairly uncommon description. However, it is the perfect description of the culmination of that battle, where the five fleeing kings hid in a cave in Makedah (*Yehoshua* 10:16)! It would appear that Moshe's additional phrase (v. 24), "No man will stand up against you," was superfluous and obvious. However, this too is a perfect insertion based on what actually happened with these kings. We read in *Yehoshua* (10:18-19) that when they were discovered in hiding, Yehoshua arranged for them to be sealed in the cave by huge boulders. He then ordered his men to leave the area to pursue the enemy in all directions rather than "stand around." (This expression sounds like they were concerned about leaving these kings unguarded, or even with a small detachment of soldiers.) Hence, in their absence, some enemy soldiers could well have sneaked back to rescue their kings. Therefore, the Torah promises that in their great fright they would not attempt to "stand up against you." In fact, we can understand perfectly the two statements about destroying the enemy that were used by Moshe. First he stated (*Devarim* 7:23), "He will confuse them mightily until He destroys them." Then (v.24) "He will place their kings in your hand and [I guarantee that] you will erase their names from beneath the heavens. [But you need not kill them immediately, for] "No man will stand up against you" [while you pursue your fleeing enemy] "until you destroy them." Thus Yehoshua locked them in the cave, rather than lose precious time with their execution, in order to pursue the enemy forces, knowing that the kings would not escape, nor be rescued. Upon returning from victory, he had them executed and "erased their names from *beneath the heavens*." [They were cast into the cave, and it was closed with boulders.] Just before the execution, he told the people (10:24) to place their feet upon the necks of the kings. I believe that this was a symbol of the promise in *Devarim* (33:29), "And you will tread upon their high places."

The perfection of Moshe's description of this military campaign, as matched in later history, indicates that Moshe had a clear vision of this battle, and provides further evidence of the Divine nature of G-d's Torah.

The next verse in *Devarim* commands that we burn their idols and must not covet their silver and gold and take of them "to bring an abomination into your home, lest you be a cursed thing (חרם) like it." It is strange that the burning of the idols is recorded in plural form, but the verbs "covet" and "take" are in the singular. I would suggest that the Torah foresaw the future, and gave a warning to Achan, the one individual who broke this commandment. In his confession, he used the term "I coveted," and he had taken gold and silver (*Yehoshua* 7:21) and stealthily sneaked these abominations into his home. He thus became *cherem* and was judged with the penalty of burning since, as the *Baal HaTurim* writes, this verse is recorded so close to the burning of the idol abominations. (In Ch.75, I will provide further proof that this section of *Devarim* speaks of Achan.

Note that in *Divrei HaYamim* (I, 2:7), Achan is called by the name Achar (עכר) (one who causes trouble, or debases), obviously based on Yehoshua's expression to Achan (*Yehoshua* 7:25), "As you have troubled us (*achartanu*), so shall G-d trouble you today The concluding verse in *Devarim* (7:26) that warns us not to bring an abomination into our homes, states that it is cursed (כי חרם הוא). How interesting that Achan is called עכר, for this is equal in gematria (290) to כי חרם הוא!

Let us now carefully examine the texts in *Devarim* and *Yehoshua* to strengthen and expand our analyses above. *Devarim* ch. 9, opened with, "Hear o Israel, you are crossing today the Jordan to come and conquer great nations, mightier than you, great cities fortified to the heavens. A great people, sons of the giants ("anakim") of whom you know and have heard 'who can stand before the sons of the anak.' But know today that your G-d passes before you, He is a consuming fire, He will annihilate them, and He will subjugate them before you; and you will drive them out and destroy them quickly as He spoke to you."

This description contrasts with that of *Devarim* ch.6 (6:10): "When G-d will bring you to the land that He swore to your forefathers... to give you great and good cities that you did not build. And homes full of good things...and wells..., vineyards and olive trees... and you will eat and be satiated." This final phrase only came true in King Shlomo's time (as expressed in *Melachim I*(4:20), and therefore this section began with the promise to our forefathers, which was fulfilled in Shlomo's era.. But ch.9 deals with the first campaigns of Yehoshua, which were not completed in his days, hence the oath to our forefathers is not mentioned there. On the other hand, the anakim are mentioned, for they were destroyed in Yehoshua's early campaigns (ch.11:21-22), which itself demonstrates that this section refers to his conquest of the

Marvels of Our Blessed G-d's Torah

land. Moshe's expression (9:3) that G-d will annihilate and subjugate them must be analyzed. Since "subjugate" implies surrender to servitude, and since we were told to totally destroy the enemy, this can only be a reference to the Givonim, who willingly surrendered to Yehoshua for servitude! Thus, the reference to annihilation was accomplished with Yericho and Aay, and then subjugation occurred with Givon, and the next two verbs ("drive them out and destroy them quickly") is a perfect description of the next two campaigns against the five kings, described earlier, followed by a campaign against Yavin King of Chatzor and his cohorts, described in detail in *Yehoshua* ch.11. These two campaigns are correctly called "quick" campaigns for they spared the army from conducting individual battles. Instead they conquered many cities and kingdoms in two quick wars, completing the conquest of thirty-one kings, as explained in ch. 12. How perfectly every expression of Moshe is matched by another battle and conquest, in correct order!

It appears that when Yehoshua halted the sun and moon (ch. 10:12-13), and the text adds that this was written "in the book of *Yashar*," the reference is to the Torah [many commentators claim that it is specifically to Chumash *Devarim*]. Various *meforshim* sought to find a reference in the Torah to the idea of stopping the sun and moon. However, it is undoubtedly the promise that we would find cities and homes waiting for us and laden with all good things. If the enemy had managed to flee at night back to their homes, they would have burnt everything to the ground to prevent the victors from enjoying the fruits of their victory, and blocked the promise that G-d made to us in *Devarim*.

We can now see and appreciate how Moshe, foreseeing all the events that would take place in Yehoshua's conquest of the land, recorded these events and battles in perfect expressions and exact verbs, in precise order. So that we would find proof in all these details that the finger of G-d hovered over every word to show us that this Torah is His, and that we must observe all His laws for our ultimate benefit.

Chapter 28

Here we will show that the Torah foresaw already at the time of the tragic meraglim event that Yehoshua (who was then forty-three years old) would only have female children.

We find in *Divrei HaYamim I* (7:27) a line of descent ending with Yehoshua.. Chazal inform us (*Megillah* 14b) that he did have daughters. This was already foreseen in the Torah (*BeMidbar* 14:24), as follows:

Kalev is given the reward that he will enter the land, and "his seed will possess it (יורשנה)." Rashi notes that this verb form (*yorish*) means to conquer, while (yirash-יירש) is the correct form for possess/inherit. Hence, he understands the phrase to mean that Kalev's children will drive out the giants and other inhabitants. Rav Yitzchak Abarbanel disagrees. He notes that Kalev himself drove out the *anakim* (*Yehoshua* 15:14).He therefore translates *yorishena* as "his seed will not only possess it, but also transmit it to their children as an eternal inheritance." However, this too is not satisfactory. The verse could have used "*yirshuha*" to indicate that they would inherit it. This term always presumes without further statement that they would transmit it to their future generations! Furthermore, the verse in BeMidbar entirely omitted the statement that Kalev would give his land to his children, leaving it understood only by implication.

We offer this solution. The phrase that his seed will transmit their land to their children is perfect when contrasted with Yehoshua. He too had a share in Eretz Yisrael (*Timnas Serach*), in which he was eventually buried, as described in *Yehoshua* (24:30). There is no mention anywhere that he too transmitted his inheritance to children. Clearly, this is so because he had no sons. His daughters inherited his land, but it was transmitted onward by their husbands to their children, not by the wives, according to the law of the Torah. Thus, the expression in the Torah is quite perfect. Kalev will merit to have his children transmit their inheritance to their future generations, while Yehoshua's daughters will inherit, but not transmit.

We may calculate the age of Yehoshua at the time of the Torah's prophecy about Kalev and his inheritance. Yehoshua died at the age of 110, after leading the people for 28 years; hence he entered the land at age 82. He spent 40 years in the desert, from which the spies were sent in the second year. Thus, he was 43 years old at the time of the prophecy to Kalev. Since the wording of this promise was the clue that Yehoshua would not enjoy similar benefits, it is clear that the Torah already foresaw that Yehoshua would have no sons.

There is only a brief reference to Yehoshua's

inheritance at the time of his passing. There was hardly any reason to dwell further on the subject. Since he received it after 14 years of war and land distribution, he acquired it only fourteen years before his passing, at the age of 96. With his passing, it transferred onward through his sons-in-law, perhaps from another tribe. This small period of time was not noteworthy. However, regarding the entry into, and conquest of, Eretz Yisrael, he and Kalev are centers of attention, as described in the Chumash (*BeMidbar* 14:30 and 38).

The expression used by Moshe in *Chumash Devarim* (1:36), "Kalev... he will see it and I will give the land that he trod upon to him and his children.....," neatly complements the expressions in *Chumash BeMidbar*. By avoiding a repetition of the term that his children will *yorishena*, it makes it clear that his sons will inherit, but not drive out the giants, for that was accomplished by Kalev himself. Thus, that term in *BeMidbar* only meant to emphasize the contrast of Kalev to Yehoshua, i.e., that Kalev's children will transmit their land to descendants, but not Yehoshua. How marvelous to note that even this detail in Yehoshua's life was already hinted at in the language of the chumash, whose author stands above time and sees the future clearly.

Chapter 29

We will show that the Torah saw that Kalev would receive Chevron as his inheritance and that he would remain with his full energies and vigor for forty years to follow [as he himself later reports to Yehoshua].

Kalev approached Yehoshua in Eretz Yisrael (*Yehoshua* 14:6-13) requesting that he be given the area of Chevron ("this mountain"). In his statement, he reviews his faithfulness to G-d in the incident of the spies, and that he has been blessed to remain physically unchanged over the forty-five years since that sad event. Yehoshua agreed and gave him Chevron. In the following chapter, he successfully drove out [killed?] the three giants Shaishaay, Achiman, and Talmaay from his land. Let us examine the Torah on this subject:

In *Chumash BeMidbar* (13:22) the twelve spies came up (the verb is in plural form of course) through the negev, and "*he* came to Chevron, (and the afore-mentioned three giants were there), and Chevron was built up seven years before Tzo-an Mitzrayim." Chazal state that the singular verb indicates that only Kalev went to Chevron alone to pray at the graves of our forefathers. However, the statement about Chevron preceding the other Egyptian city seems out of place and superfluous. If it was meant to tell of its superiority in some way, it seems that this is hardly the place to do so, especially since it was mentioned in the Torah previously several times. The spies too recognized the amazing goodness of the land when they brought the huge grapes back, so this extraneous statement is a puzzle. Let us offer a solution:

Imagine a wise king who recounts to his subjects that he recently sent out some men to scout a distant land, about which they are aware that it has bountiful, great cities. He focuses on one particular city there, giving various details about its history and beauty. He then tells them that upon returning they spoke evil things about the land, except for one scout who was ecstatic about its splendor, and that he therefore would give him one city as his reward. Can there be any doubt that they would understand that it would be that city which the king had been praising so much? Especially when we see that eventually this was indeed the city given to him, it becomes obvious that this is why the Torah discussed Chevron in the verse that mentioned Kalev's visit there.

I also find an interesting hint that the Torah foresaw that Kalev would not age at all over forty years. Reviewing the incident of the spies (*Devarim* 1:36), Moshe describes how HaShem promised to bring Kalev to Eretz Yisrael and to give him the land "that he trod (אשר דרך) upon." This unusual verb invariably implies treading with power and force, as in *BeMidbar* (24:17), *Yeshayahu* (63:3), *Shoftim* (5:21), etc. [Speaking to Yehoshua, Kalev uses that same verb describing Moshe's promise to him years before (*Yehoshua* 14:9). Only the Creator Himself could guarantee any man that he would live to claim and enjoy his inheritance, in perfect physical shape, forty-five years later!

Chapter 30

The Torah knew that Shechem will be a city of refuge, and that it will be a home for murderers; that Chevron and Kedesh will also be cities of refuge, and that Gilead will have many murderers

[The style of this chapter is by a dialogue between the writer and a questioner. We will use A for the writer and Q for the questioner]

A: As we see in *Yehoshua* (20:7), Kedesh, Shechem, and Chevron were consecrated as cities of refuge. It is also evident that Shechem contained murderers, as found in *Hoshea* (6:9) and in *Shoftim* (9:25). The Torah had already visualized the conditions in Shechem: Chazal (*Makos* 9) discuss the Torah's command that the land be divided into three parts. As described in Rashi (in the chumash) and by Chazal (in the gemara), from the southern end of the land until Chevron, from Chevron to Shechem, from Shechem to Kedesh, and from Kedesh to the northern end, all distances between sites are approximately equal. However, any one found between Kedesh and Chevron could run in two possible directions, while from the ends of the land's boundary he would run to either Kedesh or

Chevron. Hence, a killer between Kedesh and Chevron would have a shorter route than one at the southern or northern boundary of the country. The gemara was bothered by this fact, but Abaye answered that this was acceptable since Shechem had a larger number of murderers. (Wherever there are an abundance of murderers, there is also an increase in accidental killings.) Since the Torah made these arrangements, it must have known that this would be the situation in Shechem centuries later!

Q: This seems to me to be a far-fetched proof. The Torah neither mentions Shechem by name, nor any murderers there. It mentions no names of cities of refuge at all. It only states that there must be three such cities, and later Yehoshua chose them!

A. In fact, it is really quite clear. Moshe said that they should divide the land into three parts. The geographic fact is that the distances from the northern boundary to Kedesh, and from Kedesh to Shechem, and from Shechem to Chevron, and from Chevron to the southern boundary, are equal. But this creates a dilemma. For, as shown above, one who flees from the extreme boundary of the land to the nearest city must run farther that anyone fleeing from anywhere between Chevron to Kedesh, who has two choices. The only response to this point was made by Abaye, that this is reasonable because of the predominance of murderers in Shechem. Since this is the way we can understand the Torah's instructions, it must be that the Torah foresaw the entire situation and knew how and why these cities would be chosen.

Q. I find it puzzling that Moshe spoke of three sections, but there were actually four equal areas.

A. If someone gave you a large piece of material and asked that you make three tears in it approximately equal, you would have four pieces!

Q. Couldn't Moshe have meant there should be only three sections, needing only two cities properly centered?

A. You forget that he said that three cities must be chosen, thus resulting in a total of four sections.

Q. Perhaps he meant two cities at extreme ends of the land, and one in the very center?

A. This idea is ridiculous. First, because the land would only have two sections, and the Torah spoke of three. Furthermore, it would be entirely illogical for a city of refuge to be at the end of the boundary. Its purpose is to make it convenient for as many people as possible, so the more centrally located the better. Also, the verse (*Devarim* 19:2) reads, "You shall separate three cities in the midst of your land...." Obviously, they must all be in the midst of the land. Finally, remember that Yehoshua surely understood Moshe's instructions, so whatever he did is precisely what Moshe meant.

Q. Isn't it possible that the Torah meant that the two outer cities should be closer to the borders, so that any killer who had to flee to a city of refuge from any location would never need to go farther than the distance from the extreme border to the first available city? [The diagram of the two borders and the three cities would look like this:

Southern   Border-----1----------2----------3-----Northern

Border]

Actually, I am confused generally to find that the term "three" ultimately means four parts. The expression to divide the land into three, and the other expression of choosing three cities that culminate in four parts, are mutually exclusive!

A. Exactly! This was the puzzle that confronted Chazal, until they solved it by noting about the preponderance of murderers in Shechem. Thus, they understood why the distance to Shechem for anyone living between Chevron and Kedesh should be shorter. This way they understood why Yehoshua did not use the plan you suggested [diagram above]. The Torah foresaw the situation in Shechem, and so Moshe and Yehoshua knew exactly how the land would be divided for the purpose of choosing the three sites.

The prophet (*Hoshea* 6:8) records that the area of Gilead was also frequented by murderers and blood flowed freely there. This too was seen by the Torah, which called for three additional cities to be set up in the area east of the Jordan. Despite the fact that the east bank was home to only two and one half tribes, they were given the same number of cities of refuge as the other nine and one half tribes. The gemara (*Makos* 10a/b) wondered about this, and answered by reference to the verse in Hoshea. It also indicates that the situation in Gilead was much worse than that of Shechem, as mentioned there in the *Maharsha*. (The gemara also questions: Weren't there also forty-eight cites of the Leviim that could harbor killers? See the discussion there, and in meforshim [Ramban and *Panim Yafos*] who discuss this question.)

Marvels of Our Blessed G-d's Torah

For a long time I was greatly bothered by what seemed to be a major question. All these discussions concerned distances for the length of the land. What about the width of Eretz Yisrael?

At first I concluded that there is an absolute presumption that killers were rare in these areas. However, there was no problem at all, for the distances from the east and west parts of the land were actually far less than from areas in the length of Eretz Yisrael.(22)

One other additional fact about the cities given to the Leviim was noticed by the *Chizkuni*. When the Torah (*BeMidbar* 38:16-29) assigns leaders ("princes") of each tribe to be in charge of the distribution of the land to the tribes, it first lists Yehudah, Shimon, and Binyamin. This is a most unusual order, with Yosef mentioned later than Binyamin. However, in *Yehoshua* (21:4) we find that the first lot of thirteen cities given to the Kehus branch of the Leviim was taken from the territories of Yehudah, Shimon and Binyamin. Once again, the Holy One who gave us the Torah saw ahead the future activities of His children and adjusted the order of the list in the chumash to show us Who the author of our Torah was.

Chapter 31

A demonstration that Yaakov, with his Holy Spirit, saw that Rachel would be buried in the boundary of Binyamin, whose birth caused her death in childbirth, and that her grave would lie at the starting point of his territory.

Yaakov tells Yosef in *sidra VaYechi* (*Bereishis* 48:7) how Rachel died on their journey back from Padan, and how she was buried on the road to Ephras, which is Beis Lechem. This entire verse seems extraneous to the subject Yaakov had been discussing (Ephrayim and Menashe)! Sensing this problem, Rashi connects it backward to Yaakov's request of Yosef to bury him in Eretz Yisrael, and states that he was making this request despite the fact that he had not done so for Rachel, due to his vision that she would someday witness her descendants going into exile and would pray for them, as they passed her grave. However, all of this explanation is missing in the text itself! Also, as others ask, this should have been recorded immediately after the verse where Yaakov asks Yosef to bring his coffin to his homeland.

Although this vision came true, it appears that the simple meaning is the interpretation given in *Maasei HaShem* by R. Eliezer Ashkenazi:

It seems that in fact Yaakov told this to Yosef so that he should be thankful for having buried her there. We may assume that "Efras" derives from Yosef's son Ephrayim. Yaakov tells Yosef that he had a vision that that place was at the southern part of Binyamin, with Ephrayim's area at the northern tip of Binyamin's. That is why he buried her there close to the meeting place of her two descendants! The verse adds that Efras is Beis-Lechem, and some claim that Efras is named for the wife of Kalev. However, it is clear to me that there are two cities by this name, and the other Beis-Lechem is in Yehudah's portion, identified in the Tanach (*Ruth* 1:1-2) as "Beis-Lechem Yehudah." In fact, the phrase "it is Beis-Lechem" was added by Yaakov, as he told Yosef of his vision that its present name would change to Efras. Thus, Yosef now learns that Ephrayim will become an independent tribe. Abarbanel has a similar approach to this comment of *Maasei HaShem*. (23)

However, we must abandon the claim that Efras/Beis-Lechem is at Ephrayim's border. Many *meforshim* (including the Rada'k) are convinced that Yaakov is actually referring to the Beis Lechem of Yehudah. (Furthermore, the second Beis-Lechem is listed in *Yehoshua* (19:15) as being far north in Zevulun's territory!) The evidence is strongly in favor of this view. Nevertheless, since Yaakov was heading southward to Chevron, and was still a distance away from Beis-Lechem, we may presume that he was close to the future Yerushalayim. This may well have been the border between Yehudah and Binyamin. Thus, Yaakov justified to Yosef his decision to bury her at that border rather than go further into Yehudah's territory, because he wished that she be buried in the territory of her son, for whom she had given her life.

In his blessings to his sons in *parashas VaYechi*, Yaakov showed that he had clear visions of how Eretz Yisrael would be divided amongst his sons (e.g., that Zevulun would be located near the sea, Asher would have the great area of olive groves, etc.). Hence he must have seen Ephrayim and Menasheh as two separate tribes with independent territories. Had the land been divided into eleven parts, Yehudah's territory would have extended further north and engulfed the area where Rachel was buried. Now she was buried in Binyamin's area, and the next tribe to the north was Ephrayim, her grandson. This is how Yaakov justified his decision to Yosef not to continue into Yehudah's territory.(24)

Chapter 32

Just as when the Rambam or the Ri'f (Alfasi) skip a halachic statement, commentators agree that they did not accept that particular law, so too, if Moshe leaves out an expected statement, it must have great significance. Since he omitted a blessing for Shimon in his final message (Parashas VeZos HaBerachah), he surely foresaw that Shimon's area would be subsumed within Yehudah's territory, and that Shimon would have no judge or king amongst his descendants. Indeed, the Torah calculated all the future territories of the tribes, and Yaakov foresaw all these future boundaries.

It seems odd at first that Moshe completely ignored Shimon in his final messages to the tribes. We find that most of these messages of both Moshe and Yaakov involved territorial visions plus important aspects of each tribe. Thus, the silence of Moshe about Shimon speaks louder than words about the sad future of this tribe. As recorded (*Yehoshua* 19:1), "Their inheritance was within the inheritance of...Yehudah." Having no clearly defined borders, and no great future leaders, Shimon was passed over in silence.

It is noteworthy that in *Parashas Mas-ei* (*BeMidbar* 34:17-28), where the leaders (*nasi*) of each tribe were chosen to be in charge of the allotment of territories in the land, only three tribes had their representatives listed without adding the title of *nasi*: Yehudah, Shimon, and Binyamin. I believe this is because Yehudah and Binyamin were destined for greater glory, i.e., the kingship (David and Shaul, respectively). But Shimon, after the horrific act of their nasi, Zimri Ben Salu, and his execution, did not merit having another nasi at all. [They were granted a representative and no more.] This is why his only mention in the Torah (*BeMidbar* 26:14) lists him as the nasi for the *Shimoni* (spelled שמעני), leaving out the standard *vav* always found in the name Shimon. Besides, as mentioned, his territory was within the area of Yehudah, so he did not need a nasi for such a puny share (as mentioned in the volume *Paaneach Raza*).

Actually, the Torah had already envisioned the entire territory that the Jewish people would inhabit in Chumash *Bereishis*, in the great *bris* G-d made with Avraham (15:18). The area described there is identical to the territories listed in *Melachim I* (5:1-5). Only the Creator of the world could spell out these details centuries before the promise came to fruition.

At this point, Rav Shlez reviews (pp.136-137) and summarizes his findings that Moshe and Yaakov had foreseen the territories that would fall to each of the twelve tribes, as well as many other sites (e.g., the burial sites for Yosef and for Rachel, etc.). He reminds us once again that all of this astonishing material only confirms beyond all doubt that G-d was the author of the chumash, and the cynics who deny this are blind to the truth.

Chapter 33

We will examine the amazing fact that the holy Torah recorded the names of people or sites that actually received those names long after the Torah was given. Among them are Gilgal, Ashur, and Agag. We will also answer a puzzle raised by the Maharsh'a.

See the astonishing fact that Moshe records names of cities in the Torah, although they acquired these names long after Moshe was gone. We find (*Devarim* 11:30), "...opposite (the) Gilgal (25), near *Eilonei Mamre*." However, Gilgal was named later, because Yehoshua circumcised *bnei Yisrael* there (*Yehoshua*, ch.5:10) as clarified in that chapter. Looking into the future, the Torah recorded that name in the chumash! Another example is the pronouncement (*Melachim I*, 13:2) that "a son will be born to the house of David, his name [will be] Yoshiyahu." However, the case of Gilgal may not be a perfect example, since I find that someone claims that there were two places by this name in Tanach. While I am not convinced by his arguments, I leave it to the reader to decide for himself, and will record all the other relevant instances of "Gilgal" in Tanach: (*Yehoshua* 4:19, 9:6, 10:6,6.9,15, and 43), (*Shmuel I*, 10:8, 13:4, 8, 15), (*Melachim II*, 2:1). Unfortunately, I cannot prove absolutely that there was only one such site.

The Torah mentions Dan (*Devarim* 34:1), describing how G-d showed Moshe the entire land of Israel "(The Gilead) up to Dan," which is recognized as the north boundary of the land in several references stating "from Dan to Be'eir Sheva." (26) However this name was formulated many years later as recorded in (*Shoftim* 18:29), when the tribe of Dan captured Layish, expanded it, and renamed it Dan. Rashi notes that in *Yehoshua* (19:47) it was previously called Leshem, because a precious stone by that name, could be found there. Apparently it had two names at different times, and was now called Dan. Once again, the Torah foresaw the future name of that city, calling it by that name centuries in advance. We will see some other examples of this phenomenon, showing that only HaShem could have written the Torah for us, and strengthening our faith in Him and His mitzvos.

It is amazing to note that on the *choshen* (Breastplate of Judgment), there were twelve precious stones for the twelve tribes, and Dan's stone was the *leshem*!

[At this point (p.139), Rav Shlez discusses the term Gilead, which apparently has two or more meanings in Tanach. He strives to prove that when G-d showed Moshe "the Gilad", it means the Beis HaMikdash, as claimed in a midrash. Since this use of the term was initiated by Yirmiyahu (22:6), it provides another example for his thesis. However, the complete discussion is extremely confusing, and I suspect a possible major flaw in the argument. Since he has other proofs to his thesis, I have eliminated this section.]

Another example is the city Ephrasa. Yaakov buried Rachel (*Bereishis* 35:19) on the road to Ephrasa. The volume *Maasei HaShem* (by R. Eliezer Ashkenazi) offers two theories about the origin of this name: 1) from the name Ephrayim; 2) from Ephras, the wife of Kalev. Either way, this name was given after the land was conquered from the Canaanites. Thus, we have another example.

Bilaam stated (*BeMidbar* 24:7) [about the Jewish people] "And his king shall be higher than Agag." But Agag was the Amalekite king killed by Shmuel! The Ramban suggests that perhaps every king of Amalek was called Agag, similar to "Pharaoh" in Egypt. The *Maasei HaShem* extends this idea, suggesting that every great leader may have been called by this name, for we find that even in late centuries great leaders in Turkey were called Aga. However, this is not acceptable in the quoted verse. What significance is there to state the Jewish king will be higher than some important chief? It is evident that this verse referred to the mighty king of Amalek in Shmuel's time. Probably his name became a model for later kings, who were called Aga. I believe that the title "Pharaoh" for Egyptian kings, and "Avimelech" for Plishitm kings, is based on the name of the first king. However, no king of Amalek is mentioned in the Chumash, until Agag appears in *Shmuel*. I believe that the previous kings of Amalek were actually called "Amalek" in honor of their founder. When Agag took the throne, he was so mighty that this precedent was ended, and he retained the name given him at birth. Thus, in the pronouncement placed in his mouth by G-d, Bilam informs us that the Jewish king of the future will be greater than Agag, of Shmuel's time – another pre-naming example by the G-d of the universe, who stands above time and foresees all the coming generations.

Chapter 34

A discussion of names of people and of places in the Torah which reflect directly on future events that make these names so appropriate, and demonstrate how the Torah looked into the future.

As explained in the last chapter, we find many names based on future events. So too, many times a name itself is a prediction of events to come, e.g., Avraham is explained in the Torah (*Bereishis I 17:5*) as meaning "father of a multitude of nations," a promise/prophecy of a true fact. So too, "Sarah" is explained (17:16) as princess, indicating that "kings of nations will emerge from her." The name Peleg indicates (Bereishis 10:25) that "in his days the land was divided," i.e., caused by the tower of Bavel, apparently his father's prophecy. So too, "Noach" was called this name because "this one will comfort us" (or, in Rashi, "will give us rest," since he invented the plow.) How could his father know this, unless it was a prophecy.

Although Yaakov's wives gave names to the tribes, their names ultimately reflect on future events of significance, as foreseen by Yaakov in his blessings to them (*Bereishis* ch.49). "Your brothers will praise you, Yehudah" – who became king. "Dan will judge his people" – refering to mighty Shimshon. "Gad, a regiment will troop upon him, but he will troop in the end," – a fierce tribe that repelled many enemies from conquering his territory east of the Jordan. The root of "Levi" [לוה] means to accompany. The *Maasei HaShem* explains that through this tribe (represented by Moshe), G-d will accompany His people in giving them the Torah. From these examples, we may extrapolate to the other tribes as well, even if we have difficulty to explain some.

Binyamin is an exception, in that his name was not explained by Yaakov or Rachel. Rashi connects *yamin* with "south," as in the phrase (*Tehillim* 89:13) "North and south [*tzafon v'yamin*], You created them."

He then explains that Binyamin gained his territory in the south of Eretz Yisrael. But more than that, his territory touches the Beis HaMikdash at the southern part, with Yehudah at the northern part. This is the great merit that Binyamin received, as prophesied also by Moshe (*Devarim* 33:12), "And He dwells between his shoulders," i.e., at the Holy Temple.

Logically, people should receive their names before they pass away, to reflect on the life they lived. The fact is that we name them when they are born, hoping that the name will symbolize nice things that we have in mind. But the names given in G-d's Torah reflect not only the thoughts of parents, but the eventual development of that person (or place) in later years, as known to the Creator of time.

R. Ashkenazi writes in his *Maasei HaShem* that the names Levi gave to his children are also prophetically symbolic of our later status in *golus*. "Gershon" is the symbol of stranger (*ger*) and driving out (g-r-sh). "Kehas" (k-h-h) represents weakness as in (*Yirmiyahu* 31:28) "the teeth of the children weaken." "Merari" is bitterness. Thus we see so many examples of names that fit perfectly with the future lives of these people, although the parents may have had other thoughts or interpretations. So too, I believe that "Amram", father of Moshe, combines two words, i.e., uplifted nation, for in his time the Jewish people multiplied in supernatural number. Also "Moshe", named by Pharaoh's daughter because "I drew him from the water," actually translates properly as "one who draws (others)." How appropriate for the man who drew the Jewish people out of Egypt and brought them to Mt. Sinai.

It therefore appears that the name Timna, concubine of Elifaz, who gave birth to Eisav, is also in this class of names. The root of this name (מנע) means "deprive" or "prevent." Since Amalek is destined to be wiped off the face of the earth, this mother will eventually be deprived of having descendants in the world.

A marvelous thing is the perfect name given to Aharon our first High Priest. The priesthood and the Beis HaMikdash are like intertwined twins, for one does not function without the other. And the holiest part of the Holy Temple is the Holy of Holies, the center of which is the Ark of the Covenant, often referred to as "the ark" - הארן. These are the four consonants of Aharon's name, given by his parents for whatever reason they had, but eventually a perfect match to his holiest act on Yom

Kippur (entering the Holy of Holies). Surely nobody could imagine that this is a pure coincidence!

Note also that the area where the temple was built was on a mountain purchased from Aravnah the Yevusi. His name is spelled three ways in one chapter (*Shmuel* II, 24:16.18,20): ארונה ארניה האורנה! I believe this can be explained as follows: His true name was Aravnah, as in the first spelling. [The commentators have no explanation of the added "the" to his name.] The second spelling equals 266, precisely the gematria also of the mountain המוריה, where the temple was built, as described (*Divrei HaYamim* II, 3:1) using the full spelling of המוריה with the extra *vov*. The final spelling was fashioned to contain the letters of הארון (the ark) in it, and therefore this name is used regularly afterward. (27) Thus, we note that both the High Priest and the one who sold the plot for the temple have names that include the letters for the Holy Ark, centerpiece of the temple.

There is much more to say about names of people in Tanach, but I will stop with these many examples and proceed to show similar ideas about the future as reflected in the names of places.

I found that as our forefathers traveled about the holy land, the names of the locations that they visited reflect future events that would occur to their children. *Shechem*, for example, means "portion" in Hebrew, and we find (*Melachim* I, 12) that the breakup of Eretz Yisrael into two kingdoms occurred when Rechavam went to Shechem, had his confrontation with the people, and ended with him receiving his portion of the two kingdoms. (Perhaps, when Yaakov told Yosef (*Bereishis* 48:22) that he would receive "one *shechem* over his brothers," it was a prophecy that his descendant, the first king of "Israel," Yeravam, would begin his rule in Shechem. The second name of Shechem was *Eilon Moreh*, and moreh can mean rebellious. How appropriate for the city where Yeravam rebelled against G-d and His Temple. On the other hand, "*Chevron*" has the root for "joining" (chaver), and was the site where, much earlier, (after many tribes followed Yehudah and others followed Binyamin,) David had united all the tribes, and established his kingdom there for over seven years.

The city of *Aay* was burnt down by Yehoshua (*Yehoshua* 8:28) into a great heap of rubble. This root (עי) means a pile of rubble, as we find in *Tehillim* (79:1) and in *Michah* (1:6).

Ein Mishpat, which is *Kadesh* (Bereishis 14:7), as explained by Rashi, is where the righteous Moshe and Aharon were judged over the incident of hitting the rock, and (*BeMidbar* 20:13) G-d was sanctified there.

Avraham pursued the five kings to *Dan,* the root of which means judgement. In this city Yeravam built his abominable calf, worshiped by the people, which was the ultimate cause of the exile from the land, as described in Tanach (*Yirmiyahu* 52:27).

The ancient city of *Shalem*, ruled by Malki-Tzedek, is Yerushalayim. It is the city from which peace comes to the entire world and it was ruled by a king whose name stood for righteousness (*tzedek*).

The land of *Moriah* has had many interpretations, all of which fit for the site of the Holy Temple. It has been related to teaching (Torah), to the incense brought on the altar (מור - myrrh), to the element of fear (מורא) which is felt by all who come to that holy site.

Be-eir Sheva relates to the number seven, as well as to "oath", in several ways:
1) In the well-known expression "from Dan to Be-eir Sheva," it is seen as the southern end of the boundary of Eretz Yisrael, as *sworn* by G-d to Avraham.
2) Seven tribes were the primary holders of territory in Eretz Yisrael. We eliminate Reuven and Gad who settled east of the Jordan, Levi, who had only cities around the country, Shimon, whose portion was subsumed within Yehudah, Yisaschar and Asher were within the territory of Ephrayim and Menashe. This leaves Yehudah, Zevulun, Dan, Naftali, Ephrayim, Menashe, and Binyamin.
3) When Avraham made his *oath* to Avimelech there, he gave him seven lambs as a symbol that he was the sole owner of a well he had recently dug. The midrash (*Bereishis Rabbah* 54:4) says that G-d was upset over this gift, and stated that the joy of conquering Israel would wait for seven generations, seven righteous tzaddikim would be killed, seven tabernacles would be destroyed, etc. Thus, many historical events are reflected in this name.

Yaakov saw angels coming forward to greet him on his return to Eretz Yisrael. He called them "G-d's camp" and named the place *Machanayim*, which translates as "two camps!" The fact is that Machanayim in later history was the final encampment of David as he prepared to face his rebellious son, Avshalom. In this confrontation, the people had indeed divided into two camps!

After his meeting with Eisav (*Bereishis* ch.33), Yaakov goes on to Sukos, before finally entering Eretz Yisrael. This town eventually becomes part of Gad's territory. Although these booths were temporarily built for Yaakov's flocks, they were surely expanded for more permanent use by the shepherds of Gad. As explained previously in Chapter 12, by emphasizing the booths that he built, Yaakov indicated that he foresaw that the tribe of Gad would prefer this land because of its expansive grazing land over living in the holiest territory of the Jewish people, so this name reflected his displeasure with them.

Although Machanayim and Sukos are east of the Jordan, while this chapter discusses cities in Eretz Yisrael, I included them because they have the sanctity of the holy land, as discussed earlier in this volume.

As explained in Chapter 15, *Alon Bachus* is at Beis-El, and this title translates as a "tree of weeping." This city was home for one of Yeravam's golden calves, a major cause of the eventual exile, and thus creating a great weeping for generations. This was explained in detail in Chapter 15.

Beis Lechem in Yehudah was the home of David's father, Yishaay, as found in *Shmuel* I, (17:12). David fought many wars, as G-d told him directly (*Divrei HaYamim* I, 22:8), "You made great wars; you will not build a house for My name for you have spilled much blood...." When Yaakov said to Yehudah (*Bereishis* 49:8) that his hand was upon the nape of his enemy, it was a vision of David pursuing his enemies. Hence, we may say that this city was named Beis Lechem based on the root l–ch –m which means war (as in מלחמה), i.e., the city of the great warrior. So too, *Ephras*, the other name of Beis Lechem, is a clue for David, whose father is called *Ish Ephrasi* (*Shmuel I*, 17:12).

As explained in chapter 21, *MiG-dal Eider* was close to Yerushalayim. From there, people would buy and bring animal sacrifices to the temple. Thus, the term *eder*, which means a flock of animals, is a preview for the location of flocks of animals centuries later.

The Jordan River – called in Hebrew "Yarden" derives (*Bechoros* 55a) from two Hebrew words is ירד דן, i.e., goes down (from) Dan. Yet the city of Dan was called, even in Yehoshua's times, "Leshem." Here too, the Torah gave a name to that great river reflecting its future title based on a city named centuries later.

The interested reader will find many more such examples. The goal of the Torah was to clarify to us that it is G-d's own holy book, and therefore it is incumbent upon us to carefully observe all its laws and statutes for our own great benefit.

In my opinion, all these names of people and places recorded in the language of Ever descendant of Shem, who preserved the Hebrew language for us after the great dispersion from the tower of Bavel, are proof that the Torah recorded them based on the distant future. For at that time, the Canaanite nations controlled the land, speaking other languages. Hence, names like Shalem, Eilon Moreh, Beis Lechem, Efrasa, Mig-dal Eder, etc., were not the names they used. Thus, the Torah created them for our use, to observe how in later centuries these names became very appropriate. How could anyone but G-d accomplish this! This topic deserves much further serious analysis.

Chapter 35

In this chapter, we will see how the Torah knew that Shimshon, as well as Gideon, would be judges in Israel; that the Midianites would lay waste to the land in Gideon's time; that G-d would send angels to Yehoshua and to Gideon; and that unlike kings, the judges would not transmit their leadership to their children. We will analyze one verse to prove that the Torah foresaw that there would be many judges; that David and Shimshon would overpower the Plishtim, and that Shimshon would be a mighty man. The Torah also saw that the period of the judges would precede that of the kings, and previewed the expressions that the people would use in requesting a king.

Yaakov saw a vision of the tribe of Dan producing a judge, and said (*Bereishis* 49:16), "Dan will judge his people like one of the tribes of Israel." Mighty Shimshon was a judge of the tribe of Dan. How marvelous that Yaakov should see a vision of a single individual, centuries later, to fulfill this prophecy. Such a prediction could have been prevented by so many scenarios over the centuries! E.g., bnei Yisrael might have remained slaves in Egypt, or the tribe of Dan might have been killed out, or lost its individual identity, etc.

For this vision to come to pass, the people would have to choose a member of Dan to be judge. But no obstacles occurred and the vision came true, as did so many others recorded in Chumash. An aged Avraham hears that he will yet have a son who will become a great nation, and so it was. How clear it is that only the Creator Himself wrote this Torah, and no human being.

Yaakov gave the (now popular) blessing to Ephrayim and Menashe, saying (*Bereishis* 48:16), "The angel who redeemed me from every evil should bless the children...." The midrash *Bereishis Rabbah* (97:5) applies this verse to Yehoshua (from Ephrayim) and to Gideon (from Menasheh). We must understand why the midrash selected these two as the subjects of this verse. Could it not have applied to the kings who descended from Ephrayim and Menasheh?

Let us analyze Yaakov's words. Beginning with the previous verse (v.15) he says, "The G-d before Whom my fathers, Avraham and Yitzchak, walked; the G-d who was my shepherd all my life to this day; the angel who redeemed me from every evil, should bless the children...." There are two puzzles here.
1) A description of G-d's attributes should match the blessing appropriately. One might say that the G-d who heals the sick should cure this sick person, but not may the mighty G-d who destroys the wicked cure this person. If Yaakov wished to bless his two grandchildren with all

good things including G-d's eternal protection, why refer to Him as his shepherd? A shepherd provides sustenance to his flock. This could only be appropriate if Yaakov was thinking of providing food for their descendants.

2) Why change from referring to G-d and speak of "the angel"?

However, this description is perfect in reference to Gideon. As graphically pictured (*Shoftim,* ch.6), in his time, Midian had been systematically destroying Jewish land, and the people were close to starvation. Hence this phrase is a blessing for Gideon's time, that G-d the shepherd who feeds His flock, should bless Gideon to restore the people to full independence and prosperity from under the thumb of Midian. The following phrase (the angel who redeemed me from every evil) is perfect for both Yehoshua and Gideon. Both of them were directly addressed by angels (*Yehoshua* ch.5) and (*Shoftim* ch. 5), a fact not found with any other judge. (An angel appeared to Shimshon's father, but not to him.) For both of them, the angel's messages were followed by important military victories, in keeping with Yaakov's blessing.

One might ask, why the phrase meant for Gideon was first, and followed by the one meant for both Yehoshua and Gideon? Was not Yehoshua before Gideon? This is no problem. The first brachah was more limited, and then followed by the greater, more inclusive, one. The total image that emerges from this brachah confirms that Yaakov had visions here of Yehoshua and Gideon. The vision of G-d as a "shepherd" in reference to Gideon's period of great hunger, and the reference to angels, who appeared to Yehoshua and Gideon, point to a clear vision of those two leaders of Israel, and demonstrate once again the hand of G-d in writing the Torah, and in granting prophecies of the future to our holy forefathers.

(As mentioned at the beginning of this chapter), the expression by Yaakov that "Dan will judge his people, like one of the tribes of Israel," indicates that the tribes will produce judges in the future, and that Dan will be included. It is a fact that, except for Shimon, every tribe contributed judges or kings, or both. The *Midrash Tadshe* (ch. 8) explains that Shimon was punished for the horrendous sin of their *nasi*, Zimri Ben Salu, to teach us how heinous is the sin of sexual immorality.

I have explained elsewhere that Moshe Rabbeinu left Shimon out of his final blessings to the tribes, because he foresaw that this tribe would not produce any king or judge. In halachah, wherever Rabbeinu Moshe Ben Maimon left out a halachah, all commentators axiomatically conclude that he did not hold that halachah to be valid. So too, when Moshe Rabbeinu omitted Shimon, he showed that he recognized him to be inferior in this respect, finding no glorious ideas to proclaim for him. We may presume that since he did address all the other tribes, he surely saw that they would all contribute to the list of judges or kings.

It is also clear that the Torah (Yaakov) foresaw that, unlike kingship which continues from father to son, the position of judges would not be inherited by children. This is the additional meaning of the prophecy about Dan, that he would judge his people "like one of the tribes of

Israel." This implies that the position of judge would simply move about amongst the tribes, a sharp contrast to kingdom, where the Torah speaks of kings and the blessing they will receive for keeping the Torah (*Devarim* 17:20), "so that he may prolong his days in his kingdom, *he and his sons*, in the midst of Israel."

Although Rashi offers a different twist to the phrase "like one of the tribes of Israel," and renders it as "like *the special* tribe of Israel," i.e., Yehudah, therefore hinting to David, and implying that a judge from the tribe of Dan will be as unique among the judges as David was among the kings, this is not the simple meaning of the verse. As translated by Onkelos, it means that Dan will supply a judge (or judges) like any other tribe of the Jewish people, in keeping with our analysis above. (28) I will later explain why Dan was singled out over all the other tribes in reference to producing judges.

Even if we were to argue that Rashi considered the hint to King David to be the simple meaning of the verse, and thus eliminate any reference to the later judges, this prophecy would be very significant for other reasons. It is actually strange to believe that Shimshon could be viewed as the most unique of the judges, for he is surely a lesser spiritual personality than Shmuel or Yehoshua. Surely there is a vast gap between him and David. Hence, if Rashi's interpretation is taken seriously, it must be a reference to some unique matter that Shimshon and David share, making Shimshon unique in that aspect. In fact, there is such a feature! Shimshon is the only judge singled out for his special contribution of helping to rid the land of the Plishtim. As the angel prophesied to his mother (*Shoftim* 13:5), "And he will begin to deliver Israel from the hand of the Plishtim." David completely subdued them in his days, as mentioned in *Shmuel II*, (8:1). Thus, whether we view this verse through the eyes of Rashi, or through Onkelos, it provides prophetic insights into later Jewish history.

I must admit, however, that Rashi offered another simple reading,. He translates the verse as saying, that Dan will judge the people by uniting them all behind him "as one." This would eliminate both of the above analyses. However, it is far-fetched to suggest that this could stand as the one perfect translation of the verse. Could we imagine that a judge from Dan would only judge part of the people? Had the verse stated that "Dan will judge his people," who would have thought that "his people" is not the Jewish people as a whole? Surely, this is why Rashi offered additional meanings to the verse. Hence, the two interpretations with all the significant implications mentioned above, should be seen as valid and meaningful readings.

There is another marvelous implication in the verse Yaakov dedicated to Dan, about Shimshon.

Unlike other judges, leaders, or kings, Shimshon did not give orders, or organize armies for battle. By himself, he fought for the Jewish people, as is clear in reading the chapters devoted to him in *Shoftim*. Thus, the concept that all the tribes of Israel will be "like one,' i.e., united behind him is true in this sense. He personally and alone battled for all the tribes of his people, thus representing all the people. Thus, even this third reading offers insight into the future of Dan, and the people of Israel.

Whichever of the three interpretations we accept, there are prophetic messages for the future history of klal

Yisrael.

If we read the second phrase in the verse about Dan as "like the special one of the tribes," we may argue, as the Or HaChayim states, that this is not limited to King David (as argued above) but implies that every tribe will have a special person (i.e., king or judge), and Dan will be included in this feature.(29)

There are also several proofs that the Torah saw the era of the judges as preceding the era of the kings. A) Yaakov promises Yehudah that the scepter (of kingship, as explained in the Ramban's discussion of this term) will not depart from him until "Shiloh." While this will be discussed further, the fact is that had the era of the judges come after the kingdom under Yehudah was established, this prophecy would have been nullified.
B) The Torah states (Devarim 17:14) that after you conquer and settle the land of Israel, you will say "Let me place a king upon me like all the nations around me...," indicating clearly that kingship will not occur soon after arriving in the land. This actually happened at the end of the period of the judges in the days of Shmuel. In fact, at that time, the request to have a king was made in the very terms and description mentioned in the Torah, including the expression "a king like all the nations around us." Since G-d fore- saw how the request would be made, he recorded in the Torah the precise language, for otherwise this phrase is entirely extraneous. Once again, we have a demonstration of the truth of the Torah as given to us by the Creator.

How perfect is the analysis of the Baal HaTurim who wrote in Parashas Shoftim that only when the Plishtim in the south part of the land changed their system of government from "seranim" (chiefs) to kings, did the people clamor for a king to imitate them. Obviously, in the several hundred years of living in the land, they would have to have leaders. Of course these were the judges. Hence, the Torah clearly knew that the period of the judges would precede the era of kingship.

C) In the terrifying description of the calamities that would strike a rebellious Jewish nation, we were warned (*Devarim* 28:36) that G-d will exile us "and your king whom you will place upon yourselves to a nation that you do not know...." Thus, the exile that occurred late in our history would take place during the kingship period. Obviously, the era of the judges would have preceded this period.

We cannot suggest that perhaps while David would rule over Yehudah and Binyamin, there would be judges leading the other ten tribes, simultaneously. The description of Dan ruling the people [Shimshon] clearly implies that he would lead the entire nation, as indicated in the discussion of that verse earlier. Furthermore, as I will prove in chapter 36, the Torah foresaw the two kingdoms of Yehudah and Yisrael as being ruled by two sets of kings, so obviously there would not be a king and a judge at the same time. I will return to the discussion of the judges again in chapters 41, 77 and 78.

Chapter 36

In this chapter we will show that the Torah saw kings of Yehudah, and that simultaneously there would be kings for Yisrael. The Torah also hints at the three types of kings in our history: a) Kings chosen by a navi (e.g., Shaul, David, Yeravam, Yeihu); b) kingdom that will continue through descendants forever (David); c) Kings chosen by the people (only in Yisrael). It also reveals that the final kings of Yehudah who went into golus would not be entitled by Torah law to sit on the throne (e.g., Yehoachaz and his brothers).

We already know from Yaakov's prophecy that the tribe of Yehudah was destined for the kingship forever. That verse also proves that the Torah foresaw other kings from the other tribes. Otherwise we would have an unanswerable problem from a later verse (*Devarim* 17:20) which warns the king that he must observe the Torah if he wishes to have his kingdom continue "in the midst of all Israel" through his descendants. Such a warning would imply that Yehudah's hold on the throne is not absolutely guaranteed to last forever! One cannot argue that this warning may mean that if the king abandons the Torah, the entire Jewish people would be exiled leaving no king at all; since the phrase "in the midst of all Israel" clearly implies that the people would still remain in the land. Nor can we imagine that Yaakov prophesied that the kings of Yehudah would never sin, for we see that several of them (e.g., Achaz, Menashe, etc.) completely abandoned the mitzvos. Nevertheless, descendants of David never lost kingship until it was suspended with the destruction of the Second Temple and the exile of the people. Obviously, the warning in *Devarim* was meant for the other kingdom of Israel, which did see the kingdom move from tribe to tribe when the kings forsook the Torah. Thus, Yaakov's prophecy perfectly uses the term "Yehudah," which held true historically with the kingdom of Yehudah, while in *Devarim*, the warning spoke of "the midst of Israel," referring to the kingdom of Yisrael.

How perfectly Yaakov expressed the prophecy about Yehudah in the negative form. Had he said that Yehudah will rule over his brothers forever, the establishment of a second kingdom of Yeravam would have turned his words into a false vision! However, now it guarantees a continuous kingdom for Yehudah through David, but not eliminating a second one over some tribes. For this second kingdom, the verses in *Devarim* properly warn that the kingdom of "Yisrael" may move from tribe to tribe, as indeed occurred in history.

Since the term "scepter" is not an absolute term indicating kingship, several commentators wrote that it has a second implication, i.e., that a staff of beatings and tribulations would accompany the kings of Yehudah. This occurred many times, with David himself (e.g., fleeing from his son Avshalom), and with many of his descendants. Among them: Shlomo was plagued by Hadad, and lived to age 52; Rechavam lost ten tribes to Yeravam; Aviah died mysteriously after ruling only three years, and Chazal say that the phrase (*Divrei HaYamim II*, 13:20) "And G-d smote him and he died" refers to Aviah (although it could have been understood as speaking of Yeravam); Asa and Yehoram both suffered severe sicknesses; etc. etc.

The Hebrew term for "scepter" [שבט] is used also as a tool for beating someone. In the psalm of Eisan HaEzrachi (*Tehillim* 89) David is told good news and bad news. Although he is guaranteed eternal rule for his descendants, he is warned that if they abandon G-d, they will be punished "with a שבט," perfectly matching the term used by Yaakov to Yehudah! It is rather amazing that we do not find the kings of Yisrael, although wicked and sinful, suffering from such plagues and sicknesses.

<u>The Amazing Precision of the Phrase:</u> *"The scepter [שבט] shall not depart from Yehudah":*
We have seen that the term *sheivet* has three possible connotations: a) the staff of kingship b) a tribe c) a rod of punishment and beating. How intriguing that all three are correct!
A) The simple meaning is that kingship will never leave the tribe of Yehudah, since David established an eternal kingdom for himself and his descendants, which, while interrupted, will continue with the arrival of Mashiach. This was guaranteed to David several times (e.g., *Shmuel II* 7:16).
B) There is one tribe that will never leave Yehudah, for even when his rule was diminished by the establishment of the competing kingdom of Yisrael, the tribe of Binyamin never left Yehudah. Thus, "There shall not depart *one* tribe from (being with) Yehudah."

C) The punishing rod will not leave Yehudah's kings. Here the vision of Yaakov prepares us for the many tribulations many of David's descendants suffered, even as his kingship never left. While G-d had warned David (*ibid,* 7:14) that if his descendants sin, they will suffer from the "rod [שבט] of men and the plagues of people," his kingship was promised for eternity. We may well explain that the first threat implied that "men" would establish a competing kingdom (*sheivet*), while the second phrase clearly indicated plagues that would strike later kings of Yehudah. Even with all these insights we have not completed our analysis of the amazing prophecy of Yaakov to Yehudah.

<u>Further deep meanings in the vision of the *sheivet:*</u>
Since the Torah clearly warned that we might be (and indeed were) driven out of the land due to our sins (e.g., *Devarim* 4:26-27; *VaYikra* 26:32-34; etc.), we must recognize that Yaakov's promise of eternal kingship to Yehudah only applies when we are in the land. This is why the verse added "And a lawgiver...." As Chazal understood, this meant that if we were driven out, our leaders and spiritual authorities would remain descendants of Yehudah, as occurred in history, "until Mashiach comes," when the kingdom would be restored to Yehudah. Since during the exile there were no kings at all over the Jewish people, the threat in Chumash *Devarim* discussed earlier as applying to the kingdom of Yisrael proves that the Torah foresaw both kingdoms as existing simultaneously in the pre-exile period. The difference between these two kingdoms is that David was promised eternal rule, while the kingdom of Yisrael (which transferred from tribe to tribe) was not, and therefore it totally vanished from the world scene never to be

reinstituted. (Although almost all commentators and statements of Chazal claim that the ten tribes will return in the era of Mashiach, we will be one united people and one kingdom under Mashiach.)

Other Visions of the Kings of Yehudah and Yisrael

Regarding the choice of a king there is an apparently glaring contradiction *within one verse*! We are instructed (*Devarim* 17:15) to place upon ourselves a king "whom G-d will choose," while being warned not to choose a "stranger who is not our brother" as king! But of course G-d will not choose a Gentile king, and we know that only G-d can make the choice! The mere suggestion of considering a "stranger" implies that there could be circumstances where the people may choose a king without G-d's instruction!

The solution to this puzzle is clear. Many kings were chosen by G-d through his prophets, e.g., Shaul through Shmuel; David also through Shmuel; Yeravam through Achiyah HaShiloni; Yeihu through Yonah Ben Amitaay. All kings of Yisrael, except Yeravam and Yeihu, ruled without G-d's authority. Thus, the Torah instructs us to accept the kings whom G-d chose through His prophets (since G-d foresaw that some would face resistance, e.g., Shaul was originally not accepted; David rejected by Avshalom and Shimi Ben Geira; Rechavam rejected by Yeravam). For most of the kings of Yisrael the conclusion of the verse admonished the people not to allow a Gentile to sit on their throne, implying that no particular tribe had rights to that throne.

Thus, this verse contains three parts. A) Accept those

kings who are chosen by G-d through His prophets. B) A middle phase "From the midst of your brothers place a king upon yourselves" - this seemingly extraneous phrase is surely meant for the people to accept the kingship of David whose tribe of Yehudah was specifically chosen from the midst of the other brothers to have an eternal monarchy. (A marvelous comment of the *Baal HaTurim* notes that the Hebrew terms מקרב אחיך ("from the midst of your brothers" is precisely the gematria [381]of יהודה משבט ("from the tribe of Yehudah")! C) Other kings of Yisrael (except Yeravam and Yeihu) must be limited to members of the Jewish tribes, to exclude Gentiles. We should note also that the Torah foresaw the rule of Shaul as king in the phrase G-d spoke to Yaakov before Binyamin was born (*Bereishis* 35:11) "...and kings *will emerge* from your loins. Soon after, Binyamin was born. (I will elaborate on this topic in the next chapter.) All of the above discussion about this amazing verse powerfully demonstrates and proves that G-d alone could have written the Torah and hidden so many future events of later centuries in a single verse.

We can also show that the Torah foresaw that the last kings of Yehudah (before the exile) would not truly be entitled to sit on the throne by the law of the Torah. Chazal derive (*Kesubos* 103b) that kingdom is transmitted to the king's first-born as stated in *Divrei HaYamim II* (21:3), "...and the kingdom he gave to Yehoram *because* he was the *bechor*." The last kings of Yehudah were not first-born, but rather chosen by the people, as we find (*Melachim II* 23:30), "...and the people took Yeho-achaz son of Yoshiyahu and *anointed him* and made him king in place of his father." Rada'k points out that ordinarily the rightful successor to the throne does not require anointing, unless there are pretenders to the throne (e.g., Shlomo was anointed because of the attempt of Adoniyahu to be crowned). However, since Yeho-achaz was younger than his brother Yehoyakim, but was nevertheless chosen by the people against the proper system of succession, he was anointed. We know that Yeho-achaz was younger since he was anointed at the age of twenty-three, and ruled only three months, replaced by Yehoyakim who was then twenty five (as clearly stated in *Melachim II* ch.23). Although kingship was restored to the first-born, with Yehoyakim later on the throne and followed briefly by his son Yehoyachin, he was followed by Matanyah, youngest son of Yoshiayahu, placed on the throne by Nevuchadnezer and renamed Tzidkiyahu, although he should have been followed by Yehoyakim's remaining son Tzidkiya. Hence, both Yeho-achaz and Tzidkiyahu were not entitled to the throne.

The Torah warns that if we abandon HaShem, (*Devarim* 28:36), "G-d will conduct you and your king whom *you shall place upon yourself* to a nation that you do not know...." Since we have already demonstrated that this happened only with the kings of Yehudah, the verse should have stated "that He will place upon you." Hence, this implies that the Torah knew – for G-d alone stands above time – that there would be kings over Yehudah who will not be bonafide rulers, but merely chosen by popular acclaim!

Chapter 37

In this chapter we will show hidden clues in the Torah that the kingdom of Yehudah would emerge from Peretz – that there would be a king before David from another tribe – that this king would rule only a short period – that his assigned goal would be the annihilation of Amalek – that David would desist from any attack upon him, although he would seek to kill David – that David would subjugate several nations (i.e., Plishtim, Edom, Moav, Ammon) – that Shaul would not fulfill his command to destroy Amalek – that he would sin terribly at Nov the city of the Kohanim – that Shaul would sin by bringing up the soul of Shmuel through witchcraft – and other details about the lives of Shaul and David.

Before we demonstrate that the Torah foresaw a Jewish king preceding David, we must first examine the Torah's description of the birth of Yaakov and Eisav. Even if the Torah had not indicated the uniqueness of the internal struggle during Rivka's pregnancy, we would have understood that this was highly symbolic, for otherwise it would have been an irrelevant description. Once explained by the Torah, we clearly know of the eternal battle between these two nations. Thus, although the fact that

Yaakov held on to Eisav's heel is not explained there, we can understand that Yaakov's ascendency on the world scene (symbolized by his hand/power) will take place after Eisav's, for Eisav emerged first. Indeed, as we read later (*Bereishis* 37:31), "These are the kings who ruled in the land of Edom *before* a king ruled over *bnei Yisrael*." (I also believe that G-d's warning (*Devarim* 2:5) that we must not incite the Edomites into war because we will not gain any of their territory "even (עד) a foot breadth (כף רגל)" may be rendered as "*until* the king (the symbolic hand of Yaakov) steps forth who held the leg of Eisav."

Note that just as Eisav was born covered by red hair, King David is described (*Shmuel I* 16:12) as "and he was red-headed...." Thus, when the Torah stated that "one nation will be stronger than the other nation," this took place when "the red" David's army eliminated every male of "the red" Edom (*Melachim I* 11:15), yet in the days of Yehoram, Edom rebelled against the kings of Yehudah and placed a king upon themselves (*Melachim II* 8:20). Later, King Amatzya annihilated ten thousand of the Edomites (*Melachim II* 14:7). This rising and falling of power is understood by Chazal as the meaning of "one nation will be stronger than the other nation," i.e., (as Rashi quotes) "when this one rises this one falls, and when this one falls the other rises." The next phrase reads, "and the older will serve the younger." Ultimately (*Ovadia* v.21), the victorious Jewish people will rise up "to judge the mountain of Eisav, and the kingdom will be G-d's." It is noteworthy that in the previous verse (v.23), in the Hebrew terms to Rivka, the information that she bore twins, תאומים(twins) is spelled תומם, leaving out the two letters that have a gematria of eleven. I believe that this may hint at the idea that there were still eleven generations still to come, from Yaakov to David, before the "younger will gain his (first) power over the elder." These generations are (from Yaakov): Yehudah, Peretz, Chetzran, Ram, Aminadav, Nashshon, Salmon, Boaz, Oveid, Yishaay, David.

We now understand why the Torah detailed so carefully the births of Peretz and Zerach, and the motive of Yehudah in giving their names. This is not found with any of Yaakov's other grandchildren, (except for Yosef for whom the Torah did so because his two sons became recognized as separate tribes). The name Peretz is no mystery for us, for it offers a glimpse of the future when David and his royal descendants would break forth and rule over the tribes. Peretz breaks out before Zerach, just as David bursts forth to take the kingdom over (even) his older brothers. Furthermore, this chapter interrupts the story of Yosef as he is being brought to Egypt. The Torah is telling us that just as he is soon to become a prime minister in Egypt and "ruler" over his brothers, in keeping with his dreams, so too Yehudah will become king in keeping with Yaakov's prophecy that the staff of kingship will eventually be with Yehudah. So too, just as Esther becomes queen to prepare the solution for the Jewish people *before* the threat of Haman to destroy them (as the Talmud always reminds us that the "healing" is prepared before the "plague"), the Torah tells us, in effect, that the eventual kingdom of Yehudah over the Jewish people is already in progress before their descent into Egypt to centuries of temporary, cruel slavery. As we find in a midrash, "The tribes were busy with selling Yosef, and HaShem was busy with creating the 'light' of Mashiach." Another midrash (*BeMidbar Rabbah* 2:21) states that wherever HaShem was engaged in establishing a nation or

Marvels of Our Blessed G-d's Torah

a chain of important pedigree, He records the family tree... as we find etc... and for two people He recorded their pedigree, one for the kingdom and one for the priesthood as explained there: (Peretz and Aharon). It is quite clear that in the account of the birth of Peretz, the Torah already foresaw King David's reign.

Note that we often find with our prophets that they are instructed to do an action, or give their children a chosen name, to serve as a prophecy for the future. E.g., Hoshea (ch.1) was ordered by G-d to marry a prostitute, and Yeshayahu (ch. 8) was told by G-d to name his son *Maher Shalal Chash Baaz,* etc., for symbolic reasons. So too with Yehudah, his son's name "Peretz "symbolized his power as a king who may halachically break forth into private property to make a path for his army. Thus his name is equivalent to calling him "king,." just as the struggle in Rivka's womb was a portent of the eternal battle between Yaakov and Eisav.

Note: The chapter about Yehudah and Tamar creates an interesting question: When Yehudah goes out to establish his family, he marries the daughter of Shua, and she is thus called Bas-Shua. Why is her own name never given in the text? A true mystery is found in *Divrei HaYamim I* (3:5) where Shlomo is called one of the sons of Bas-Shua rather than Bas-Sheva! I am convinced that here the Torah looked into the distant future, that Bas-Shua would bring forth David and the entire kingdom of Yehudah. Although her first son (Eir) and his brother (Onan) both died, the birth of Peretz [and Zerach] to Yehudah and Tamar brought back [by reincarnation - *gilgul*] Eir and Onan, respectively. Many commentators have claimed that Peretz was, in fact, Eir. Hence, Bas-Sheva is called Bas-

Shua in *Divrei HaYamim* to hint at this secret. Thus, Yehudah's wish to "establish a name for Eir," as he stated to Onan, took place by Eir's return as Peretz. Perhaps, this was also hinted by the midrash which states that "Bas-Sheva was suited for David from the six days of creation."(31)

Further Analysis of the Yehudah-Tamar Incident

It is clear that the Torah's insertion of these events in the life of Yehudah came to point to the eventual rule of David (from Yehudah) as king, descending from Peretz. This represents a marvelous and exalted wisdom on HaShem's part. He knew that eventually His children would find (in *Megillas Rus*) the pedigree of David descending from Peretz, and presented this story in detail, giving many clues to the ascendency of Peretz as the primary son of Yehudah.

A) The fact that, unlike the other sons, there are so many details presented with Yehudah's family;

B) That later on, Yaakov would clearly state that the "scepter shall not depart from Yehudah," leading the logical reader to review this chapter and recognize that this would take place through Peretz.

C) The insertion of this story in middle of the description of Yosef's life, obviously to show that just as Yosef's adventures are precursors to Jewish history leading to his descendant, Shaul, establishing the monarchy, simultaneously Yehudah begins the process leading to the eternal kingdom founded by David.

D) When we note that Yaakov referred to Yehudah (*Bereishis* 49:9) as a "young lion," (the king of the animal world,) who "rose from the prey of my son," by saving Yosef from the plan of Shimon and Levi to kill him immediately, we realize that at that instant he "became" the young lion who would receive the kingdom.

E) People would surely note that after a previous chapter (ch.36) that listed the kings of Edom "before a king ruled amongst Bnei Yisrael," it is logical that soon afterward in the tale of Yehudah's life, the Torah would prepare us to see the eventual kingship in Bnei Yisrael as emanating from Yehudah, and that just as Edom was a twin who preceded Yaakov in birth, but would eventually fall to the Jewish people, so too, his kingdom preceded ours, but would be outlived by the eventual rule of Mashiach. In Yehudah's case too, Zerach wanted to exit first, but was pushed back by Peretz, for royalty can break forth with power. All of the above shows that G-d the author gave us a glimpse of the future of the Jewish people, as only He could do, standing above time and foreseeing all the events of Jewish history.

Additional Observations in the Story of Yehudah and Tamar

We must now interpret the wonders in the birth of the twins. We read (38:28) that Zerach extended his hand and the midwife tied a string to his hand, saying that "this one came forth first." Some worthy questions:

1) In all world literature this is astonishing and unique. But, what is the purpose of such an occurrence anyway? If the Torah described it, it must be very significant.

2) Why is the description worded, "*He* put out his hand," instead of "One of them put out his hand"?

3) Why did the midwife hurry to tie the thread without waiting for him to be born? [Did she imagine that he would withdraw it, if this never occurred in history?]

4) The wording is peculiar. Translated literally it reads,

"And the midwife took, and tied on his hand, a thread," instead of "took a thread...."

5) The next verse: "And it happened, as he was withdrawing his hand, and *behold* his brother came out," should have stated, "He withdrew his hand, and afterward his brother came out."

6) The midwife exclaimed (v.29), "How you have broken forth upon yourself a breach," yet *he* called him Peretz. Also, the expression "upon yourself" should have been "upon *him* (Zerach)."

7) When Zerach came out, why did the Torah have to repeat the obvious fact that he was the one with the string on his hand? And in v.28, the midwife tied a thread to his hand *saying* "this one came out first."   Why was the extra word "saying" necessary here?

Let us examine this chapter and try to answer all these questions.

At first thought, it seems that the midwife did something meaningless. Why not wait until he is born, and mark him in some way to show he is the *bechor*? If he were to retreat and be born second, the thread would not declare him as the *bechor* anyway! Furthermore, why did the Torah describe this entire incident?

Obviously, in this unusual situation of a hand appearing, the midwife, who realized that there were two babies in the womb, understood that he might not be born first. She wanted to be able to prove whether this baby was actually born first or second. Without the thread, if he withdrew the hand and later a baby emerged, nobody could determine which baby he was. While this might have been mere curiosity on her part, the fact that the Torah carefully recorded this tells us that HaShem wanted us to see great significance in it.

It surely means the following: Since we have already shown in detail that the prior emergence of Peretz foretold that he would be king, the appearance of the hand must symbolize that before Peretz rules, a hand will rise to form a first kingdom to precede Peretz's descendant. This would be the kingdom of Shaul! The hand means that this kingdom would be only a passing, temporary phase in Jewish history. Thus this entire event foretold that a kingdom would arise in Israel, followed by a full and permanent kingdom ruled over by descendants of Peretz.

The obvious objection is, why would Shaul's kingdom be foretold by Zerach, who is not from Shaul's tribe?

Should this not have been foretold in connection with the birth of Binyamin's children? However, this is no true objection. We already have found prophecies of both Yehudah's kingship, as well as Binyamin's rule, in Yaakov's visions before he died (as explained there by Rashi). Binyamin is seen as a wolf and Yehudah as a lion, the king of the animal world. With Zerach and Peretz, the only further point was to show that the other king's rule would precede Yehudah's. Yaakov's vision revealed that this other king would be from Binyamin. Had the incident of Zerach showing a hand not occurred, and a prophecy about Binyamin been given with Binyamin's children, we would not have been certain about the order of precedence. Now we know that the hand of another kingdom will be raised before the ruler from Peretz will take the throne forever. (Besides, the Torah could not even suggest that a prior king would arise from Zerach, and then be replaced by Peretz' line, since once any king of Yehudah takes the throne it must be his forever, based on

Yaakov's prophecy for Yehudah.)

We can now answer question 2, above. "*He* put out his hand," rather than "one of them..." indicates an unidentified hand, hinting at the possibility that it does not represent a hand from a descendant of Yehudah!

How appropriate is the name Zerach (named for the shiny thread on his hand!), which means to shine. For ultimately he represents Shaul, who rose [as Rashi describes in Parashas *VaYechi* (49:27)] at the dawn and "first shine" of Yisrael.

I also find it fascinating to note that when a hand is mentioned in the Torah, it typically is the right hand, *yamin* in Hebrew. Thus the *yad-yamin* of Zerach, even if he is actually from Yehudah, could point to *Binyamin*. I believe that Yaakov may have meant "son of my right," for the right symbolizes strength. Of Rachel's two sons, Yosef is the ancestor of the wicked Yeravam, while from Binyamin came the righteous Shaul, one of the transmitters of our *mesorah*.

According to Kaballah, Peretz reincarnates Eir, and Zerach is *Onan*. Since Zerach's hand is ultimately Shaul from Binyamin, how fascinating that Rachel called him Ben-*Oni* (Onan). (32)

Further Thoughts about Zerach's *Hand*

In Tanach, the hand symbolizes/means many things, all of which can be applied to the kingship in Jewish history. 1) It means legal authority, as in (*Bereishis* 41:35), "under the *hand* of Pharaoh," i.e., his control and authority. 2) It means power, as in (*Devarim* 32:36), "He will see that their *hand* (power) is gone...." This use implies rulership or kingship, as in the expression *yad ramah* ("upraised hand.") 3) It means dealing in partnership as with the sinner who lies about an object he was guarding, or he was partner with another, called (*VaYikra* 5:21) *tesumes yad* (i.e., he gave his hand in a pledge to the other). So too, Shaul became a "partner" to David in kingship. 4) It means a part of a whole, as in (*Mishlei* 13:11), "He who gathers little by little (*al yad*) will increase." So too, Shaul ruled over a part of the Jewish people for only two years. 5) It also means nearby, as in (*BeMidbar* 13:20), "The Canaanites dwell (*al yad*) *by* the sea and *by* the Jordan." So too, the kingdoms touched geographically. 6) Finally, it symbolizes an act of trespass, as in (*Shemos* 22:10), "He shall take an oath that he did not *stretch forth his hand* upon his neighbor's property." Combining all these meanings, the hand of Zerach, which symbolized Shaul, as analyzed earlier, tells us that Shaul will have a monarchy, partnering with David, but only over a small portion, bordering on David's territory, and will eventually rebel against G-d's instructions regarding Amalek, losing his power to David (Peretz) who broke out over him in power. Thus, the added term (v.28) "saying" really means that this act *says to us who read the Torah* that this emergence of a hand speaks volumes about future Jewish history.

The term for the thread *"shani"* can be read *sheini* i.e., the number "second" or "two." It is interesting that both Shaul and his son Ish-Boshes each ruled for two years! By placing this word *with "his hand"* it implies that the power would last two years. This answers question 4, above. Might we also suggest the following intriguing idea: In David's song (*Shmuel II* ch.22) repeated later (*Tehillim* ch.18) there are some interesting changes in terminology. In the later version he speaks of being saved from (v.1)"the hand (*yad*) of Shaul," a small variation of the original in Shmuel (22:1) where he used *"the kaf"* of Shaul. Although this also means "hand," the change to "yad" echoes of the hand of Zerach, the symbol of Shaul in later history.

We can now clarify a strange expression in *Shmuel I* (15:12) [when the navi went to seek out Shaul after his war with Amalek to inform him that he would lose the kingdom for not obeying the command of G-d to leave no survivors.] Shmuel is told that "Shaul has come to Carmel and is setting up a *yad*" (a commemorative monument?). We find many commentators wondering about this expression. However, it seems quite appropriate to match this phrase with the outstretched hand of Zerach. Perhaps Shaul also conceived that the hand of Zerach symbolized his own rise to the kingship, and his erection of a monument, which is called a *yad* in Tanach, was his way of proclaiming a vision of his hope for an eternal throne. In his mind this was earned by him for his successful war against Amalek. We find that when Shmuel was told about Shaul's whereabouts, the verse states that it was told to Shmuel "saying" (לאמר). Why is this word needed? This echoes the *leimor* we noted in question 8, above. We may say that Shmuel is told (by G-d in a Divine message) that Shaul imagines that he is the king, prophetically indicated by the hand of Zerach to indicate an eternal monarchy.

It is noteworthy how often the term *yad* is found in reference to Shaul's hand in Tanach (see *Shmuel I* 23:17; *Shmuel II* 12:7; *Tehillim* 18:1).

We can now appreciate the absolute perfection of the

expression in *Chumash Shemos* (17:16): And he [Moshe] said, "For a *hand* [is raised, i.e., an oath exists] upon the throne of G-d [G-d has sworn], there is a war of G-d with Amalek from generation to generation." Since Shaul is represented by a hand, behind the simple meaning of this expression lies a deeper interpretation: the hand of Shaul will precede (על) that of David, whose kingdom is called "the throne of G-d" (as we find with Shlomo (*Divrei Hayamim I* 29:23) who "sat on the throne of G-d."), to conduct G-d's war with Amalek. Thus, the hand of Shaul will begin the eternal war with Amalek ("*from his generation*") to (the final) *generation* of Mashiach Ben David. (32) (Without this deeper meaning, the expression would have been "dor dor" rather than "midor dor." The additional "*from* generation" implies that it will begin at one time and then be completed at another generation.)

Further Wondrous Points in the Chapter about Yehudah

The term for the thread "shani" indicates something colored red, as in the term *tolaas shani* used frequently in *Chumash VaYikra*, and in *Yeshayahu* (1:18), "Come....if your sins be like scarlet (*kashanim*) they shall be white as snow...." We also know that red often indicates the spilling of blood, as the midrashim explain Eisav's red hair. Hence the red thread on Zerach's hand becomes an additional hint of the destined use of Shaul's hand to spill the blood of Amalek (as we indicated above that Rachel's descendants were chosen for this task), who is the grandson of "red" Eisav. However, the withdrawal of Zerach's hand foretells that Shaul will draw back from completing his task by sparing Amalek's king Agag! The expression we quoted earlier, "And it happened *as he was withdrawing his hand, behold, his brother came out....*"

seems to say that *because* he withdrew his hand (i.e., Shaul did not complete his mission), Peretz came out to replace him (David gains the kingdom). (Of course the midwife had no notion whatever of all this. It was the spirit of G-d hovering over all these events to show us visions of the future.) This helps explain (question 5 above) the term "and behold," indicating the immediate consequence and direct result of that withdrawal was the powerful emergence of the true kingdom of the Jewish people.

Understanding all of the above, we now can appreciate the curious expression of the midwife (v.29), "How you have broken forth *upon yourself* a breach," rather than "upon him."

This act is significant. It represents or symbolizes King David
taking the kingdom from Shaul. But David never attacked, or rebelled against, Shaul in any way. On the contrary, even when he could have killed him in his sleep, he was careful not to do so, but exclaimed (*Shmuel I* 26:11), "G-d forbid that I should strike G-d's anointed." Hence, even if this expression of the midwife was quite awkward, [a slip of the tongue?], she could not say the intended words, which would have been incorrect in later history. Instead, it is as if he broke forth to kingship by the strength of his own soul and faith in G-d. This answers question 6.

In question 7 we asked why the Torah added, after Peretz was born, that the brother came out "that the thread was on his hand." Wasn't this obvious? However, this is very significant. The appearance of Peretz represents the establishment of David as king. After the war with

Amalek, Shaul was told clearly and absolutely that he had lost the kingdom for not annihilating Amalek as ordered, leaving Agag and their flocks alive. Nevertheless, even after this stage of Jewish history being foretold, Shaul *later* proceeded to wipe out the Kohanim of the city of Nov (*Shmuel I*. ch.22), in effect, using the "bloody red thread" improperly. This is the perfect symbol of "*afterwards*, his brother came out" – after David is already declared to be king – and "the thread of blood is on his hand" – to kill innocent people, rather than those whom he should have killed earlier!

(I can also suggest a positive symbol in this red thread called *shani*. After Shaul was killed, David exclaimed in his eulogy (*Shmuel II* 1:24), "Daughters of Israel, weep over Shaul, who clothed you in *scarlet* (shani) and other delights...." This may be an additional "prophecy" of the midwife.)

To answer question 7: Note that although Leah named her first two sons, "*he* called him Levi." As the midrash (in Rashi) explains, the angel Gavriel brought him before G-d, and He gave this name for he would be accompanied with the gifts of priesthood and the gifts of the Leviim. Thus, for an important name with great meaning for the future, "he" gives the name. Here too, since the birth of the twins symbolize so much as the future history of the Jewish people, the Torah changes to the male form for naming both sons. Perhaps we may say that here too, the names were given by G-d!

Now let us concentrate our minds on this phenomenon. The Torah recorded two sets of twins in *Chumash Bereishis*. Rivka gave us Yaakov and Eisav, who produced Edom and Amalek. Yaakov is progenitor of two kingdoms, Binyamin and David. Binyamin (Shaul – and later Mordecai) becomes the great adversary of Amalek, while David and several of his royal descendants war with Edom. David subdued Edom (*Shmuel II* 8:14) and they remained in subjugation until their rebellion against King Yehoram (*Melachim II* 8:20). Later, King Amatzya won a great war against Edom (*ibid.* 14:7), and his son Azaryahu (14:22) captured Eilat from Edom and built it up. Later (ch. 16:6) Eilat was recaptured, and settled by Edom again. Thus, the battle of Edom and Yisrael continued, and will end with the arrival of Mashiach.

Thus, the second set of twins becomes "a twin" to the first set! We may interpret the response Rivka received during her difficult pregnancy a new way (*Bereishis* 25:23): There are two nations (Yaakov and Eisav) in your womb, *and* two kingdoms will separate *(from each)* from your bowels; [since the term le-om implies kingdom:] Shaul and David from Yaakov, the kings of Edom and Agag of Amalek from Eisav. Tamar's twins provide further clarification, that a raised hand of Zerach would be the temporary king Shaul to vanquish Amalek, and Peretz (David – and mashiach) would judge Edom in the final days.

All of the above analyses point clearly to the only author who could have recorded these events with such prophetic perfection – our G-d in heaven!

Further Discussion of Yehudah

Reading *Shmuel II*, from ch.8 through ch. 12, we find that David subdued the people of Edom, Ammon and

Moav. This was prophesied by Bilaam (*BeMidbar* 24:17-180) where Moav and Edom are specifically named. The ending expression in v.17 is ("and destroy all the sons of *Sheis*" [שת]. Since this term in Hebrew refers to the buttocks, I believe it means Ammon, hinting at the ugly way he was born through incest. Thus, these conquests of David are envisioned in these verses by Bilaam.

We already recorded earlier (ch.36) that the Torah foresaw David subduing the Plishtim, based on Yaakov's prophecy that "Dan will judge his people (i.e., that Shimshon will subjugate the Plishtim) like the [great] one (David) of the tribes of Israel," (i.e., just like David will do unto them). Even if we agree that there are other interpretations to this verse, we showed in ch.19 other indications of David overpowering them:

I recall reading in some volume a story (I believe it was about Julius Caesar's birth) that a pregnant woman suddenly gave birth as she walked in her home, and the baby fell out to the floor upon an engraved image of a lion. The wise men predicted that he would be mighty like a lion, and he indeed became an emperor.

So too, Yehudah impregnated Tamar on his way up to Timnah. This was surely a sign that the child born from this event, Peretz, would bring into the world a descendant (David) who would conquer the people who inhabited Timnah, and as we know from the life of Shimshon, it was Plishtim territory. The Plishtim were the last people to be conquered in keeping with the promise that Eretz Canaan would be ours How appropriate that this final battle in the conquest of the land was carried out by a descendant of that man who was born from a meeting that occurred in

Plishtim territory at Timnah.(34) I think that G-d's promise to Avraham at the Akeda (*Bereishis* 22:17) that "your seed shall conquer the gate of his enemies" was directed to this final conquest of the Plishtim, who resided at the "gate" of Eretz Yisrael, as we saw in *Chumash Shemos* when HaShem directed Moshe not to go through their territory in a straight line to the promise land. Taking all these events into account, it is as if the Torah was telling us that a descendant of Peretz, King David, will complete the conquest of Eretz Yisrael in his final subjugation of the Plishtim.

Note how the Torah added the information that Sheilah was born in Keziv, about which I showed elsewhere that it was outside Eretz Yisrael (35). Thus, all three of Yehudah's sons from Bas-Shua were unworthy of kingship over *Am Yisrael* in the holy land. However, Peretz, born in Eretz Yisrael at the territory of the Plishtim was the destined one to give us a descendant who completed our acquisition of the entire land for G-d's people.

We may also note that the Torah, in effect, saw that Shaul would not accomplish the complete annihilation of Amalek. In *Chumash Devarim* (ch.21) we are directed to wipe out the memory of Amalek. Why then did G-d state to Moshe (*Shemos* ch.13), "*I will* wipe out the memory of Amalek....," and that furthermore G-d's war will continue "from generation to generation" indicating that it would continue forever? Clearly, this implies that the Jewish people will not complete this task until Mashiach's arrival.(36)
The Torah foresaw Shaul's transgression with the "sorcerer", known in Tanach as a "*baalas Ov.*"

Shaul sought a *baalas Ov*, who summons souls to come down and communicate with living people.(37) The Torah forbids going to them (*Vayikra* 19:31) by stating,"Do not *turn* to (them); do not *seek* to be defiled by them...." Why were these unusual verbs used, rather than simply saying "do not go to them"? Especially puzzling is use of "seek to be defiled"! Surely, anyone who seeks their help is not really *seeking* to be defiled! It is simply a consequence!

However, these terms are perfectly chosen in the situation that Shaul found himself. There (*Shmuel I* 28:5-7), Shaul was terribly frightened of the Plishtim army, and G-d did not respond to his attempts to communicate with Him. In desperation, *he turned* to a final avenue, e.g., a *baalas Ov*, asking his servants to *seek out* such a practitioner for him. Both the term *turn*, which implies an attempt made after others failed, and the term *seek*, fit his situation perfectly. It is as if the Torah addressed him and said, "Shaul! Although you will find yourself in desperate straits, do not turn to a *baalas Ov*, and do not seek one out, for you will become impure as a consequence of such a pursuit."

It is noteworthy that the Torah places this admonition directly after the mitzvah, "Observe My Sabbaths and fear My holy objects" (*VaYikra* 19:30). The Talmud teaches (*Sanhedrin* 65b) that in certain cases the Ov practitioner cannot function on Shabbos. Hence, by observing Shabbos, we recognize that Ov is a vain practice, for G-d's Shabbos overpowers it. Perhaps "fear my holy objects' may have been an admonition not to disturb the holy prophet Shmuel, as we see indeed that he was very disturbed with Shaul for raising him up (v.15).Note also, that when the Torah warns again (*Devarim* 18:11) against seeking out Ov practitioners, it uses the verb שואל - "inquiring of Ov"– containing the four letters of the name "Shaul." In later chapters, we will return to Shaul and show that the Torah foresaw all of his sins and shortcomings.

Chapter 38

In the chapter we will show hidden clues that the Torah foresaw the kings who will emerge from Binyamin (Shaul) and from Ephrayim and Menashe (from Yeravam thru the dynasty of Yeihu). It also saw that David would take the throne from Shaul. We have already shown that the Torah knew that David would start his monarchy in Chevron, but that Yerushalayim would be the seat of kingdom forever.

In the last chapter, we demonstrated that the Torah knew that David would descend from Peretz, and in chapter 43 I will show that it also saw Shaul, a member of the tribe of Binyamin, as king. Now we will show that the Torah saw kings of Yisrael emerging from Ephrayim and Menashe.

In a vision to Yaakov (at which time Binyamin was in Rachel's womb), G-d revealed (*Bereishis* 35:11), "I am Almighty G-d; be fruitful and multiply; a nation and a company of nations will be from you, and kings will emerge from your loins." Rashi explains that "a nation" refers to Binyamin, while "a company of nations" refers to Ephrayim and Menashe, who were not yet born, and would become counted as tribes of Israel. Simply understood, these three tribes would produce the kings referred to in the next phrase. This is precisely what occurred, for Shaul came from Binyamin and most of the kings of Israel were from Ephrayim (Yeravam, Nadav, Omri, Achav, Achazyahu, Yehoram), and Menashe (Yehu, Yehoachaz, Yehoash, Yeravam, Zechaya). However, we must respond to a possible objection that might claim that this vision of future kings only meant Shaul and Ish-Boshes from Binyamin.

Actually, we later find that Yaakov referred to this vision (*Bereishis* 45:4-5) as he spoke to Yosef, and after mentioning the promise of "a company of nations," he says (v.5), "And now, your two sons....Ephrayim and Menashe, will be to me like Reuven and Shimon." Obviously, this decision was how Yaakov understood G-d's wish to turn them into the "company of nations." Thus, the three tribes referred to in the phrase "a nation and a company of nations" will be the ancestors of the kings who will emerge from Yaakov's loins. This phrase cannot imply that Yaakov will produce in the future any new sons, for at this time Binyamin, his last son, was already stationed in Rachel's womb.

It surely is the fact that because, a) G-d said to Yaakov that kings *will emerge from your loins* and only Binyamin remained to be born, b) and Yaakov understood that this *company of nations* referred to the future birth of Yosef's two sons, – therefore Yaakov understood that he should recognize Ephrayim and Menashe as full-fledged sons. This explains the precise statement that Ephrayim and Menashe will be "like Reuven and Shimon," i.e., figuratively "sons" of Yaakov. Thus, we are fully justified to say that in these verses the Torah revealed that in the future these three tribes will be the primary source of almost all the kings of Yisrael, while we already know that Yehudah will be the exclusive source for all the kings of Yehudah.

In *Bereishis Rabbah* 82:4), R. Berachya (and others) say, that "kings will emerge from your loins" refers to Yeravam and Yehu. The midrash then asks how could the righteous Avner decide that Ish-Boshes should succeed his father Shaul? They answer that he understood this phrase as referring only to Shaul and his son, since "kings" is in the plural. Obviously, Avner did not interpret this phrase as including Ephrayim and Menashe, while the others did. While Avner surely knew that the kingdom will ultimately belong to Yehudah forever, he understood that this verse only meant a temporary kingdom will emerge first to be ruled by more than one person, because of the plural "kings." This is why we find in the Talmud (*Sanhedrin* 20a) that Avner was punished because he held up David's kingdom by two and a half years (since David should have ruled unopposed when Shaul died). As Yaakov actually foresaw, the "kings and company of kings" would rule simultaneously with the kingdom of Yehudah, but should not have blocked David from taking the crown as soon as Shaul died.

Further Analysis is Necessary in the Words of Yaakov

We must still understand (as the Or HAChayim asks) how Yaakov was so certain that when G-d told him that "a company of nations" would emerge from him, He meant Ephrayim and Menashe. As Or HaChayim says, could not the intention have been for two others, e.g., Peretz and Zerach?

However, Yaakov surely understood that a company of nations refers to precisely two such nations, for otherwise the number is entirely unclear. The minimum plural is two! Realizing that no other son had exactly two sons except Yosef, Yaakov concluded that this vision pointed to Ephrayim and Menashe.

Furthermore, we cannot imagine that the company of nations promised to Yaakov could be two grandchildren born after Yaakov arrived in Egypt, for the following reason: The promise of gaining a company of nations was made before the sale of Yosef. After more than two decades later, on his way down to Egypt, G-d appears to Yaakov with words of encouragement. If the intention of two nations was for later grandchildren, why did G-d not wait for the later vision to impart this information, rather than many years before? Obviously the "company of nations" was born in the intermittent period between the two visions. This is why Yaakov emphasized in speaking to Yosef (*Bereishis* 43:3) that G-d appeared to him "in Luz, in the land of Canaan..." with the promise of a company of nations. Hence, he must have meant Ephrayim and Menashe, the two brothers born after that vision, before Yaakov headed down to Egypt. This is why Yaakov emphasized that Ephrayim and Menashe were born to Yosef (48:5) "before I came to you to Egypt." Other sons of Yosef would be subsumed under Ephrayim and/or Menashe. (38)

Based on the above points, one might ask why Yaakov had to add that the vision took place in Luz, if the main point was that it occurred in Eretz Canaan? However, this too is a marvelous indicator of the future!

We have noted many times that the place where something significant occurs is crucial to the event itself, for the very stones stand as witnesses. Yaakov was in Shechem when G-d told him (35:1) to go to Luz and erect an altar, and there He told him about the three nations that would emerge from him. We discover in *Yehoshua* (18:11-13), as specifically mentioned by Rashi (*Bereishis* 28:17), that the town of Luz (called Beis-El) was situated at the northern border of Binyamin and Menashe/Ephrayim. There could be no more perfect place for HaShem to inform Yaakov that kings would emerge from Binyamin, Ephrayim, and Menashe! Surely, Yaakov had visions of this future and emphasized the town where this vision was given to him. The location was itself a demonstration that the company of nations would emerge from Ephrayim and Menashe, just as the "nation" would be Binyamin.

(How fascinating is the observation of the *Baal HaTurim* that the terms "goy u'kehal goyim yih'yu mimeka" [a nation and a company of nations will emerge from you] is equal in gematria to "Yeravam and Yehu" – and the gematria of "ben poras" Yosef [a fruitful son is Yosef] equals "Menashe and Ephrayim"!)

I know full well that Luz was on the boundary of Ephrayim, but *not Menashe*. However, since Menashe's territory was contiguous to Ephrayim's, it is still the boundary of "the company of nations," and there is no better location for G-d to grant this vision.

Some Further Observations on Yaakov's Statement to Yosef

As Yaakov describes to Yosef the death of Rachel on their way home (*Bereishis* 48:7), he says "Rachel died by me in the land of Canaan *on the road* when there was a little way yet to come to Efrat...." Why was the obvious expression "on the road" necessary here? It was obvious in the context! Indeed, many commentators ask about the purpose of this entire description. It seems to have no connection to the topic.

However, as Yaakov immediately adds (*ibid.*): "Efras which is Beis-Lechem." Her death as they approached Beis-Lechem, the home of David and his father's family, symbolized that the kings emerging from her line (Binyamin, Ephrayim, and Menashe) would fall to the royal line that comes from Beis-Lechem. This is an additional meaning to the name Rachel gave to Binyamin - Ben-Oni ("son of my pain") – as she died in childbirth (35:18). In the days of the righteous king Asa (of Yehudah), when he reinvigorated the spiritual life of his people (*Divrei HaYamim II* ch.15), we find that many members of the ten tribes came over to Yehudah territory (v.9) to join in this religious revival. We also find that after the dispersion of the ten tribes to Ashur, many were brought back by Yirmiyahu under King Yoshiyahu. In the "end of days," Yeshayahu sees the return of those who were lost in Ashur (*Yeshayahu* 27:13), and Yechezkel follows this vision as well (*Yecheskel* 37:21-24), concluding with (v.25) "my servant David will rule over them." Thus, in various periods, "Yehudah" was in control over "Yisrael," which is symbolized in the death of Rachel (mother of the major tribes of Yisrael) as she failed to reach Beis-Lechem, birthplace of the first king from Yehudah. Once again, the geography explains why she died at that particular place.

When Yaakov informed Yosef that his two sons would be treated like full tribes, in effect, making Yosef into a *bechor* in place of Reuven, Yosef should have wondered if they would also receive the kingdom. Therefore, Yaakov immediately inserted the verse about Rachel dying on the road to Beis-Lechem, which was the sign that her children (although they would also produce kings) would be superseded by the man born in Beis-Lechem. (39)

Thus, Reuven lost all rights of a *bechor* by his arrogant act with Bilhah; Shimon and Levi also, because of their killing the inhabitants of Shechem. Yaakov might have given kingdom to Yosef, just as he gave him the rights of a first-born by turning him into two tribes. But the death of Rachel near the entrance to Beis-Lechem showed him that the Divine will was to have a man of Yehudah, born in Yehudah's town of Beis-Lechem, become the eternal king, leaving Rachel's descendants with only a temporary kingship.

All these vision of the future were previewed here for us by the only One who could have seen so far into the future – G-d, the Divine author of the Torah.

Chapter 39

In this chapter, we will analyze the two great pillars that Shlomo built into the Holy Temple, with the right one representing the First Temple, and the left one representing the Second Temple. We will also review the astounding statistical facts that R. Yitzchak Abarbanel noted about the kings of the Jewish people and time sequences in this long period of Jewish history.

Tanach records (*Melachim I* 7:21), "He erected the pillars...he set up the right pillar and called (it) Yachin; ...and the left pillar and he called (it) Boaz." We find (*Divrei HaYamim I* 28:11-19), "David gave to his son Shlomo the pattern of... the houses, etc., All in writing by the hand of G-d instructed to me; all the works of this pattern." Having been given by G-d, these instructions contained many secrets and mysteries. We also find much discussion of the terms Shlomo chose – Yachin and Boaz – for the two pillars. The height of the right pillar is listed (18 *amos*), but not of the left one (7:15). On the other hand, *only the left one has the width* given (circumference of 12 *amos*) in the text (7:15)! Why?

I have an explanation. During the first temple, eighteen kings ruled who were descendants of King David.

The complete list actually finds twenty-one names.

However, Queen Asalya ruled by force and cruelty and is not to be counted, and the three sons of Yoshiyahu – Yehoachaz, Yehoyakim, and Tzidkiyahu - are of one generation and should be counted as one. Although Tzidkiyahu ruled after Yechonya, he was actually an uncle of Yechonya. Thus, Yechonya should be viewed as the eighteenth generation. His other name is rendered as Yoyachin! We also find in *Maseches Yoma* that eighteen Kohanim Gedolim functioned in the first Holy Temple. Thus, how appropriate that the right pillar a) stood eighteen *amos* high, symbolizing both the kings and the Kohanim of that era, and b) was called Yachin, as a prophecy that Yoyachin would be the eighteenth king of David's descendants to rule in the First Temple period.

Our *meforshim all agree that the Second Temple* was only a temporary aspect of Jewish history to give the people an opportunity to strengthen themselves in Torah in order to survive the centuries of golus which G-d had decreed for us. The volume *Yaaros Devash*, among others, wrote extensively on this topic.

We are taught that there are three crowns: of Torah, of priesthood, and of kingship. We have shown that the 18-*amos* right column, Yachin, represents both priesthood and royalty. We can now support the idea that "Boaz" represents the great crown of Torah. Chazal taught that the short-lived Second Temple was needed to strengthen *klal Yisrael* in their dedication to Torah that would carry them through the long, bitter golus. The name "Boaz" breaks into two words: bo az [בו עז] — "in it there is strength." As we recite frequently, "HaShem gives His nation *(oz)* "strength," which is understood by all to mean the Torah. Unlike the other two crowns which were limited to the tribes of Levi and Yehudah, the crown of Torah belongs to all twelve tribes of the Jewish people. Hence, its width is *twelve amos*. (40)

Marvels from the Generations of the Kings

It is amazing to contemplate the following facts: the kings of Israel proceed through three distinct situations. In the first, the kings from Shaul to Rechavam ruled over all the Jewish people as one nation. In the second and third situations, there was a kingdom over Yehudah and Binyamin, and another kingdom over the ten tribes. Abarbanel, in his introduction to *sefer Melachim* notes that there were nineteen kings over the kingdom of Yisrael, from Yeravam to Hoshea, in a period of 241 years. So too, from the reign of Rechavam to Tzidkiyahu, there were nineteen kings over Yehudah (Asalyah is not counted for she usurped the throne illegally, and was not of David's lineage).This period lasted 393 years according to his account. (I will show in a later chapter that it was actually 373 years.) G-d's plan was that the Davidic kingdom should last longer for its nineteen kings because, unlike the ten tribes who were ruled only by wicked kings, many of David's descendants on the throne were righteous. As we read in *Tehillim* (10:27), "the fear of G-d adds years." This precise match of nineteen and nineteen is clearly part of a Divine symmetry, as Abarbanel claims.

I wish to add to this analysis. I find that from their arrival to Eretz Yisrael, from Yehoshua through the reign of Shlomo, there were also nineteen leaders/rulers over the Jewish people! They were: Yehoshua, Asniel, Ehud, Shamgar, Devorah (w/ Barak), Gid-on, Avimelech, Tola, Yair, Yiftach, Ivtzon, Eilon, Avdan, Shimshon, Eili,

Shmuel, Shaul, David, and Shlomo. This era lasted 477 years, for leaders who were all righteous, with one exception only: Avimelech, who took control for three years. How perfect in this pattern of three sets of nineteen, lasting for different amounts of years, with the more righteous continuing for more years. Surely, G-d made this arrangement to show that He is the ruler over everyone and everything.

Drawing on the verse in *Shemos* (12:2), "This month will be for you the first of the months...," the *Yalkut Shimoni* (*Divrei HaYamim I*, remez 1082) states: "When you merited, you counted as it [the moon] increased – Avraham, Yitzchak,... Shlomo; when you did not, you counted as it decreased – Rechavam, Aviya, Asa,... Yoshiyahu – and Tzidkiyahu was blinded, thus the decrease [of the moon]." This midrash counts a 30-day lunar month, viewing the first set of fifteen days as positive, leading up to Shlomo and the building of the *Beis HaMikdash*. The second one begins the decline, and heads for total darkness. Yoshiyahu is seen as the fifteenth, for he represents the last spark of light for the disappearing moon. In the subsequent period, his son Yehoyakim is exiled to Bavel, the situation collapses with the last kings likewise exiled to Bavel and the kingdom crumbles. This is the total darkness when the moon is not visible at all

Now, consider the following amazing account. Just as from Avraham to the arrival of Tzidkiyahu's rule there passed thirty generations (a full 30-day lunar month), so too from Avraham, Yitzchak, Yaakov, Levi to ... Aharon... to the last Kohen Gadol (Yehotzadak), 29 generations are listed for the priesthood, i.e., a short lunar month. How amazing that G-d measured out the generations of the monarchy, and of the priesthood, to precisely equal solar months.

Furthermore, Levi's son Kehas, and Yehudah's grandson Chetzron, both came down to Egypt with Yaakov. Chetzron is part of the chain of kingship, and Kehas of the priesthood. These two chains are only one generation apart, as each chain completes its "solar month" many centuries later. How many? Adding 210 years of the Egyptian exile, plus 480 years from the entry into Israel until the First Temple was built, and 410 years later when it was destroyed, we are dealing with 1100 years of history! This pattern was part of the beautiful handiwork of our Creator, whose hand is so visible to all who carefully study the Torah "day and night" to marvel at His designs in our history. All the patterns reviewed, and the marvelous statistics presented in this chapter, point to the hidden hand of our G-d, to show us so clearly that He is the ruler and manager of history.

Wonders from the Time of Jewish Settlement on the Land

From the year of entry to Eretz Yisrael until the exile of Gad and Reuven [and Menashe] 709 years passed. Eight years later all of the ten tribes were exiled, after 717 years in Eretz Yisrael. Here are the statistical details: From the entry to the land to the building of the *Beis HaMikdash 440 years* passed. Shlomo began building it in his fourth year as king. Since he ruled forty years, we add *thirty-six* to our account. Yeravam ruled *twenty-two* years, Nadav for *two* years, Basha for *twenty-four*, Eilah *two*, Omri *twelve*, Achav *twenty- two*, Achazyahu *two*, Yehoram *twelve*, Yeihu *twenty-eight*, Yehoachaz *seventeen*, Yehoash *sixteen*, Yeravam *forty-one*, Menachem *ten*, Pekachya *two*, Pekach Ben Remalyahu *twenty*, and Hoshea *nine*. These figures (given in Tanach for each king) add up to 717. (Since the two and one half tribes were driven out eight years earlier, their stay was of 709 years.) The *Baal HaTurim* notes (*Shemos* 6:4) that in G-d's expression to Moshe that he established a covenant with our forefathers to give us "the land of their wandering אשר גרו בה" ("wherein they sojourned"), this Hebrew phrase equals 717 in gematria.(41) The *Baal HaTurim* also finds hints of the exile of the two tribes eight years earlier: In the chapter describing their approach to Moshe about living east of the Jordan, the expression "the sons of Gad and the sons of Reuven" appears eight times.

Note that a midrash quotes a verse from *Mishlei* (20:21) (and interprets it as referring to Reuven and Gad) which states: "An inheritance may be gotten first in "haste" [מיוחלת], but in its end it will not be blessed." All commentators agree that the term "mevocheles" is actually meant as "mevoheles" – the ח symbolizes the number eight – the earlier date that these two tribes were sent into a hasty exile.

Let us calculate: A lunar month is 29 & 1/2 days + , which is equal to 708 hours, plus the fraction 793/1080 of an hour, totaling very close to 709 hours. How amazing that the two tribes were exiled in their 709th year of living in the land, giving a new meaning to the verse that G-d said to Moshe (*Shemos* 12:2), "*This month is for you...,*" with each hour representing a year in Eretz Yisrael..Let no one suspect that the breakdown of a day to twenty-four hours is a human convention. I have already demonstrated in my volume "Yadav Emunah" that the secret of the lunar month (29 &12 days, plus 793/1080 *of an hour*) was presented only to the Jewish people directly by G-d (42), confirming that the unit of hour was Divinely chosen. Such symmetry cannot be coincidental, but shows the hand of G-d in all of history.

We must note, however, that another opinion claims that our figures need a slight adjustment, because the ten tribes actually remained in the land two additional years. By this account, they were in the land 719 years. In thirty days, there are 720 hours. Even in this account, the symmetry is accurate for they were exiled at the very end of the 719th year. *Yirmiyahu* (15:9) records, "The unfortunate one, bearer of the seven, has given up her life, her sun has set while it was yet day...." The Talmud (*Gittin* 88a) interprets this verse as referring to the seven evil kings of the Kingdom of Israel who worshiped idols. Thus, the prophet foresees the exile as coming just before the darkness, as day 30 turns to night, and "our month" comes to a tragic end. Clearly, the hand of G-d hovers over all these events. May He soon restore our ancient glory.

From the generation of Avraham, who traverses the land to take possession of it for his descendants through the era of King Tzidkiyahu, whose people were exiled, thirty generations passed, as reviewed earlier in this chapter. This may explain the large "lamed" (ל) in the frightening description of G-d's fury (*Devarim* 30:27) concluding with "He cast them out (וישליכם) to another land....," since it is 30 in gematria. Adding the ten generations from Adam to Noach, and the ten from Noach to Avraham, there were 50 generations from Adam to the exile. As the *Kli Yakar* points out, this can be found in the opening verse of *Lech Lecha*, when G-d tells Avraham to "Go forth from your land," which can be rendered thus: "You will have *lech* (לך = 50 in gematria) generations before you will be sent out "from your land" into exile!

Chapter 40

Here we will note the astonishing fact that the ten tribes remained in the land according to two counts – one equivalent to the solar year and one to the lunar year. This was the design of the Creator of both sun and moon. We will see that this was already alluded to in the Torah itself.

Note the amazing fact that the ten tribes lived for 719 years in the land. Adding the 365 days of the solar year with the 354 days of the lunar calendar, we get this precise number. Thus, they gained a year for every day of the solar and lunar years combined. This number was measured out by the creator of the sun and the moon. Although I recorded earlier another account of 717 years, I will return later to these statistics in a special chapter to show that 719 is the correct figure. We can see the hand of the great guardian of time and history, measuring out precise order in the events of Jewish history.

Even if there were no further hints of this phenomenon it would be marvelous to see here the works of G-d in history. How much more so when we will now note that the Torah hints of this special number of years in a hidden way, in Parashas VaYechi, as noted and recorded by the *Baal HaTurim*.

Marvels of Our Blessed G-d's Torah

In the prophecies that Yaakov pronounced to his twelve sons, if we add up the gematria of all the *first letters* of the *first* words *following their names*,

בכורי אחים אתה לחוף חמר ידין גדוד שמנה אילה בן זאב

the total **is 365!** –

and the gematria of the *last letters* of these twelve prophecies **is 354!** They are:

עלה בישראל מחלב צידון עובד יק עקב מלך שפר אחיו שלל

The *Baal HaTurim* relates this phenomenon to the verse (*Yirmiyahu* 31 35-36), "Thus says G-d, who gave the sun to light the day, the ...moon and stars to light the night: if these laws will pass from before Me, says G-d, so will the seed of Israel cease being a nation before Me for all time."

How marvelous that Yaakov left this hidden clue for us to note that he foresaw the years the ten tribes would be in the land, a year for every day of the solar and lunar years combined, and knew that they would then be exiled for centuries. He therefore placed the sun and moon in his prophecies, not only to hint at the solar and lunar years, but as witnesses that nevertheless just as the sun and moon are eternal, so will the Jewish people be His eternal people for all time.

(Note also that the center word of the eleven words in the first list above is ידין and in the second list it is the name of G-d. It seems to tell us that *G-d will judge* the ten tribes and sentence them to exile. In fact, the primary source of the idolatry for the tribes was the city of *Dan* [is], where Yeravam set up his golden calf.)

I explained much earlier that the verses in *Devarim* (4:26-27) that threaten us with exile for grievous sins refer to the ten tribes. They include the phrase לא תאריכון ימים עליה ("you will not have length of days upon it." The term "yamim" is often used for "years," and the minimum of years is two. We may find a clue in this terminology, that your first "year" of 365 (years) will be followed by a shorter second "year" of 354 (years). I.e., you will not merit two long "years" (365 x 2) of 730 years, but rather 719 years.

These signs and clues were given in the Torah to show us that the Creator of the sun and moon had already measured out the precise time span for the ten tribes to remain in the land, so that we would recognize who the author of the Torah is.

(I would interpret the following verse as an additional clue: (*Devarim* 32:8) "...He set the boundaries of the nations according to the count of the sons of Yisrael." I.e., G-d set the time-boundary of the Canaanite nations occupation in Eretz Yisrael according to the (concealed) number-count hidden in the words of Yisrael to his sons.)

In his introductory verse to his sons, Yaakov stated that he was about to tell them what would happen to them in "the end of days," – אחרית הימים. The two words אחרית הימים equal 719 in gematria! A more powerful use of this same phrase is found in Moshe's message to the people (*Devarim* 32:29) that he foresaw their abandonment of G-d which would lead to evil befalling them in *the end of days*. Thus, the evil exile would come to them after 719 years in the land!

How many amazing clues are hidden in the words and letters of the Torah, emanating from the Throne of Glory in Heaven!

Chapter 41

The Torah reveals that eight kings of Israel will rule over Edom (i.e., Shaul, Ish-Boshes, David, Shlomo, Rechavam, Avihu, Asa, and Yehoshafat). Edom revolted during the reign of Yehoshafat's son Yehoram. We will explain the prophecy of Yitzchak to Eisav (Bereishis, 27:40), "And when you will gain dominion, you will break his yoke from your neck." Because Yaakov called Eisav "my master" and bowed to him seven times, Edom was saved from servitude to fifteen kings. The Torah also reveals that there will be fourteen judges in Israel, and that Yosef will be the ancestor of six righteous ones of them. There are also clues that the eleven kings descended from Yosef will all be sinners. An interpretation will be offered about his dream of the sun, moon, and eleven stars bowing to him.

It is amazing that the Torah saw eight kings of Israel having dominion over Edom, after which Edom would revolt against Yehoram. For it is difficult to understand why the Torah recorded (*Bereishis* ch. 36) the names of the eight kings who ruled Edom before there was any Jewish king. Why was this description needed? (43)

Obviously, HaShem lovingly revealed to His beloved nation that while the older son would produce eight kings before Yaakov would have kings over his descendants, eventually the son who held on to the heel of the elder would acquire dominion over him by his own eight kings. Thus, although Eisav's kings did not rule over the Jewish people, Eisav, having produced eight kings, was dominated by eight kings of Yaakov's descendants in keeping with the promise to Rivka that "the elder shall serve the younger." How can anyone not realize that the list of Eisav's kings was only included in the Torah so that we could see the hand of our Creator preparing us for the later rise of Yaakov over Eisav to prove to us the Divine origin of our holy Torah.

Furthermore, as I understand it, this point was already hidden earlier in the Torah in *Parashas Toldos*. There, Yitzchak said to the weeping Eisav (after Yaakov "stole" his blessings) (27:40), "You will live by your sword and you will serve your brother; and it shall come to pass when you will dominate (*ka-asher tarid*), you will break his yoke from your neck." The *Tur* explains (as do others) that *tarid* means to rule and dominate over Yaakov when he abandons proper observance of the Torah. However, the following phrase about breaking his yoke seems entirely superfluous. If Eisav will dominate over Yaakov, of course the yoke is broken! There are several other interpretations of this term, but all have difficulties in logic or awkwardness in translation.

I am convinced that the following interpretation is best: Yitzchak prophesies that Eisav will have to serve Yaakov, and adds his vision of how long this will continue. *Vehaya* – so it shall be and last *ka-asher tarid,* i.e., "just like" your rule will stretch through eight kings, his dominion over you will end after his eight kings – and then you will break his yoke! With this interpretation we can understand why the Torah bothered to enumerate all the eight kings of

Edom, which would otherwise be a perplexing and extraneous chapter in the Torah.

Additional Interesting Matters Between Yaakov and Eisav

Rabbeinu Bechaya and the *Baal HaTurim* quote a midrash that Eisav had eight kings before a monarchy was established by Yaakov because Yaakov had referred to Eisav as "my master" eight times in *Parashas VaYishlach*. (Similarly, we find (*Divrei HaYamim II* 16:7) that the navi Chanani condemned King Asa for placing his trust in the King of Aram rather than upon G-d.) Adding the seven times that Yaakov bowed to Eisav, we have fifteen offenses of Yaakov being subservient to Eisav. Presumably, had these acts not been committed by Yaakov, Edom would have been subservient to the Jewish people until the destruction of the First Temple. It is amazing to note that the release of Edom from Israel's dominion occurred exactly before the period of the final fifteen rulers of the Jewish people, from Yehoram to Yehoyachin, after which the destruction occurred during the abridged reign of Tzidkiyahu. (44)

We also find interesting points about the number of animals Yaakov sent to Eisav (15:32-33). V.32 contains eight words, all ending in ים, the plural ending. The *Baal HaTurim* points out that we find (*BeMidbar* 29:33) a similar case with seven words that list offerings for the altar. He finds this an allusion to the idea that because of Yaakov's excessive fear of Eisav in offering 550 animals, we were required to bring 550 *additional* sacrifices (*musafim*) each year, beyond the daily *temiddim*. (45)

When Yaakov politely turned down Eisav's suggestion that they travel together, he added (33:14) "until I will come to my master to Sei-ir." I believe that he foresaw the time when the Jewish people will overtake the Edomites at Sei-ir and dominate them through a period of eight kings. When Eisav responded that he would leave some of his followers with Yaakov, he may have meant that Yaakov should rule *over them* in place of any future domination. Yaakov responded, "Why this – (why such a tiny domination over a few servants) – Let me find favor in my master's eyes" – please let me do it my way!

Rabbeinu Chananel writes that Eisav's monarchy preceded the first king of Israel by 550 years – precisely the number of animals Yaakov delivered to his brother!

The *Baal HaTurim* also notes that the eight kings of Eisav plus his eleven listed *alufim* (dukes/leaders) match the eleven judges of Israel and their eight kings up to Yehoram, symbolized by Eisav's expression (33:12), "And I will go *before you*." Actually, there were 16 judges from Yehoshua to Shmuel! However, I believe he meant that we only find the title "judge" (*shofeit*) with eleven of them.

We can find various hints in the Torah about the judges and kings of Israel. When Yaakov blessed Yosef's sons (*Bereishis* 45:20), we read, "And he blessed them on that day saying (לאמר): Yisrael will bless [their children] by you, saying, 'may G-d make you like Ephrayim and Menashe.'" The *Baal HaTurim* notes the rare ו in the term לאמור, and states that in this section the name Ephrayim precedes Menashe six times, and this also hints at the six righteous judges who will descend from Ephrayim. This is why Yosef's brothers, angrily responding to his dream of their bundles of wheat bowing to his, exclaimed, "Will you reign (המלך) over us, or dominate (משול) us?" Since domination is a lower level than ruling, this word with its unusual ו alludes to the six righteous *judges* descending from Ephrayim and Menashe (Yehoshua, Gideon, Avimelech, Ya-ir, Yiftach, Avdon), while the term המלך (*hamaloch*) has no ו, for all the kings from Yosef were wicked. (46)   Although the *Baal HaTurim* says that the righteous judges came from Ephrayim, they included two from Menashe. Possibly the term ממנו (from him) should be corrected to מהם (from them), or the term "from him" refers to Yosef. The additional remark of the *Baal HaTurim* that Yosef also produced six wicked judges is a mystery to me. I searched in all the sources and could not find six wicked judges at all. He could be referring to kings, for Yosef produced eleven kings (six from Ephrayim and five from Menashe), none of them righteous.

When Yosef objected to Yaakov's crossing his hands, Yaakov used the term ידעתי twice (45:19): "*I know* my son *I know* that he (Menashe) will be a nation." *Baal HaTurim* notes that this word equals in gematria "חמשה מלכים" (five kings)! How appropriate to explain the repetition of this term with a gematria.

How clear it is that by adding the unusual ו to the verb משול and leaving the matching verb המלוך in its usual spelling, G-d was showing us so many clues of the future history of His people as so cleverly noted by the Baal HaTurim and demonstrating that He alone is the author of the Torah.

I also find it intriguing that in speaking of kings, the brothers spoke of kings ruling *"aleinu" (over us)*, while with the judges dominating, they used *"banu"* (*in us*). Since the kings from Yosef were wicked, in their arrogance they would rule *over* their subjects, but not so the righteous judges, for whom *banu* is more appropriate. (47)

[I omit the last paragraph of this chapter which appears quite incomprehensible to me, in which the author expounds on ideas about the sun and the moon, as representing Yosef himself!]

Chapter 42

In this chapter we will be able to make marvelous discoveries and deductions from the absence of two words, and thus prove that the Torah foresaw many powerful future events. Behind this omission hovers King Yoshiyahu, and we can demonstrate that the Torah saw kings before him, like Menashe, and the kings after him to Tzidkiyahu, recognizing the destruction that would follow, as well as other details of that period.

In the previous chapter I discussed matters pertaining to the first kings in Yehudah. Now we will proceed to the later kings. In the second of the ten commandments, we were warned not to have other gods, not to make idols, not to bow or worship them, and to remember that G-d is vengeful, remembering the sins of the fathers upon children, third, and fourth generations who are His "enemies." By mentioning the fourth generation, the Torah indirectly revealed when the *churban* would occur, for it occurred in the reign of Tzidkiyahu, the fourth generation of King Menashe (Menashe, Amon, Yoshiyahu, Tzidkiyahu). HaShem had said (*Melachim II* 24:3) that the terrible sin of Menashe's idolatry was the ultimate cause for the decision to destroy the Beis HaMikdash. Thus, G-d visited the sin of the father (Menashe) upon the fourth generation who continued to be an enemy of G-d.

One may ask, how can we be certain that this verse was directed specifically at Menashe. The fact is that the Torah showed this to us very clearly. The second of the Ten Commandments states (*Shemos* 20:3): "You shall have no other gods *before Me* [עַל פָּנַי]. The literal expression is "by My face," implying in the very presence of G-d. Here, G-d foresaw the abominable act of Menashe, the only Jewish king who dared to place his idols in the sanctuary of the Holy Temple (*Divrei HaYamim II* 33:4-5). It seems evident from that chapter that Menashe brought the *asheirah* (worship-trees) into the Temple which Yoshiyahu removed (*Melachim II* 23:6).

If one might question this analysis with the following argument: Perhaps the Torah spelled out this terrible scenario with no particular historical future event in mind, but Menashe simply fulfilled it. In that case, this is not an example of the Torah foreseeing Menashe's reign. However, logic dictates that the precise accomplishment of this Torah admonishment indicates that it was directed to that moment in history. In fact, there is more to this situation. Actually, there was a golus in the days of Yehoyachin, who was a *fifth* generation from Menashe. If the Torah foresaw Menashe in these verses, why did it stop at four generations?

However, as already noted earlier, the other version of visiting sins upon progeny does include a fifth generation. In (*Shemos* 34:7) we find, "He visits the sin of the fathers upon sons, and upon grandsons, upon third generations and fourth generations." Here, since grandsons are a third generation, "third" and "fourth" are actually the fourth and fifth generations. This would be the prophecy regarding

Yehoyachin. But we must reconcile this with the other version which limits punishment to the fourth generation.

Marvelous Solution from Two Missing Words

I found that there is a debate over the above observations. In the *Tur* commentary on the Torah, he quotes Ibn Ezra's interpretation of the verse in *Shemos* (20:5) where "grandsons" was omitted, that "sons" includes grandsons as well. This is his answer to the contradiction, so both quotations included a fifth generation. But the Ramban disagrees and insists that the Torah only spoke of four generations. Even where the text read (*Shemos* 34:7) "and on grandsons, on third [generations] and on fourth...", Ramban insists that "third" is a repeat of grandsons, remaining a third generation from the father. Hence the Torah never referred to a fifth generation. Thus, Ibn Ezra and Ramban have divergent opinions over any fifth generation.

While I hesitate to question the holy Ramban, and I would kiss his feet, in this matter I am forced to strongly object to the idea that the Torah wasted two totally extraneous words. Why mention "*benei banim*" [grandsons] and then write "third" in a unnecessary repetition! The Torah could have used the same expression as used with the spies in *BeMidbar*, quoted earlier, and in the Ten Commandments, "the sin of the fathers upon sons, upon the third [generation] and upon the fourth..."! It is clear that Ibn Ezra is correct in declaring that such an additional expression must add a fourth and fifth generation.

In fact, we may prove this contention from a quote

regarding King Yeihu (*Melachim II* 10:30), who was promised to have "fourth-generation children" on his throne. Indeed, this promise played out with the fifth generation (Yeihu, Yehoachaz, Yoash, Yeravam, Zecharya).

Nevertheless, we must face the dilemma that the Torah, in its descriptions of these attributes, sometimes includes and sometimes excludes the term *bnei banim*. It is very difficult to accept the argument of Ibn Ezra that where it was left out, the term *banim* was meant to include grandsons, because the Torah would be inconsistent, sometimes adding these two words and sometimes deleting them.

However, there is a marvelous explanation for this phenomenon. Once the Torah included *bnei banim* in the listing of the Thirteen Attributes, it established that *shileishim* must be the next generation - the great-grandchildren, whom we call the fourth generation. Hence, in the Ten Commandments, this is also true. Thus, when *bnei banim* was deleted there, it actually proceeded from the second to the fourth generation, omitting the grandchildren entirely. This is in fact exactly what the Torah was doing for good reason, as follows:

We explained earlier that the second commandment's reference to having "other gods <u>before me</u>" was pointed at Menashe, the king who installed idols right in the Beis HaMikdash, before G-d. His son was Amon, an idolater who was killed after two years on the throne. Thus, the sins of the father were "visited" upon the son. His son was the righteous tzaddik Yoshiyahu, therefore his generation is omitted from this list! The next generation - *shileishim* -

are Yoshiyahu's three sons (Yehoachaz, who ruled for three months, Yehoyakim and Tzidkiyahu, who each ruled for eleven years), all of whom were idol worshippers. The *ribei'im* generation is Yehoyachin, son of Yehoyakim, who in his very short reign of three months is also described (*Melachim II* 24:9) as a wicked king. Thus, the omission of grandchildren in a list that alludes to Menashe is absolutely perfect and a breathtaking demonstration of how precisely Hashem wrote His Torah for us, to prove His authorship for all to see.

One might ask: Since the sins of fathers is visited upon the children only when they themselves continue in wicked ways, in what way do the sins of the fathers count in punishing the wicked sons? We may suggest two ideas. 1) Since the son has clearly chosen the evil path of his father, G-d need not wait for him to do so for many years before he receives his punishment. Thus, for example, Amon followed his father Menashe and sat on the throne only two years.(48)

Another objection must be addressed. The fact is that the Talmud (*Sanhedrin* 103 considers Tzidkiyahu to have been righteous! However, the gemara adds that his entire generation was wicked and he did not try to improve them in any way. In fact, in the name of Chazal, the *Seder HaDoros* lists him among the seven wicked kings of David's descendants! There is another point to consider:

In the fifth year of the exile of Yehoyachin, G-d tells the prophet Yechezkel (4:6) to sleep on his right side for forty consecutive nights, to "carry the sin" of the forty sinful years of the kings of Yehudah. Rashi explains, from Chazal, that this includes the twenty-two years of Menashe's reign, two years of Amon, eleven years of

Marvels of Our Blessed G-d's Torah

Yehoyakim, and the five years of Tzidkiyahu's reign up to the time of this prophecy. Hence, while the precise status of Tzidkiyahu is somewhat unclear, his generation is surely seen as a wicked one.(49)

Besides, in those forty years, the shmittah was not observed. This alone is cause for exile, as the Torah indicates in Parshas Bechukosai.

Since Menashe and three generations of his descendants (excluding Yoshiyahu) worshipped idols, it is interesting that in the second of the Ten Commandments, which we have argued is directed to Menashe, we find negative commands about idol worship listed four times (*Shemos* 20:3-5) under the heading of commandment number two. Perhaps these are four statements for four generations of Menashe!

Of course, for those who see the words of Torah as somewhat haphazard, the presence of *bnei banim* in one listing and its absence elsewhere will mean little or nothing. But for those who are sensitive to every word of G-d's Torah, the points we made in this section are powerful indicators that show the hand of our Creator in every phrase of His holy Torah.

A Further Proof

How marvelous is the description of the Torah in *Devarim* (4:25), "When you shall beget children and children's children, and shall have remained long in the land...." One must wonder why "children's children" was necessary since the verse clearly speaks of passing generations. How many times the Torah only mentions "children" and clearly means many generations! However, here too, we may argue that this is a vision of Menashe, his wicked son Amon, his righteous grandson Yoshiyahu, and only after that generation the verse continues, "and you shall become corrupted and make a graven image...and do evil...." This vision includes all the generations after Yoshiyahu that led to the destruction of the Mikdash. The double expression of the destruction (*avod toveidun*) may well be a hint of the two generations after Yoshiyahu, as enumerated earlier.

In the Thirteen Attributes pronounced by G-d in Parshas Ki Tisa (*Shemos* 34:7), He states that "He visits the sin of the fathers upon sons, and upon grandsons, upon 'third' (great-grandsons) and upon 'fourth' (great-great-grandsons) [generations]." We may suggest that this means either-or, e.g. sometimes one, sometimes the other, and sometimes all. For example, the sins of Yeravam and of Basha were "visited" upon their sons, Nadav and Eilah, respectively, each ruling only two years. The sins of Omri were visited upon his grandson Yehoram, who was assassinated and left unburied in the field of Navos (*Melachim II* ch. 9), while Yeihu's sins were visited upon the fifth generation - Zecharia (assassinated less than one year on the throne) Ben Yeravam Ben Yehoash Ben Yehoachaz Ben Yeihu. Remarkably, no less than four sons of wicked kings of Yisrael kept the throne for only two years: Nadav Ben Yeravam, Eilah Ben Basha, Achazyahu Ben Achav, Pekachya Ben Menachem, while some others ruled for even less time.

In the chapter of the spies (*BeMidbar*, 14:18), where grandsons are left out (as in the Ten Commandments) of this pronouncement in Moshe's prayer for the people,, there too the intent is the generation of Menashe whose grandson was the very righteous Yoshiyahu. This is very appropriate, since the report of the spies led to the great weeping on the night of Tisha B'Av, when G-d decided (as found in the well-known midrash quoted in Rashi) on that date for the destruction of the Holy Temple, and Menashe's sins led to the absolute decree of the *churban*, as spelled out clearly in *Melachim II* (21:11-14). Thus, Moshe says, in effect, why punish them now when it is already determined in history that there will be a great destruction in the future because of Menashe and his wicked descendants, excluding his grandson.

David writes (*Thillim* 106:24-27), "They despised the pleasant land...and He lifted His hand against them to cast them down in the desert and to scatter them in the lands." However, we don't seem to find in the chapter of the spies a reference to scattering them into exile. As mentioned more than once in Chapter 14, only their death in the desert is spoken of! Indeed, if that had taken place, there could not be any exile anyway! David can only mean that G-d, standing above time and knowing that this would not happen, already looked ahead in time and decided upon their eventual exile from the land. But how did David see this in the chapter itself, where there is no such hint to an exile?

I believe that David saw this in the expression HaShem used in His first response to the people's rejection of Calev's plea that they keep their faith (*BeMidbar* 14:12), "I will strike them down with the plague and drive them out, and make you into a greater and mightier nation than they." Here is the allusion to the terrible warning (*Devarim* 28:21) that the plague will attach to the people to destroy them and drive out (those who remain) to other lands. Even if we interpret the plague as referring to their death in the desert during the forty years of wandering, the expression "and I will drive them out" must refer to a future exile, for once they are destroyed this expression is meaningless! Thus, Moshe begged G-d to hold up this retribution to the future generation of Menashe. When G-d responded, "I have forgiven as you say," He meant that this forgiveness was already granted before Moshe requested it, and postponed for Menashe's descendants. This explains the expression G-d used, rather than the Torah informing us, as it does after the sin of the Golden Calf (*Shemos* 32:24) " and G-d relented over the evil that He spoke of about His people." Thus, David correctly added that G-d was prepared to "scatter them in the lands," if not for Moshe's prayers for them.

The well-known statement of Chazal that G-d can relent about an evil decree that He made must be analyzed. In my opinion, they did not mean to say, Heaven forbid, that G-d would decree and then change His mind! He would never issue a decree that does not take place. Rather, that when He seems to reverse a decree, it was never made as an absolute and irrevocable edict. Thus, He says to Moshe (*Shemos* 32:10), "And now, let me alone...and I will destroy them," keeping this punishment dependent upon Moshe. Similarly He says to Moshe and Aharon (*BeMidbar* 15:21), "Separate yourselves from this congregation and I will destroy them instantly." But they did not separate themselves and the decree was thus nullified. However, when G-d said that He would strike them down by plague and drive them out, no further condition was added, making this edict irreversible. According to our analysis, it did indeed occur at the time of the *churban*. In fact, the additional phrase, "and I will make you into a great nation" also took place in history, as we find (*Divrei HaYamim I* 23:17) that the descendants of Moshe's grandson Rechavyah Ben Eliezer "increased greatly." When HaShem said (*Shemos* 33:1), "Go and arise from here, you and the people whom you led out of the land of Egypt , to the land that I swore to Avraham, to Yitzchak, and to Yaakov, saying 'I will give it to your seed'," it should not be understood as promising Moshe entry to the land. Rather, "saying" is equivalent to ""that is to say,"

and really means that it will be given to Moshe's descendants. The following verse (v.2) Adds, "And I will send before you a messenger (or angel)" can refer to Yehoshua (the messenger) and might be a hint to the angel G-d sent to Yehoshua (*Yehoshua* 5:13-15).

Chapter 43

This chapter will discuss King Shaul, demonstrating to anyone of intelligence that the Torah already spoke of him hundreds of years earlier, and saw his transgression with Amalek. It apparently also saw his terrible sin at Nov, the city of the kohanim, and his sin with the female practitioner of Ov. We will also show hints about Esther and Mordecai in the Torah, and some other amazing clues.

Up to this point, I have discussed in several chapters the kings of Yehudah and Israel in general terms. Here I will explain more specifically how the Torah foresaw them individually. Intelligent people can see that the Torah spoke of Shaul centuries before his birth. Yaakov predicted for Binyamin that (*Bereishis* 49:27) he will be "a wolf that ravages", a reference to the historical event that took place at the end of *Shoftim* (20-24) when it was arranged for the remaining six hundred males of Binyamin (after the devastating civil war which wiped out thousands of their tribe) to seize wives at the annual festival in Shiloh from the maidens who danced in the vineyards. As Yaakov continues in that verse, "In the morning he will devour the prey" - a reference to Shaul, the first king of the Jewish people in the dawn of their history - "and in the evening he will divide the spoils" - referring to Mordecai and Esther who took over the wealth of Haman's house, in an "evening" period of Jewish history, during the exile brought about by Bavel. It is noteworthy that Chazal say that Shaul was himself one of the six hundred remaining males of Binyamin. The *Tur* (Rabbeinu Yaakov, son of the Rosh) explains that the reign of Shaul is comparable to a ravaging wolf, because wolves kill their prey but quickly leave the area of the kill, just as Shaul ruled for only two and a half years. On the other hand, David who ruled for decades is seen as a lion (in Yaakov's prophecy to Yehudah) for lions remain with their prey until it is consumed. I see another reason for the comparison of Shaul to a wolf. The Talmud notes that there is a period in the year when wolves are exceptionally violent and powerful (*Bava Metzia* 93b), just as Shaul had a short period of great military successes in the early part of his short reign. In contrast, David (the lion) had many great successes over many years. The Torah also saw Shaul rising over Agag, king of Amalek, in Bilaam's prophecy (*BeMidbar* 24:7), "and his king will be higher than Agag...." The commentators agree that this was a prophecy about the rise of Shaul. Even in chumash *Bereishis* (35:11) G-d says to Yaakov, "A nation and a company of nations will come forth from you and kings will emerge from your loins." This was expressed in the future form, and Yaakov's only additional son was Binyamin, who produced two kings, Shaul and IshBoshes. (I discussed this topic at length elsewhere.)

There is no doubt that the Torah itself saw the eventual failure of Shaul to annihilate Amalek. Let us use the following parable:

A king sends out his chief general to destroy a nearby nation and demands that he leave not a single person alive.

The king, who is himself the master military man of the kingdom, had whispered to a trusted servant days before that he will have to carry out this task himself. The servant is confused, having heard the general promise to accomplish the king's wishes. Why would the king have to go forth to vanquish a destroyed nation? However, soon the general returns and it is discovered that he allowed the son of the enemy's ruler to survive. Years later, people find that this survivor has had offspring and that the vanquished nation is rebuilding itself. Now the servant realizes that his king had great foresight and knew that his boastful general would not complete his task, and that the king would have to do it himself.

So too, G-d commanded (*Devarim* 25:17-19) that we never forget the vicious attack of Amalek, and that we must wipe out them and their memory from the earth. Yet, he had already told Moshe to record in the Torah and whisper to Yehoshua that He swore to wipe out Amalek and to continue that war forever ("from generation to generation"). Clearly, HaShem already knew that we would not succeed to carry out the command given in *Devarim*, which was assigned to Shaul. Hence, Shaul's failure was already foreseen in the Torah!

It cannot be argued that G-d's pronouncement of His war against Amalek meant in the period before Shaul ruled: a) The expression "from generation to generation" means forever. b) Furthermore, the fact is that there were no wars or battles versus Amalek in the entire period of the judges. Only after Shaul defeated the nations surrounding the Jewish people, i.e. Moav, Ammon, Edom, Plishtim (as the Torah had written: (*Devarim* 25:19) "When G-d grants you rest from all your enemies around ..blot out the memory of Amalek from under the heaven....."), did Shmuel instruct him to proceed to carry out this command. Hence, Shaul's failure to do so successfully, was already predicted by G-d in His statement to Moshe in *Shemos*, as clarified above.

Indeed, the victory over Haman may be seen as a war of G-d, who manipulated behind the scenes all the events leading to the downfall of Amalek in that miraculous period. (Of course, there too there was no total annihilation of Amalek, which will only occur in the end of times.) In fact, the Or Hachayim suggests that the double expression of G-d, "Machoh emcheh" (I will surely wipe out) is probably an allusion to the two great battles against Amalek by Shaul and by Mordecai, while the phrase "from under the heaven" means in the final encounter that is destined to take place.

I feel that in the great tumult made by the children during the reading of the megillah, we hear the sound of that great final battle with Amalek. Just as "remember the Sabbath day" requires of us a physical action (making a kiddush recital), so too "remember what Amalek did to you" also demands an action, and this is the noise of the grogger when Haman's name is pronounced. Since Amalek attacked (*Devarim* 25:19) the weak stragglers, so too our weak and tender children gain the mitzvah of drowning out Amalek's memory. As they turn their noisemakers round and round, they remind us that the battle against Amalek goes on and on forever.

How interesting that the *Baal HaTurim* noted that "מחה אמחה" equals "זה המן" in gematria (107), while "from generation to generation" – מדר דר - is 448 - gematria of

לימי משיח (for the days of Mashiach).

Returning to Shmuel, let us note how he turns away from Shaul (*Shmuel I* 15:27), after informing him that he will lose the throne because he did not annihilate entirely the flocks of Amalek, as well as the king Agag. Shaul reaches out to stop him, but seizes only Shmuel's coat and it is torn. Shmuel says that [this symbolizes] G-d has torn the kingdom from him this day and has "given it to your neighbor who is better than you." We may ask, in what way was David better? Except for this one transgression, Chazal claim that Shaul was free of sin entirely. Shmuel's next statement (v.29) is unusual in his use of a new term for G-d, referring to Him as "Netzach Yisrael" (the Strength/ or Eternity/ of Israel). Why this new term?

However, we may find here a marvelous prophecy in Shmuel's terminology, hinting at the miracle of Purim. We know that by extending Agag's lifetime for a while, his seed produced offspring from which Haman eventually descended, threatening the continuity of Am Yisrael. On the other hand, David spared the life of Shimi Ben Geira, who might have been properly executed by David for cursing the king (*Shmuel II* 19:22). Mordecai, who made up for the sin of Shaul, was descended from Shimi. How appropriately Shmuel said to Shaul that his extending the life of Agag, would place the Jewish people in great danger, but David, by sparing Shimi, helped bring Mordecai on the scene, to save them from that terrible threat. Thus, he was indeed "better than you." And thus the Eternity of Yisrael will be preserved by the Eternal One of the world, who did not speak falsely when he declared that your kingdom will be taken away.

(It is possible that when Shmuel began his rebuke of Shaul when he returned from his war with Amalek, saying (*Shmuel* 15:14), "And what is this sound of the sheep... that I hear?," he may have been alluding to the Jewish people, who are called G-d's sheep frequently by the prophets, and was prophesying about the great anguish and weeping of the people and Mordecai when the destructive decree of Haman was first announced, a situation made possible by Shaul who did not immediately execute Agag!)

Note that only after Shaul tore Shmuel's garment, did the navi add that his kingdom was given to a better man, although he had already twice stated (15:23,26) that his reign was forfeit! Why did he not add this point earlier? Observe also, that when David clandestinely cut a part of Shaul's garment while he slept (*Shmuel I* 24:5), and later chastised Shaul for pursuing him improperly, a penitent Shaul remarked (v.21), "And now, behold I know that you will rule......" It seems that he *now* had come to that conclusion. Why not earlier? Rashi comments (based on a midrash) that Shaul had been given a sign that one who cuts his garment will take the
kingdom! When was this sign given?

I believe that when Shaul tore Shmuel's garment, the navi's reaction really meant that his kingdom would be given to one who would tear Shaul's garment, and that is why it was not mentioned earlier. Shaul understood the hint, and so he said to David that *now* he knows that David will rule the people.

I also found one commentator who interpreted the verse in Sidra *Balak* (24:7), "...his king shall be higher than

Agag, and his kingdom shall be exalted" very differently. His translation is "And his king (Shaul) shall be *lifted away* (i.e., removed) *because of* Agag, and his kingdom *carried off.*"

A further hint of Shaul's error with Amalek comes from Rabbeinu Bechayei's analysis of (*Shemos* 17:16), "For a hand [is upraised] upon the throne of G-d, war by G-d will be with Amalek from generation to generation."

He explains that G-d pronounces an oath *upon any king who sits on the throne of G-d* that wars against Amalek must be purely a *war for G-d*, i.e., not for spoils or booty, forever. (This is why *Megillas Esther* emphasized two times (9:10 and 15) that they did not take any booty.) (50) Thus, Rabbeinu Bechayei's unusual interpretation provides a further condemnation of Shaul for taking Agag alive, as well as countless animals.

I see even further ideas in this verse. The term "hand" is often used in the sense of stretching out a hand against someone or something, as in the two references (ibid.) from *Megillas Esther*. Hence we may read the verse that God has stretched out His hand against (he who sits) upon the throne of G-d (because of the) war of G-d against Amalek (and what will occur there - a vision of Shaul). We do find that a Jewish king who sits on the throne is seen as sitting on the "throne of G-d" in (*Divrei HaYamim I* 29:23) referring to Shlomo.

Rav Yitzchak Abarbanel wrote that comparing Binyamin to a "ravaging wolf" may be understood as a rebuke to Shaul. Just as a wolf roams, viciously seeking to attack weaker animals as its prey, so too, Shaul attacked

Amalek in a manner unbecoming a royal king of Israel, intent on taking the spoils of his war, as Shmuel rebuked him when he said (15:19), "And you swooped down upon the booty." I explained in chapter 37 that the tribe of Binyamin was the appropriate one to war with Amalek, and only for this reason Shaul became king ahead of the destined tribe of Yehudah. (51)

I found in the Torah allusions to Shaul's transgression with the practitioner of *Ov* (bringing back the dead), as well as his command to kill the kohanim of the city Nov. The chapter about choosing a king in *Devarim* (17:14-20) is immediately followed by two sections: the proper treatment of kohanim (and leviim) in the Temple (18:1-8), and prohibition of all kinds of necromancy, including Ov (9-13)! It appears that G-d, foreseeing Shaul's sins, immediately warned the kings of Israel about giving proper treatment to the kohanim, and avoiding black magic of all sorts. The warning against *Ov* is expressed with the verb *sho-el* (שואל). How interesting that these are the letters of "Shaul"! (52) Other hints of the Torah's recognition of Shaul's involvement with *Ov* were already mentioned at the conclusion of chapter 37.

Another amazing matter about Shaul in the Torah

I believe that Torah foresaw the terrible punishment Shaul received (seven of his sons were executed) from the Givonim in revenge for his mistreatment of them (*Shmuel II* 21:1-2). They demanded this execution, and David agreed, in order to end a great famine that was caused by Shaul's actions.. In that chapter we find that they were not buried for a long time, remaining covered on the ground until the rain season arrived. How could David ignore a clear command of the Torah to bury even executed criminals the same day that they are executed (*Devarim* 22:23)?

However, we must examine that text carefully. We will find that the Torah itself gave permission! It adds a reason for this ruling, namely (ibid.), "for one who is hanged is cursed by G-d." It is unusual for the Torah to add reasons for a particular mitzvah. Furthermore, how does this explanation clarify the need for his removal?

However, Onkelos translates this awkward Hebrew phrase differently, "since, he was hanged over [the fact that] he was guilty against G-d." This justification also needs analysis.

One thing is clear. The requirement that he be buried quickly is connected with his guilt. Thus, if an innocent person is hanged, this law does not apply. But in Jewish history, the only case of innocent men being hanged is the case of Shaul's sons! David had to comply with the demand of the Givonim to end the great famine!

I believe we may explain everything perfectly. The reason for quickly burying a truly guilty sinner is that the longer he hangs the greater is the profanation of G-d's name. People passing by would comment about how terrible this person was, how he abused the Torah and his G-d. In the case of Shaul's seven sons, the reverse reaction occurred. Seeing them on the ground, passersby would note that these royal princes were executed for the crimes of the king, their father, and would be impressed that in the Jewish kingdom absolute justice prevails. Everyone is held accountable and must pay the price for crimes. What a sanctification of G-d's name! Since the Torah's additional explanation applied only once in history, it is obvious that G-d inserted the phrase to demonstrate that He stood above time and gave us his Torah steeped in hints about future events in Jewish history. This additional phrase justified David's apparent disregard for the Torah's command.

According to the *Or HaChayim*, the Torah also foresaw Shaul's error in not waiting for Shmuel as instructed by him (*Shmuel I* 10:8). This was another meaning in Yaakov's pronouncement comparing Binyamin to a ravaging wolf. Just as the wolf does not tarry over its victim but speedily goes on to find another helpless animal, Shaul did not wait patiently for Shmuel but proceeded with haste to sacrifice the animals. The navi scolded him (13:13-14) and indicated that his reign would not last long. (53)

There is a well-known statement of Chazal that Esther is hinted at in the Torah in the phrase where G-d says (*Devarim* 31:18), "And I will hide (*astir*) My face on that day for all the evil that they will have done...." I think that Chazal were alluding to the absence of G-d's name in the entire megillah, as He hid in the shadows but manipulated the events. We know how His name is hidden in the last (and first) letters of several phrases to remind us that He was always present and active. The *Baal Haturim* noted that in the previous verse (31:17), the five Hebrew words that spell out "and I will hide My face from them and they shall be devoured," the last letters of each equal the gematria of Haman (95). Also, in *Shemos* (18:14) where G-d tells Moshe to record in writing, and whisper to Yehoshua, that "I will wipe out the memory of Amalek from beneath the heavens," in the four Hebrew words "*k'sov zos zikaron basefer*" (record this as a memorial in the book), the middle letters are "Esther." (54)

Further Precious Hints in the Torah [About Amalek and Binyamin, etc.)

I already recorded in my volume *Yadav Emunah* in the name of the volume *Paaneiach Raza* a marvelous explanation of why the Megillas Esther has precisely 166 verses. There are two chapters in the Torah about annihilating Amalek. A count reveals that together they contain exactly 166 words! The author also offers kabbalistic explanations of the significance of this particular number.

The author of *Panim Yafos* (Rav Pinchas HaLevi Horowitz - Baal Haflaah), offers two interesting clues from the Torah and Nach about the future of Amalek.

He discusses the brief phrase (*Shemos* 17:12) "until sunset," recording the long period that Moshe held his hands upward while Amalek was being defeated. [The literal translation is "until the sun (*shemesh*) comes."] He says that this (sh-m-sh) hints at three future leaders who will "come" to continue the eternal war against Amalek: Shaul - Mordecai - Shiloh (a term for Mashiach, from Yaakov's blessing to Yehudah.) (55)

He also focuses on the verse in *Tehillim* (75:11), " All the horns of the wicked I will cut off, the horns of the righteous shall be exalted." The term for horn (*keren*) also means corner, as in the Torah which speaks of the horns/corners of the altar (*Shemos* 29:12) and in numerous

Talmudic references. The "corners of the wicked (רשעים) are the reish and the mem - רמ - and of the righteous (צדיק) are the tzadi and the kuf - צק. These are equal in gematria, respectively, to 240 and 190. Amalek in Hebrew is 240 - those who will be cut off, and 190 represents the end of times - >e - as in *"keitz hayamim,"* (end of days) when the righteous will be uplifted.(56)

The *Kli Yakar* notes that Moshe's era represents the dawn in Jewish history, as compared to the times of Mordecai and Esther, who lived in a period of "sunset." Hence, Moshe's steady hands against Amalek should be understood as his merit which helped us during the sunset period to overcome the machinations of Haman.
As Rashi noted at Yaakov's blessing to Binyamin, "evening" symbolized the era of Mordecai and Esther.

Commentators have noted that Yosef gave his brother Binyamin five suits of clothing to symbolize the five royal garments that Mordecai wore after the Jewish victory over Haman (*Esther* 9:15). The *baal haturim* also notes that G-d's pledge to destroy (מחה אמחה - I will annihilate) Amalek equals in gematria *"zeh* Haman" - 107. [As Yirmiyahu predicts (*Yirmiyahu* 30:9), King David himself will rise to serve as Mashiach. Hence] the "hand" - יד (equal 14) - that G-d places on the "throne of G-d" may be understood as דוד (14) sitting on his throne to conduct the (final) war against Amalek.

Rabbeinu Bechayei notes the placement of *Sidra Yisro* immediately after the war with Amalek. This shows the wickedness of our blood relative who came from the distance to stage an unprovoked war with the Jewish people, as contrasted with the Midianite Yisro who came to us and continued with us to show the way through the desert, whose descendants (the Keini) dwelt among us at the border with Amalek. His reward was that Shaul urged the Keinites to depart before his war with Amalek (advice which they accepted) so that they should not be affected during this war. The Torah hinted at this future event by placing Yisro's story next to the war with Amalek.

I think that we might read this idea into the opening phrase of the sidra : and Yisro "heard","(i.e., he sensed the future events in Shaul's time.)

Chapter 44

In this chapter we will note how the Torah saw all the important events in the life of King David: his great strength, his battle with Gulyas, his rule over Yehudah alone followed by his acceptance by all the tribes, that his tribe would provide most of the great commentators on the Torah, etc. It is also clear that Yaakov and Moshe foresaw facts about his kingdom, as well as all his tribulations and his exile from the land. His conquest of Edom, his sad experience with Avsholom, and the plague that struck during his reign, are all found by analysis of verses and expressions in the Torah.

Yaakov's blessing to Yehudah contains many phrases that build on the clear implication that he would be the ancestor of the kings. It is strange that so many phrases were used for the same ultimate purpose. As we examine them, we will answer other questions that might be raised about these phrases.

Yaakov begins (*Bereishis* 49:8-11) with "Yehudah! You - your brothers will praise you." Without "you," the next two words translate as "your brothers will praise you," making "you" entirely extraneous! However, it indicates the manner in which his reign will begin. There was a vast difference between Shaul's rise to kingship vs. David's rise. The people saw nothing in Shaul to elevate him to rule. In fact, at first many ridiculed the choice proclaimed by Shmuel (*Shmuel I* 10:27). In contrast, David's popularity was immense after his defeat of Gulyas and some further military exploits, causing the people to sing of his accomplishments (18:7). His might, which was the greatest among the tribes (*Divrei HaYamim I* 5:2) was G-d's gift to him so that the people would love and respect him as king. Hence, the added "you" says, in effect, that by your special attributes you (symbolizing David) will be praised and admired by all to be the chosen king. The term for praise (yoducha) also means "to admit," and may be understood also as alluding to the admission of all the tribes that the kingdom should be given to David.(57)

The next phrase, "your hand will be upon the nape of your enemies," is a perfect description of David's defeat of Gulyas. The text (*Shmuel I* 17:49) describes that as he died he fell forward on his face. Normally, as the stone lodged in his forehead, he should have fallen backward! Thus, when David severed his head, it was by way of the nape, as Yaakov foresaw, and as explained by the *Panim Yafos*. Since David came toward him without a sword, it is so appropriate that this phrase speaks only of "your hand."

As Gulyas fell forward at the feet of David, he drew out his victim's sword and severed his head. This might have been the hint of the verse (*VaYikra* 26:8) that describes the defeat of our enemies by "your enemies will fall before you to [receive] the sword," since Gulyas' head was at David's feet, while, had he fallen back, David would have been forced to run past his huge bulk to reach his head.

The next phrase is "the sons of your father will bow to you." matches the fact that David first ruled over the tribe of Yehudah in Chevron, as the text emphasizes (*Shmuel II* 5:5), " In Chevron he ruled over Yehudah seven years and six months, and in Yerushalayim he ruled thirty three years over all Israel and Yehudah." Here too, the personal pronouns "you" and "your" are not directed at Yehudah himself, but at David who represents the tribe. Thus, "your father" is the ancestor of David, namely, Yehudah. At this point, Yaakov describes Yehudah as a cub-lion (gur aryeh). This is surely a description of David who started as a cub, ruling over one tribe, and eventually as a lion, king of all the people. Continuing, "From the prey (teref), my son, you rose up" can be rendered many ways. Since David replaced Shaul, who was described (above) as a (ze-ev yitraf) - ravaging wolf - I would suggest, "my son (David), you rose above the man (Shaul) who identified with the root t-r-f.

It might also be understood differently. "My son David, your rose up (spiritually) from teref - i.e., from killing Shaul when he was in your power in the cave, not knowing that you were there in the depths of that cave (*Shmuel I* ch. 24), and a second time when he slept (ch. 26). In such a reading, using the term teref gives a strong hint that Shaul is the one being discussed, since this root is associated with him. David "rising" from this situation could also hint at his right to rise to the kingdom itself. This would lead neatly into the next verse.

The next phrase describes David as "he crouched, and couched like a lion, and like an old lion, who can budge him?" This verse symbolizes three stages: a) David crouched (in a temporary position) on his knees, when he started his kingdom in Chevron, at which time Shaul's son Ish-Boshes was still holding on to the position of king.

b) Then he became fully established in Yerushalayim like a mighty lion comfortably lying in his den.   c) Finally, Shlomo, although weaker than David, like an old lion, established his throne and was respected by all the surrounding kingdoms.

I realize that some might argue that the phrase about rising from teref refers to Yehudah's advice that saved Yosef's life. However, I believe that this may be a second interpretation, but not the only one. If it were, it should have followed immediately the opening statement that gave the kingdom to Yehudah. [I.e., Your brothers will acknowledge you and accept you as king because you rose above the ravaging of my son Yosef.] However, with our interpretation, the phrases are in proper order, all of them discussing David.

Having concluded with Shlomo, the next verse (v. 10) states, "The staff shall not depart from Yehudah...."

This is a perfect description for the reign of Shlomo's son Rechavam. Since the Hebrew term for staff is "sheivet," which also means a tribe, is foretells that even with the division of the people into two kingdoms, Rechavam would retain one tribe (Yehudah) which would not "depart" from him! Indeed, in *Melachim I* (11:36) we find the prophet Achiyah saying to Yeravam in the name of G-d, "And to his son I will give one sheivet...." Thus, all the verses to this point detailed the rise of Yehudah to kingship, over one tribe, and then over all Israel, and then only over his own tribe. The next phrase continues the order: "... nor the lawgiver (or, ruler's staff) from between his feet..." In the Midrash Rabbah (*VaYechi*, 98:8), Chazal interpret this phrase (and the previous one) as representing the period after the destruction of the second temple, when the chiefs of the Sanhedrin (sheivet) and the scribes of the judges (mechokeik) were descendants of the tribe of Yehudah, e.g. Hillel, descendant of David, who is the ancestor of 'Rebbe" (R. Yehudah HaNasi) - and the midrash proceeds to list many other examples of leaders descended from the tribe of Yehudah. I understand the term "from between his feet" to mean that this will continue even in the period when the Jewish people will be barely able to stand as they gradually proceed to "fall" into centuries of decline. The beginning of that decline was the destruction of the first temple, and these families were leaders during the second temple. HaShem gave us this period just to organize, develop the study of Torah on a high level (especially the Torah shebaal peh), and prepare for the long exile. This should serve as an excellent allusion to the importance and authority of the oral Torah, which was truly needed to carry us through our many centuries of exile.

Many ask (58), if the staff will not depart from Yehudah, how is it that we do not have a king today from Yehudah? There are many correct responses. Some say, that this does not mean that at no time will the staff depart even temporarily, for the Torah itself warned (*Devarim* 28:36) that if we sin - we and our king will be led off into exile. The phrase means only that it will not depart forever, so that when it returns, it will be through Yehudah. Some believe that even today our leaders are from Yehudah (even if we cannot recognize their ancestry). I think this is in fact hinted in the verse itself by mentioning "between his feet," indicating during the time that we are close to falling and barely able to stand, just as the feet are at the bottom of the body.

This phrase also has a more fundamental meaning, namely, his children will supply the law-givers (similar to the expression (*Devarim* 28:57) "and towards her afterbirth which comes out from between her legs"). The next phrase ("until (ad) Shiloh comes") has been translated dozens of ways. The term *ad* also means forever in many references in Tanach. Hence we may connect it to the previous phrases to mean that this situation will continue forever, "because" (kee) Shiloh (i.e., Mashiach) will come, as Rashi has explained, who will be from the tribe of Yehudah, reaffirming that tribe as the eternal king of the people. The final phrase of this verse then states that the people will be obedient to him.

The first two phrases in the next verse (49:11) can be best understood as referring to the abundant blessing of wine produced in Yehudah's territory: [as Rashi explains, "He will tie his foal to the vine, and his young donkey to the choice vine" - i.e., they will fill a complete load without moving from one position.] However, the final two phrases ["he washes his garment in wine, and his clothes in the blood of grapes"] must have deeper interpretations.

I believe these phrases return to David, who will win great victories in war. Here, "wine" and "blood of grapes" is a symbol of the blood of his enemies, as used several times in Tanach, e.g., (*Yeshayahu* 63:2), "Why is your apparel red, and your garments like one who treads in the winepress?" As the prophet indicates immediately afterward, he speaks of the blood of enemies.

The final verse addressed to Yehudah by Yaakov

(49:12) states, "Eyes that sparkle from wine, and whiteness of teeth from milk." I believe that "teeth" symbolizes soldiers at war (pictured as tearing enemies with their teeth) as found in *Shir HaShirim* (6:6), "Your teeth are like a flock of sheep...", which Chazal interpret to mean that although your soldiers are fierce and ravage the enemy with their teeth (symbolically), they are as righteous and fair as a flock of sheep. Here too, although their eyes are bloodshot from the fierce war and shedding of blood, the soldiers are whiter than milk in their purity and righteousness.

This verse might also be alluding to the redheaded David himself, if we can interpret "wine" as a symbol of the Sanhedrin (since *yayin* - יין equals 70 in gematria, the number of members of Sanhedrin). Thus, *from* the point of view of the Sanhedrin, David 's eyes sparkle with righteousness, and his teeth ("warriors") are whiter than milk in purity

Note that both Yehudah and the tribe of Dan (*Devarim* 33:22) are described as young (*gur*) lions. Later in Tanach we find that David killed a lion (*Shmuel I* 17:36) and Shimshon, of the tribe of Dan, did likewise (*Shoftim* 14:6). Perhaps in both descriptions, we might interpret "gur" as "fear" (as in *Devarim* 18:22) to imply that lions will fear them!

How Moshe Viewed King David

While Yaakov foresaw so much of David's future as ruler, Moshe prophesied about his tragedies and dangers. In his single verse for Yehudah, Moshe says (*Devarim* 33:4): And this is for Yehudah, and he said, "Hear, G-d, the voice of Yehudah, and bring him to his people; his hands should contend for him, and be a help against his enemies." This verse has many interpretations and I wish to offer my own carefully considered reading. I believe that David is the subject of this verse. When we examine all the generations in Tanach from the very beginning, we find no person who was involved in so many difficulties and dangers as David, from which HaShem saved him every time. We may enumerate thirteen great dangers, for which he owed G-d a special blessing each time he was saved:

1) His battle with Gulyas, the giant who terrorized the entire Jewish army, and his astounding victory with a slingshot - a clear case of G-d's intervention;

2) Escaping twice from spears hurled at him by Shaul (*Shmuel I* 18:11);

3) Shaul's plot (which he confided to Yonasan and other servants) to kill David, which Yonasan foiled with his heartfelt plea to his father (*ibid.*, 19:1-7);

4) Shaul's second failed attempt to kill David, causing David to flee from the palace to his home (*ibid.*, v.10);

5) Another attempted assassination in David's home, foiled by the help of his wife Michal (*ibid.*, 11:17);

6) When Shaul discovers that David is with Shmuel in Naios, he sends soldiers to kill him but they are overwhelmed with a prophetic spirit until he comes himself but is likewise overwhelmed while David escapes (*ibid.*, 19:24);

7) Fleeing fromShaul, he finds himself in Gass, Philistine territory, where the king's servants tell him that David is their mortal enemy. David feigns insanity, and Achish is fooled while David moves on (*ibid.*, 22:11-17);

8) The Ziphites informed Shaul that David was hiding among them, and as Shaul was closing in on finding him,

a messenger came and told him that the Plishitm had invaded the land, so he returned (*Shmuel I* 23:14-28);

9) Again, Shaul was pursuing David in the Ein-Gedi wilderness and entered a cave wherein David and his men were hiding in its depths. David surreptitiously cut his cloak, and later informed Shaul that he could have killed him. Shaul weeps, and returns home (*Shmuel I* ch. 24);

10) Once again, Shaul pursues David in the area of the Ziphites, and sleeps at night surrounded by his men. David and Avishaay creep into the circle and take his spear and water jug, proving to him the next that they could have killed him, and Shaul returns home;

11) The incident at Tziklag, where Amalek had taken all the women and children captive, and upon his arrival there, David was in danger of being killed by the embittered men of Tziklag. However, he pursued the enemy and eventually brought back all the captives.;

12) the well-known confrontation with his rebellious son Avshalom, who sought to assassinate him, but was killed (*Shmuel II* chs. 15-18);

13) In another battle with the Plishtim, David was almost killed, but saved by Avishai. Thenceforth they prevented David from going forth to battle any longer (*Shmuel II* 21:15-17).

Thus, David faced thirteen great dangers to his life, prayed to G-d each time and was saved, and recorded his prayers and praise of G-d recording them for future generations. Regarding Shaul, see Psalm 7 and 18. In the latter, he refers to being saved "from the hand" of Shaul, apparently referring to Shaul's hurling his spear at him. Psalm 34 speaks of his feigning insanity before Avimelech (Achish) and how G-d saved him (60). Psalm 54 praises G-d for saving him from the Ziphites who colluded with

Shaul. Psalm 57 [and Psalm 142] present his prayers to G-d while hiding in the cave from Shaul. Psalm 59 records his thanks to G-d for saving him in the event described briefly above in danger number five.

Surely in reference to all of the above, Moshe prayed for "Yehudah" (David), saying, "Hear HaShem the voice of Yehudah (*Devarim* 33:7)... and be a help [to him] from his enemies." The second phrase in that verse, "and bring him to his people," refers to David's being forced to leave his homeland and find refuge in Plishtim territory (*Shmuel I* ch.23), which bothered David greatly, and he considered it equivalent to worshiping other gods (*ibid.*, 26:19). So too, his flight to Achish, and his flight from Avshalom, are additional events that may be subsumed under Moshe's prayer that he be brought (back) to his people. The third phrase, "let his hands contend for him," must refer to his battle with Gulyas which he won with the power of (G-d and) his hand. (61). Of course this phrase may include his other encounters with adversaries who sought to kill him. These many incidents are also included in the final phrase where Moshe prays that G-d be a help to him from his enemies. Indeed, the *Yalkut Shimoni* on *Chumash Devarim* (remez 954) includes most of the above ideas as one of its interpretations.

Moshe's verse regarding Yehudah has precisely thirteen words, perhaps to indicate the thirteen dangers in David's life, enumerated above. His successful encounters with a lion and a bear, as he recounted to Shaul, are of a different nature, not included in this list, just as his victories over enemies with his soldiers are excluded.

I believe that David actually understood that he was the

subject of Moshe's message to Yehudah. When David recorded in *Tehillim* (63:3), (at a time that he was seeking refuge in the wilderness of Yehudah), "Indeed, I saw you in the *kodesh* (sanctity?), to view Your power and Your glory," I believe he was referring to the "holy book" - the Torah. He meant that he would escape his dangers and witness G-d's great power in preserving him from his enemies. He adds in the next verse (v.4) "For your kindness is better than life; my lips shall praise you." G-d's *kindness* (the cause) sustains David's *life* (the effect). Ordinarily, the effect is more important than the cause that brought it about, for it is the goal of that cause. But David says here that the wondrous fact that G-d looks down upon him to watch over him and protect him, as foreseen already by Yaakov centuries earlier, means more to him that his very life itself.

Lest one might think that he does not properly appreciate the life that was given to him through G-d's protection, he adds (v. 5), "Thus will I bless You in my lifetime.... (perhaps, *for my life)*." In a similar fashion, I heard an interpretation of the difficult verse (*Tehillim* 116:10), "I believed (*when I was in danger I had faith*) that I will speak (*about that period in my life, after I am saved and at peace, that*) I was greatly afflicted (*at that time*). (62)

Let us now examine the opening of Yehudah's verse - "And this to Yehudah." There are many explanations of this phrase, i.e., what is the meaning of "this?" I believe I may offer my own as well.

The tribe of Reuven on the east side of the Yarden River had two problems. 1) They were endangered by possible enemies, since they were separated from the primary area of the Jewish people. 2) Perhaps the tribes in the heartland would distance themselves from them, feeling that they had abandoned the Holy Temple and the king to live in isolation. In fact, we find a reference to this idea in *Yehoshua* (22:21-29) where the tribes of Reuven and Gad express their concern that a day might come when the other tribes would see them as strangers who abandoned the Jewish people. Let us examine the context of the verses preceding Yehudah's.

(*Devarim* 33:5-6): "And there was a king in Jeshurun (Israel), when the leaders of the people gathered together with the tribes of Israel. Let Reuven live and not die,; and may his men be of number (i.e., many)."

I believe the second verse for Reuven refers to the previous one. May Reuven live and thrive in these periods of Jewish history: when there will be one king in Israel (e.g., Shaul, David and Shlomo); when leaders of the people gather to rally them (the period of the judges); and when the tribes of *Israel* come together (to break away from Yehudah, and become a separate kingdom). Throughout these periods may Reuven continue to thrive and be counted in the family of the Jewish people, and be part of all decision-making and activities of the tribes. *However, This* (previous statement of kingdom in verse 5) is *for Yehudah* (to whom the kingdom belongs exclusively). [The balance of that verse then focuses on David and his tribulations, as outlined earlier.]

The Torah [through the mouth of Bilaam] also foresaw an event in the campaigns of David. Bilaam sees (*BeMidbar* 24:17) that "a tribe/scepter [*sheivet* - the term used by Yaakov for Yehudah and David] shall rise from Yisrael and smite the *corners* of Moav...." "Corners' is an enigmatic term! However, when David overpowered Moav (*Shmuel II* 8:2), he had the captives lie on the ground, choosing two to die and one to survive. [While the precise description is a bit obscure, it appears that] each surviving Moabite lay between two condemned men, each at his side. Hence, these are the men at the "corners" visualized by Bilaam!

As Rabbeinu Bechaye explains, this verse refers to David, who lived four hundred years after Bilaam. Thus, he had correctly stated at the beginning of that verse, "I see him but *not now;* I behold him but not soon...." The phrase following "the corners" of Moav may be rendered "and destroy (*karkar*) all its foundations" (i.e., totally annihilate Moav, with the term "sheis" (שת) understood as the root for "foundation" - see Psalm 11:3). Bilaam adds two further verses (vs. 18-19) describing the destruction of Edom by one who will rule (וירד) from "Yaakov" (a Jewish king - David). Hence, we have found that all the major events in the life of David were foretold in the chumashim, and only one who refuses to open the Torah and look would deny these conclusions.

The *Panim Yafos* (by the author of the famous *Haflaah*) interprets the second phrase "and "destroy"[perhaps uproot?](63) all the sons of "Sheis" (in effect, all of mankind, descended from Adam's third son Sheis). I.e., at the end of *maseches Yadayim*, R. Yehoshua's opinion (the accepted one) is that Sancherev mixed the populations of the entire world's people. However, we also find in *maseches Megillah* (12b) that Moav is definitely an exception to this claim (see the Tosafos there). Hence, in our verse, Moav is very appropriately separated from the rest of mankind and has a special phrase describing its destruction.

The *Yalkut Shimoni* (*Bereishis, remez* 159) comments on Yaakov's opening praise to Yehudah, and expands on all the glory of this tribe. Yehudah's kings will rule in both worlds, and in *olam haba*, as we find (*Yechezkel* 37:25), "And my servant David will be their king *forever.*" Descendants of Yehudah include Elisheva Bas Aminadav, mother of the kohanim (as wife of Aharon); her brother Nachshon, leader of the *nesiim* and of the first tribe to go forward in all travels; his descendant Betzalel, who built the *mishkan* and its vessels; Asniel Ben Kenaz, the first of the judges; the builders of both the first Temple (Shlomo) and the second one (Zerubavel); and Mashiach, who will build the Third eternal one. The number four recurs often with Yehudah, the fourth of Yaakov's sons. Speaking of Mashiach, David writes (*Tehillim* 89:37), "His throne is before me like the sun," which was created on the fourth day. Just as "David" begins and ends with ד, the fourth letter, so too he begins the true kingdom in Israel and will be the final one. Four tzaddikim of Yehudah were saved from certain death in one era (Daniel from the lions' den, and Chananyah-Mishael- Azaria from a fiery furnace). In Tanach, Yehudah was declared the leader of the tribes in four places.

The *Baal HaTurim* records most of the items in this paragraph: In *BeMidbar* (ch. 7), where all twelve tribal heads brought their sacrifices on alternate days, with verses that repeat the description twelve times, Nachshon's section contains two added "vavs" (ו) missing with all the others: in verse 13 - וקרבנו, and in verse 17 - עתודים. This fact points to the number 6 by *gematria*. In

Midrash Rabbah (*BeMidbar* 13:10-11) various explanations of "six" are given: a) Nachshon's descendant David was blessed in six ways enumerated in *Shmuel I* (16:18) - musician, powerful, clever, etc. Since the root for he-goats [עתד] also means to stand up (as in *Mishlei* 24:27 - and in *Iyov* 15:28), the additional vav in עתודים could symbolize the rise of David, blessed with his six special attributes. I believe the hint of six is found with Nachshon, because from him to David there are six generations, as recorded at the end of *Megillas Ruth*. The *gematria* of יהודה is thirty, and David began his rule at the age of thirty. Hence, it is interesting that the final verse in *Devarim* (17:20) of the chapter dealing with choosing a king begins and ends with a *lamed*, (= thirty) in *gematria*. Two phrases in Yaakov's blessing to Yehudah begin with letters that equal fourteen in *gematria*, the same as the name דוד: אחיך ידך בעורף אויבך (*Bereishis* 49:8), and (v.9) גור אריה יהודה .

The *Baal HaTurim* also found a hint for David's rebellious son Avshalom. Since he was a captured woman's (*yefas toar*) son, who usually grows up to be, as Chazal tell us, a rebellious son (*ben sorer umoreh*), it is appropriate that the term *sorer* (סורר) equals in gematria [466] זה אבשלום בן דויד. (We should note that "David" is consistently spelled דויד (with the xtra *yud*) in Divrei HaYamim. The *Paaneiach Raza* also notes that the Torah's description of a condemned man being hung (*Devarim* 22:22) begins with "Should there be a man...," the Hebrew words of which (וכי יהיה באיש) equal 379, the gematria of אבשלום, who died by hanging.

Another Event with David Foreseen by the Torah

A marvelous demonstration of how only G-d could have written our Torah comes from an amazing warning in *Chumash Shemos* (30:12) that counting Jews must be done by using coins, not bodies. If they are counted by head, they are subject to a plague! What human writer would have imagined such a strange punishment for a seemingly ordinary act as taking a census, something done by many countries throughout the centuries with no evil results? Yet, hundreds of years later, David foolishly ordered a census of the people (*Shmuel II* ch.24), and the result was a plague that took seventy thousand victims. Only by direct dictation by G-d could Moshe have issued this dire warning against a Jewish census! I will soon show that the Torah's warning was in fact directed specifically at David's decision, by noting some further details of David's census.

Why did the Torah warn against a head-count? I believe this may be the reason: HaShem promised our forefathers that we will be as countless as the stars, and like the dust of the earth. If we count the Jewish people and reach a specific number, it appears that G-d did not keep His promise and it is a chilul hashem. Actually, in truth, this is not really so, for it is our fault. Chazal noted the seeming contradiction in *Hosheia* (2:1), "The number of the children of Israel..." vs. "that cannot be numbered..." in one verse! They answered that one case deals with the situation that they do not observe His commandments properly (hence they are a finite number), while they cannot be numbered when they are a righteous people. Thus, a successful count [such as the one ordered by David] proves that they are not fully observant, and results in a plague. Therefore, the only proper census must be by a donation of a half-shekel which is itself an act of atonement. This is why the half-shekel is called (*Chumash Shemos* 30:15) "an atonement for your souls."

I believe that a half-shekel was used for it symbolizes something incomplete. Each Jew demonstrates that he is only a fraction who must join his fellow Jews to be complete. We argued above that evil will only befall a counting of the *entire* people. So wrote also the *Sifsei Chachamim* at the start of Parashas Naso in the name of Rav Eliyahu Mizrachi to explain why it was permissible for David to count his soldiers, dividing them into three groups, as he prepared for battle against Avsholom's army (*Shmuel II* 18:2). However, one could argue, why was there a plague at David's later count of the people? We find (*Divrei HaYamim I* 21:6) that Yoav left out the tribe of Binyamin and the Leviim from his count! I believe that since David had intended a total count, and the great majority of Jews were in the census, this exclusion did not change the Torah's decree against such an undertaking. This is quite logical. Once someone begins such an attempt, he shows that he defies G-d's pronouncement that it must not be done, hence Yoav's decision not to finish the count is irrelevant. Of course, if nobody makes a count, even if in fact it could succeed because the people are not fully observant, it means nothing for this sad fact remains hidden and unknown. Note the precision of the Torah's expression:

(*Shemos* 30:12) If you (Rashi: *decide to*) take the sum of the children of Israel *by their number* (i.e., if you wish to know the total population), you must do so only by means of the half-shekel coins *"in counting them"* (i.e., from the very beginning of the count, as long as the goal is to complete it); so there will not be a plague upon them *in counting them* (i.e., the plague would strike only if a count is undertaken, but not if merely planned and never started). Since in Jewish history, the only attempted goal of counting the Jewish people for no real purpose (such as going to war, etc.) other than pride, occurred with David, and was unfinished by Yoav, it seems obvious that the Torah foresaw this sad event and was alluding to it in this chapter by its awkward text.

We should note that all questions can be answered differently by means of a midrash (*BaMidbar Rabbah* ch. 2) that states that the Torah's dire warning only referrs to a census without significant purpose. David's census was the only such case in our history.

The fact that precisely seventy thousand died in that plague is itself highly significant. That number in Hebrew is recorded as שבעים אלף. The first letters spell out the Hebrew term for "count" (שא). This is a reminder that the plague was no natural phenomenon, but was brought about by the unnecessary counting of the people.
The two letters are in the command form: "Count!" This is like the father who catches his young son drinking wine, and beats him with his cane again and again. Then he says," Drink!" by which he means, "Go ahead - I dare you" - still holding the cane in readiness. Here too, the "*sa*" says to us: if you didn't learn your lesson yet, go ahead and *count*!

Chapter 45

How the Torah foresaw the assassination of Amasa by Yoav, and Yoav's attempt to avoid retribution.

It is clear that the Torah saw the murder of Amasa by Yoav, in *chumash Shemos* (21:14):

"If a man comes intentionally upon his friend/neighbor to kill him with trickery, take him from My altar to die." Two verses before, we already find the death penalty for murder! That verse could have ended with the rule that the altar does not save a murderer, and this verse would have been extraneous! [Furthermore, why only "a friend" and only by "trickery?"] It is obvious that this verse prepared us in advance for the precise method by which Yoav killed his "friend" Amasa, by feigning a kiss with his right hand while he stabbed him with his sword using his left hand (*Shmuel II* 20:9-10). In later years, Yoav was condemned to die, and fled for refuge to the altar. By Shlomo's instructions, Benayahu killed him there (*Melachim I* 2:28:34). The verse presented in perfect detail all that transpired with Yoav and Amasa. Indeed, had the Torah meant to emphasize that there is no escape from a death penalty, it should have used the more likely scenario of the murderer fleeing to a city of refuge! Clearly, the Torah intended to give a preview of the death of Yoav, and only G-d Himself could have written such a text. In fact, many commentators have written that Yoav was not actually guilty of a death penalty, since there was no warning (*hasraah*) as the Torah requires. However, his act of fleeing from Shlomo to the altar can itself be viewed as a rebellion against the king, a capital offense. Thus, we may read the expression "from My altar" as "because of My altar take him to die." I will show in other texts (ch. 52, ch. 53, ch. 56, etc.) that the Torah used unusual expressions to match events that took place later in history. As I showed in ch.3, for example, the stones upon which were recorded the blessings and curses at the mountains in Shechem were left on Mt. Eival because that was the spot where, centuries later, the people transgressed these decrees.

Chapter 46

We will see how Moshe's instructions about kings are written as if Shlomo stands before him to hear them - and that he will marry many (unworthy) wives. Also, that many good tidings would occur in his era, including the building of the First Temple. The Torah also foresaw the kingdom of Rechavam and his errors, some of the problems faced by Shaul and David, the splitting of the kingdom into two, that David and Shlomo did not sin, and some other items as well.

I have explained several times that when mortal kings record laws for their followers they cannot know who or when these laws may be broken. G-d, however, records His Torah with an eye towards future events, and hints at them with the text by which these laws are recorded. Following are some potent examples:
1) The rules for a monarch include (*Devarim* 17:16) not accumulating too many horses. One can almost feel that Shlomo is facing Moshe as he pronounces these limitations, for they all apply to him. E.g., we find (*Melachim I* 5:6) that he had 40,000 stables for his horses. While the Torah adds that he should not send his people to Egypt to buy horses, we read in *Melachim* I (10:28-29) that his buyers brought up from Egypt horses and chariots at specified prices. The Torah continues (v.17) that he must not have many wives, while Shlomo had (*Melachim*

I 11:3) seven hundred wives, plus three hundred concubines. The Torah explained that G-d was concerned that they would "turn his heart" (from the Torah), and the cited verse adds: his wives turned his heart. While the Torah warns that he must not have excessive gold and silver, Shlomo had so much gold (10:14:21) that silver was considered worthless in his time. Since these excesses are the ones enumerated in *Melachim* exactly as the Torah warned, it seems evident that these admonishments were directed to him.

2) Furthermore, even the order of these admonishments is perfect. Logically, the Torah should have addressed the excess of gold before the others, for it is the source for almost all excesses, followed by the accumulation of wives, and of horses. However, the Torah lists horses first, for we indeed find in *Melachim* that the huge number of stables for his horses is the first item on the list of his excesses. Although the abundance of gold by Shlomo precedes the mention of his many wives, his marriage to the daughter of Pharaoh comes much earlier (*Melachim I* 3:1), which may explain why the Torah places wives before the accumulation of gold.

3) The Torah's additional explanation that the king should not have many wives to prevent them from "turning his heart" away from G-d obviously presumes that they would be foreigners [with dubious conversions]. This already points to Shlomo who married women from Moav, Ammon, Edom, etc. (*Melachim I* 11:1). Jewish wives could increase his arrogance, but it is not logical to say that they would turn his heart away from G-d!

4) As the Torah concludes its admonishments regarding the king, the text reads (*Devarim* 17:20) "...that he should not turn aside from the commandments to the right or to the left, so that he shall prolong his days over his

kingdom, he and his sons, *in the midst of Israel*." This final phrase is incomprehensible and perplexing. But this too is a message from G-d that should Shlomo ignore the Torah's warnings against excess gold, horses, and wives, his descendants will not continue his kingdom in "the midst of Israel" but find themselves ruling over one or two tribes in a split kingdom, as happened to his son Rechavam. (Even in Shlomo's own lifetime, Yeravam began his rebellion against the kingdom, and since Shlomo lived only fifty two years, he did not succeed to "prolong his days over his kingdom.")

5) Another interesting demonstration of the Torah directing its view at Shlomo: When the Torah speaks of the nations that must be driven out of *Eretz Canaan*, it mentions only six names (*Shemos* ch.3, ch.23, ch.33; *Devarim* ch.20). However, in *Devarim* (7:1) it lists seven names – Chiti, Girgashi, Emori, Canaani, Prizi, Chivi, and Yevusi – *followed by the command not to intermarry with them*. All halachic authorities agree that the prohibition of marrying non-Jewish wives is universal, and not limited to the Canaanite peoples. Why was this verse written just after listing these seven names?

We find that these seven nations were gradually eliminated from Israel, as the Torah promised (*Shemos* 23:30) ("little by little I will drive them out...."). Shlomo completed this action, as we find (*Divrei HaYamim II* 8:7-8): "All the people remaining of the *Chiti, the Emori, the Prizi,* etc....who were not killed, Shlomo assigned them to pay tribute to this very day." Thus, the Torah foresaw that Shlomo, who would complete the elimination and subjugation of these people, would be the king who would marry forbidden women. Therefore, this command follows the list of these nations. Although Chazal tell us that he had them all converted, the Tanach records his marriages as if this did not take place, for it was highly objectionable anyway. We may suggest a special reason why in this list, the *Chiti* is mentioned first, an unusual order. Of all the foreign wives that Shlomo married (see *Melachim I* 11:1 for the list), only the *Chiti* is of the seven Canaanite nations.

6) After Avraham successfully passed his greatest test in binding Yitzchak, G-d made him a series of beautiful promises (*Bereishis* 22:17-18): a) to increase his seed like the stars and the sand; b) they would conquer their enemies; c) all nations would be blessed through his seed. [These are pronounced right after Avraham prayed that this would be the site of the Holy Temple of G-d.] These blessings all occurred during Shlomo's reign, as recorded in *Melachim I* (chs. 4 and 5). Chapter 6 proceeds to describe how he built the *beis hamikdash*. Chapter 10 describes how all the nations honored Shlomo, and came to visit Yerushalayim to hear his wisdom. Thus, the Torah was describing Shlomo's era centuries before, in the chapter of the *Akeida*.

We might add some small points on the Torah's chapter about the monarchy that hint at Shlomo:

1) The admonishment not to have too many horses begins with the word רק (only) and seems awkward. These letters equal 300 in gematria, the same as Shlomo's first letter;

2) The description of how the king would sit on the "throne of his kingdom" recalls the fact that Shlomo's throne was totally unique of all the thrones in ancient days;

3) In the command that the king always read from his personal Torah "יקרא בו כל ימי חייו", the first letters of the four words beginning with "*bo*" equal 40 in gematria, the precise number of years that Shlomo sat on the throne,

from age twelve to fifty-two.

The Torah points at King Rechavam

It is likely that when the Torah warned the king (*Devarim* 17:20) not to be arrogant and despotic, and not to turn away from the "mitzvah," this was prophetically directed at Rechavam. In his insolence, he ignored the wise advice of the elders who counseled him to be yielding and respectful of the people and their wishes, and accepted the foolish judgment of the youngsters to address the people with arrogance and contempt (*Melachim I* 12:13-14). The Torah states that he must not turn from the "mitzvah" rather than the "mitzvos" because it is directed to the specific mitzvah that the elders reminded him of, i.e., not to be arrogant. By following the Torah's rules, he would live long on his throne with his descendants succeeding him "in the midst of Israel." Having ignored these rules, it resulted in his ruling over Yehudah alone, no longer "in the midst of Israel." The three elements reviewed in this chapter all point to Rechavam, as the object of the Torah's description.

Interestingly, the number 17 dominates in *Melachim I* regarding Rechavam. The wise advice of the elders (chapter 12:7) referred to
above are expressed in seventeen words; the warning that his heart not rise above his brethren (*Devarim* 17:20), expressed in four words, contains seventeen letters; the hope that he would reign for long years (*ibid.*) is also expressed in four words containing seventeen letters; having failed, Rechavam ruled for only seventeen years. Together with Shlomo's forty years, the total is fifty-seven. From the point where the Torah pictures the happy

possibilities of a righteous kingdom (17:18), i.e., the second word in that verse (which we explained earlier refers to Shlomo), to the end of that entire section (v.20), we find precisely 57 words.

Also, where the Torah urges that we seek the counsel of a father and of elders (*Dvorim* 32:7), the first letters of *sh'al aveecha v'yagedcha zekeinecha v'yomru lach* equal 320 in gematria, which is also the gematria of רחבעם.

Reviewing the chapter on monarchy in the Torah, we can find further allusions to Shaul and David, as well as to their opponents. After declaring (*Devarim* 17:15) that G-d must choose the king who would rule, the verse continues with the warning that we must not allow a non-Jew to rule! Is this not obvious? Would G-d choose (through a navi or by the *Urim v'tumim*) a non-Jew? This question was already raised in the *Tur* on the Torah in the name of the Ramban.

However, in actual fact, history shows that both types of kings sat on the throne(s). Shaul, our first king, was chosen by G-d, and crowned by His prophet Shmuel, as was David later on. So too, the first king of the Kingdom of Yisrael, Yeravam, was appointed by the prophet Achiyah haShiloni, and Yeihu also was appointed by a messenger, Yonah Ben Amitaay, sent by the Navi Elisha. On the other hand, Omri was chosen by the people on their own authority (*Melachim I* 16:16, 22). In the kingdom of Yehudah too, we find that the people chose Yehoachaz BenYoshiyahu as king (*Melachim II* 23:30).

The Tanach records that Shaul had opponents (*Shmuel I* 10:27), and David had many of them, beginning with

Avner, who crowned Ish-Boshess (*Shmuel II* ch.2) in opposition to David. Seeing these future events, the Torah commanded that we *place* upon ourselves the king chosen by G-d. The use of a double form (tasim som for "place") surely implies that having been placed by a navi, we must confirm the choice by our acceptance of the navi's choice. Afterward, the Torah adds that, whenever *we make the choice ourselves*, he must not be a non-Jew. The seemingly superfluous phrase (*Devarim* 17:15) "who is not your brother" that follows "you must not place upon yourselves a foreign man" is clearly directed at Asalyah, who was not foreign but was a "sister", not a "brother." Thus, we observe that all the expressions in this chapter outline all the situations that arose in history regarding the kings of the Jewish people.

When the people first asked Shmuel for a king, it was immediately after the Plishtim chose their first king, replacing the earlier system of having officers only. The Torah precisely foresaw that the request would be "place upon us a king to judge us like all the nations around us," exactly as they expressed it to Shmuel, after the Plishtim had chosen a king. Only G-d could express the request for a king with such terminology, as He looked into the future. The chapter in *Devarim* began with "When you come into the land that your G-d gives to you and you will inherit and will "sit" (וישבתה) in it, the additional "h" is grammatically incorrect. (*Baal haTurim*) It is probably meant as a hint that the request for a king would (and did) occur after they lived five generations in the land.

We can clearly see the absolute truth of the Tanach, for it favored nobody, always stating the precise truth. After describing the brilliance of Shlomo in the loftiest terms, as the wisest of all men, it did not spare him from condemnation for allowing his wives to turn him to idolatry. We must understand this precisely, for it cannot mean that he actually worshiped idols. The text can be explained properly.

(*Melachim I* 11:4): "And in his old age, his wives turned his heart after other gods; and his heart was not whole with G-d like the heart of his father David." The astounding puzzle created by this verse can best be understood with a matching enigma. Imagine a description that reads thus: This man was so poor that he had not a morsel to eat, walking barefoot through the streets, and searching for left-over scraps. He did not have millions of dollars nor mansions and vast estates. This last sentence makes no sense!

So too, after telling us that Shlomo went after foreign gods, one of the greatest sins of the Torah, it added that his heart was not complete with G-d?! Amazing! Chazal therefore understood that the sin of Shlomo was that he did not interfere with the activities of his wives, whose conversions were proved to be insincere. Hence, the text condemned him with terms that sounded even more egregious than the actual facts. To clarify this intention, the additional phrase explained that his own heart was not as whole with G-d as David's had been, due to the evil practices that he saw and tolerated around him. It was now clear that he did not actually turn to idol worship, for which he would have been written out of Jewish history and totally condemned. Thus, Chazal wrote emphatically that anyone who imagines that Shlomo actually sinned (by idol worship) is mistaken but since he should have condemned the practices of his wives and did not, the text describes it as if he sinned himself.

The fact that the Tanach describes fully the weaknesses and errors of our great heroes is proof of its truth. Indeed, Shlomo is called *Yedidyah* - friend of G-d! By extension, we may conclude that David was not guilty of adultery with BasSheva, for he would have been forbidden to take her as a wife later, and (if he did so in a forbidden way) how would G-d have allowed their son Shlomo to rule with His blessings? Both had done seriously wrong and deplorable actions, but not as serious as many might think. Nevertheless, the Tanach condemns their actions with powerful words, as is reasonable, for we expect our great spiritual people to be on the highest ethical and moral levels.

Chapter 47

Here we will speak of King Uziyahu, of whom the Torah foretold about his leprosy.

The forecast of Uziyahu's sin and punishment is spelled out in *BeMidbar* (17:4-5) where Eliezer took the censers that had been offered by [Korach's] burnt followers and spread them as covering for the altar as a memorial... that no "stranger" (non-kohen), come near to offer incense before G-d, that he not be like Korach and his company, as G-d had spoken "by the hand of Moshe" *about him* (לו). (When the term "spoke" is followed by the proposition "לו" rather than "אליו", although theoretically these both mean "to him," there is a principle throughout Tanach that it acquires the meaning of "about him." About whom? Rashi says it means about Aharon, i.e., that burning incense is reserved only for Aharon and his descendants. Rashi's second interpretation is that it refers to Korach, and warns that one who improperly acts as a kohen will suffer leprosy, as happened to Uziyahu. Ramban explains that the verse is now understood as follows: one who improperly brings incense to the altar will not be treated like Korach and his group but rather like the hand of Moshe (which became leprous as sign for him to show the

Jewish people (*Shemos* 4:6) that he was their redeemer.) This idea is stated in the *Midrash Tanchuma* (in Parashas *Tzav*): "He shall not be like Korach to be swallowed into the earth or like his company who were burnt, but rather like Moshe... at the bush, as it is stated, 'Place your hand in your bosom, and he brought it out, and it was leprous like snow', i.e., he will become leprous."

The warning of the Torah could have meant that nobody should act like Korach and his company, or that one who does so will not be treated like Korach and his people were treated but rather they would become leprous. If we examine the language of the above midrash, we can note that it is supports the second interpretation. The first one leaves us with a question: Why did the Torah state "... like Korach and like his company" rather than "like Korach and his company?" Our midrash noted this little point by explaining "like Korach to be swallowed *and* like his company to be burnt." This was meant to support the second interpretation that an improper approach to the altar with incense will not be punished by either of these acts of retribution, but by the one symbolized in the "hand of Moshe" i.e., by leprosy. Hence, the Torah foresaw the actions of Uziyahu that resulted in his leprosy (*Divrei HaYamim II* 26:16-20).

Despite this analysis, the fact is that the extra term "לו" seems entirely extraneous. If left out, the verse would read very smoothly. Even with Rashi's grammatical clarification, it should have been recorded next to the verb "spoke" rather than at the very end of the verse. I believe that we can find an interesting solution by noting the text in *Shemos* (4:2-11) where G-d gave Moshe three wondrous signs to prove to the people that he was truly sent by G-d to redeem them. Within these verses, we find four expressions of "G-d said," all addressed to Moshe. For saying "to him," the Torah twice uses "אליו," the usual standard. Only in v. 6, when G-d tells Moshe to place his hand in his bosom, which turned leprous, the Torah uses "ויאמר ה' לו." We may reasonably say that in our verse in *BeMidbar* (17:5) the placement of "לו" at the end of the verse alludes to the time when G-d spoke to Moshe through the leprosy of that hand "לו". Unlike the many places in the Torah where the "hand of Moshe" has a different meaning, in this verse it visualized the time it became leprous, and serves as a warning to any non-kohen who would offer incense on the altar. Thus, we have found another situation in which the Torah foresaw an act (Uziyahu) that would take place centuries later.

Note that after detailing the tragic death of Nadav and Avihu in *Parashas Shemini*, the Torah did not continue with *Parashas Acharei Mos* which seems to be the precise connecting chapter. In stead it interrupts with two Parshios, *Tazria nd Metzora!* Why is this so? Actually it is a logical continuation. Having described these two deaths, resulting from an improper offering of incense, the text wished to detail the laws for lepers, a condition that results from such acts, so it recorded all other laws associated with impurities. Thus, already in *Shemini* it inserted the laws of kosher and non-kosher animals and impurities of various crawling insects followed by all the other situations of impurities, including leprosy. A key verse in that section (*VaYikra* 13:46) is the requirement that a leper must stay outside the camp in isolation, a condition precisely described about Uziyahu, (*Divrei HaYamim II* 26:21) ,who was forced to live alone in a separate house until he died. Its description as "house of freedom" is explained in the Talmud *Yerushalmi* as being located at the cemetery, for departed people are called "free from mitzvos."

From all of the above, it becomes evident that the Torah pronounced this unusual punishment for offering improper incense in the *Beis HaMikdash* as a preparation for the foolish act of Uziyahu and his retribution. We should note that the Torah's warning is recorded in the singular form that included two seemingly extraneous words (*BeMidbar* 17:5) "so that no strange(r) *man* should approach, not of the seed of Aharon *is he,* to burn incense...." Any Hebrew reader can see that the two words "man" and "he" are not needed in this verse. They emphasize that this warning will be necessary for one man alone. Uziyahu is the only one recorded in Tanach to have done this vile act in the *Beis HaMikdash* after being warned directly to desist. It is noteworthy that, unlike the description in *Divrei HaYamim* where he is called Uziyahu, in *Melachim* (15:1-8) he is called Azaryah or Azaryahu! I believe that the extra "r" placed after the "z" produces the Hebrew word "זר" (stranger, i.e., non-kohen) - the very term the Torah uses to warn the non-kohen not to offer incense! This name itself thus hints at his sinful act.(65) All these clues point to the conclusion that the Torah foresaw the act and pounishment of Uziyahu in later history. Refer back to the parable I recorded in chapter 23 to appreciate more fully the significance of the above analysis.

The symbol given to the people not to improperly offer incense was the flowering of Aharon's staff and its production of almonds (*BeMidbar* ch. 15) which all the people witnessed. Uziyahu, who obviously did not believe in this warning, was appropriately punished with leprosy upon his forehead which everyone could see. There may be another explanation of his punishment. G-d had chosen Eretz Yisrael, the kingdom of the house of David, the location of His temple, and the eternal priesthood of Aharon, for eternity. Having broken through this "fence" of authority and acted like a kohen himself, his own fence as king was shattered and his monarchy taken from him irrevocably in his lifetime.

Chapter 48

Here we will see that the Torah foresaw events in the lives of many later kings, including Menashe, Asa, Yehoshafat, Chizkiya, Yeravam and Achav. Most notably, that Achaz would give of his seed to the Molech, and produce a copy of the altar that he saw in Damascus.

An analysis of the Torah's text regarding giving children to the *Molech* idol will show that it was aimed at King Achaz. We read (*VaYikra* 20:2-5), "...Anyone... who gives of his progeny to the Molech shall be executed; the people shall stone him. (V.3) And I will set My face at that man and cut him off from the midst of his people...(v.4) And if the people will hide their eyes from that man... not to kill him. (V.5) I will set My face at that man and his family and I will cut him off and all who go astray after him, to stray after the Molech from the midst of their people."

Presumably, verse 3 speaks of a case where he was not stoned by the people. But if they looked away, this is the situation of verse 4! If they did not look away, they stoned him, so what is the purpose of verse 3? We cannot argue that even after being stoned, this verse adds that He will also receive *kareis*, since the Halachah rules that any death administered by the court removes the punishment of *kareis*. Nor can we say that this verse refers to one who did this act secretly and must be punished by G-d, for it ends with the condemnation that he has "profaned My Holy Name." The other phrase that he has sullied "My temple" is strange. Does this law only apply when the temple is standing? Furthermore, why were these two phrases omitted in verse 5? Also, why is "his family" only included in verse 5 but not in verse 3?

It is clear that verse 2 refers directly to King Achaz. In his case, the people did not look away, but were nevertheless helpless to act against their king. Hence G-d declares his punishment, for he contaminated the sanctity of the temple, producing a terrible *chillul haShem*. In fact, Achaz died at the age of thirty-six [the reason for his early death is not explained in the Tanach].(66) Since this verse was directed at Achaz we can understand the additional phrases about contaminating the temple and profaning G-d's name, while in other places and times it is not relevant.

We can now review these verses. Verse 2 condemns a worshiper of Molech to death by the court, or, if this is not possible, by a public stoning. Verse 3 speaks of a unique situation where everyone is helpless because the crime was committed by the king (Achaz), so G-d must punish him but not his family, for they too are helpless against his power. Verse 4 speaks of any citizen whose Molech worship is ignored for any reason by the people and he is unpunished. In verse 5, G-d "sets his face at him and his family" (Rashi: not necessarily killing the family, but rather appropriate suffering for not forcing him to desist) and carries out the full retribution upon him and any followers. The justification of stoning in verse 2, that by giving of his seed to the Molech he has sullied the sanctity of the temple and profaned G-d's name may be seen as also referring to Menashe, especially since he did this for the specific reason of willfully acting against G-d. It is clear that this section of the Torah was pointing a finger at Achaz long before he lived, by our great G-d who stands above time.

When the Torah demands (*Devarim* 12:3-4) that, when we conquer the land, we smash their altars, break their monuments, burn their worshiped trees, smash their idols, and destroy their names – it adds "Do not do so to your G-d." This warning seems a bit strange. I think we can interpret it as referring to the altars that we smash, and says "Do not *make* similar ones for your G-d," i.e., do not copy their style of altar, foreseeing what Achaz was destined to do. So too, burning their trees is a preview to Menashe, who built images of the *asheirah* in the temple, as described in *Melachim II* (ch.21). Hence, the wickedness of Achaz and Menashe may have been foreseen in these verses.

When Achaz saw the fascinating altar in Damascus, he studied it until he knew all the precise dimensions. Then he instructed the kohen Uriyahu to copy it for the *Beis HaMikdash* (*Melachim II* ch. 16). It is interesting to note the unusual text in the Torah (*Devarim* 18:9), "Do not *learn* to do the abominations of the gentiles." Achaz learned and Uriyahu did. That section continues with a list of many abominations (bringing children to the Molech, practicing various forms of necromancy, etc.) which eventually were done by Achaz (partially) and by Menashe (totally), for these abominations of the gentiles caused their exile from the land. The implication is that if we do these acts, we will also bring about our exile. Near the end of *Melachim II* (24:3), the exile of the Jewish people is blamed primarily upon Menashe.

A midrash(67) states that Moshe's prophecy for Yehudah (*Devarim* 33:7), "HaShem, hear the voice of Yehudah..." refers to three kings – Asa, Yehoshafat, and Chizkiyah. "The voice of Yehudah" hints at Chizkiyahu, whose prayers to G-d cancelled his imminent death and extended his life for over twenty years. The *Panim Yafos* noted that the word "kol–קול" itself is the gematria (136) of חזקיהו! The phrase (ibid.) "may his hands be sufficient (רב) for him" may be interpreted as referring to Asa, who won a glorious victory over an enemy that outnumbered him by almost two to one (*Divrei HaYamim II* ch.14).(68) The final phrase in that verse ("and be a help from his enemies") can refer to the great battle of Yehoshafat against Moav, Ammon, and Edom (*Divrei HaYamim II* 20:22-23) in which these enemies fought each other and brought about their defeat! Thus we may interpret the phrase differently: and there shall be help (i.e., *it shall come*) from his enemies! The *Baal HaTurim* notes that the first three words in Yehudah's verse (above) "HaShem, hear the voice... is equal in gematria to Yehoshafat.

In the census in *Parashas Pinchas (BeMidbar ch. 26)*, each tribe is introduced with the phrase "the sons of (בני)" except for Ephrayim and Dan, for whom we find "*these are* the sons... אלה בני)". The tribe of Ephrayim produced Yeravam who set up the two golden calves for idolatry in his kingdom of Israel. Thus the term "eileh" is reminiscent of the cry of exultation for the original golden calf (*Shemos* 32:4) "eileh are your gods o Israel." One of Yeravam's calves was set up in the territory of Dan (*Melachim I* 12:29), explaining this added term for these two tribes (*Baal haTurim*).(68) Perhaps we can connect to this "eileh" the expression of Yaakov to Yosef, when

(Menashe and) Ephrayim stood before him, "Who are eileh?"

This expression also has a mystic connotation. In Kaballah we find that the twelve tribes are matched with the twelve constellations, which gave them certain intangible spiritual elements. When Yaakov told Yosef that Ephrayim and Menashe would be considered as Reuven and Shimon (full tribes) (*Bereishis* 48:5), this caused a significant spiritual change in them to convert them into tribes. When Yaakov then notices them standing with Yosef, he senses they are spiritually two tribes, and so he says (v.8), "Who are these?" Yosef responds that they are his sons (even presuming Yosef understood the deeper meaning, he meant that in this physical world they are mine). But Yaakov then says (v.9), "Bring them to me and I will bless them," i.e., they are now mine, spiritually just like Reuven and Shimon, and I will bless them myself.

Chapter 49

In this chapter we will see how the Torah foresaw the discovery of the Torah scroll in the days of King Yoshiyahu; the exile of the kingdom of Yehudah in the days of his descendants; as well as the earlier exile of his grandson Yehoyachin.

The Torah describes (*Devarim* 29:17-27) a frightening description of moral decline resulting in the exile of the Jewish people. It begins with an image of one man or woman (or family or tribe) (v.17) turning to idol worship, unafraid of retribution. G-d would not forgive "that man" but would wipe him off the face of the earth (v.19). Verses 21-23 describe a later (or last) generation amazed by the vast devastation of the land, and wondering what caused it! This sounds like the entire land could be devastated by the sin of one man! Isn't there a missing insertion that if this terrible decline spreads to all the people of the land, the result would be devastation and exile? I have seen some commentators struggling with this puzzle, but I find their solutions unacceptable and do not wish to discuss or analyze them further.

I believe I can shed light on this issue. We must first

note an astonishing second puzzle in these verses. After clearly portraying the final punishment of this individual in terrible terms (v.19), i.e., "G-d will erase his name from beneath the heavens," the next verse continues with a further retribution to this person, "G-d will separate him for evil of all the tribes of Israel ...." He was already erased! Besides, what other evil could he now suffer that was not previously intimated?

I believe that these verses speak of two separate situations, i.e., sins of an individual, and sins of an entire tribe, with descriptions of each given separately. The punishment of the individual idolater is completed in verse 19, by erasing his name from beneath the heavens. Verse 20 ("G-d will separate him/it for evil") speaks of an entire tribe, as the phrase correctly continues, "of all the *tribes*...." An entire tribe cannot be totally erased from Jewish history.

Hence they will only be "separated for evil." It is also very appropriate that the verse addressed to the individual man (v.19) speaks of "the 'curse' [in singular form] recorded in this book" (of *Devarim*), where the entire frightening *tochecha* of Parashas *Ki Tavo* is written in the singular form. The next verse addresses a tribe that is separated for evil like all "the curses" [plural] recorded in this "book of Torah" (implying other books, and thus including the *tochecha* of Parashas Bechukosai, written in the plural form).

Having gone on to the idolatrous tribe, who will suffer all the curses of the *tochecha* in *Chumash VaYikra*, which describe destruction and exile, verses 21 and forward fit perfectly to the end of this section. One might still ask, why should all the people be exiled for the idolatry of only one tribe? However, the fact is that this is precisely what actually happened! The exile of Yehudah came after the other tribes had already been dispersed. Binyamin is always seen as blended with Yehudah as if they were one, as in *Melachim I* (11:32,36) where they are called "one tribe." As earlier noted, the sins of Menashe, King of Yehudah, were the final cause of the exile. One mighty question stands in the way. If these final verses speak of Yehudah, how can we justify the expression (v.20) "of all the tribes of Israel," after they had already been exiled long before? This expression would indicate that those tribes are in much better condition! This enigma confounded me for hours! (However, if one studies his Tanach seriously and recognizes a difficult question as a mighty wall blocking the way, he looks for, and finds, a great cannon that can breach the wall and smash it down.)

Upon reflection, it is clear that the final exile was far worse than the exile of the ten tribes and their king Hosheia. He was merely imprisoned by the Assyrians, who drove the people to other cities to the east (*Melachim II* 17;4-6). [There is no description of massive killing or destruction.] This contrasts sharply with the exile of Yehudah, accompanied by pillage and destruction on a colossal scale. The king was blinded after his sons were executed before his eyes. Worst of all, the Second Temple was burnt to the ground and never rebuilt. Hence, this phrase is perfectly acceptable. This is confirmed in *Yechezkel* (23:32-34) where the retribution of Yehudah ("*Ahalivamah*") is pictured as far worse than that of the kingdom of Israel ("*Ahalah*").

However, another obstacle remains in clarifying this

chapter. We have claimed that verse 21 is attached to verse 20 which began an analysis of the kingdom of Yehudah and the curses which will befall it. It would therefore apply to the era of Tzidkiyahu, during whose kingdom the *churban* of the Holy Temple took place. In that case, what does verse 21 mean by "the later/last generation will say?" It is that generation itself which will see the destruction and wonder why they deserved such retribution! Why speak of "your children who will rise after you"?

A marvelous response to this point requires a very small adjustment to what we have written to now. The separation of that tribe for evil times in verse 20 (Yehudah, as discussed above) actually refers to the era of King Yoshiyahu, grandson of Menashe. In *Melachim II* (21:12-15) G-d had already proclaimed the imminent destruction of the kingdom and the temple because of Menashe's idolatry. Only because Yoshiyahu had instituted a great repentance after finding in the temple the original Torah written personally by Moshe, he was promised by the prophetess Chuldah (22:19-20) that the terrible annihilation would be postponed during Yoshiyahu's lifetime. The people of Yehudah under Yoshiyahu were merely "separated" for the evil which was destined for them, but not intended to occur immediately. Thus, the later generation in verse 21 is the generation of Yoshiyahu's sons Yehoyakim and Tzidkiyahu and his grandson Yehoyachin. The evil Yehoyakim ruled eleven years, replaced after his death by his son Yehoyachin. Three months later, Nevuchadnezer took him into captivity and placed his uncle Tzidkiyahu on the throne for eleven years, until the *churban*.Thus, there were two exiles, known to this day as *golus*

Yehoyachin and the final *golus*.

We may now observe the perfection of the text of verse 21.
"The last generation will say" – this is Yehoyachin *grandson* of Yoshiyahu; "your *children* who will rise after you" – Yehoyakim and Tzidkiyahu, *sons* of Yoshiyahu; "and the foreigner who will come from a distant land" – the invading enemy; "they will see the plagues of that land... like Sedom and Amorah...etc. – the churban.

How perfectly the verse first spoke of the last generation (grandson of Yoshiyahu) and then "your children who will rise after you" – since the children of Yoshiyahu did rise *after* the grandson to rule over the kingdom; for Yehoyakim and Tzidkihayu were the uncles of Yehoyachin, and ruled after him. Thus, they are recorded in the plural form of "your children."

After explaining the reason for the destruction and exile (namely, the abandonment of the Torah and the mitzvos), the next section offers consolation (30:1-6). Eventually, we will repent wholeheartedly, and G-d will (v.3) return (ושב) the captives with mercy, and He will "return" (ושב) and gather us from all the lands of our dispersion. He will bring us to our land, increase us, bless us, and turn our hearts to love Him with all our power so that we may live. The repeat of "return" in v. 3 can be explained nicely. The first is directed at the exile to Bavel that will return seventy years later. The second refers to the much greater exile across the world centuries later (as clearly indicated in the text) that will end with the ultimate and final redemption.

Marvels of Our Blessed G-d's Torah

Any reader who examines this chapter carefully and reflects upon it, can now see how it visualized the period before the terrible *churban*, and the glorious end of times, in such perfect terminology that only G-d could have used, standing above time and seeing our future history. As we read in *Pirke Avos* (5:25), "Delve, and delve into it (הפך בה) for everything is in it." First we delve to discover the questions, and then we delve further until we clarify and solve all the problems we encountered, and perceive that everything is revealed in the Torah.

I know that some may object to the above analysis based on the Talmudic statement (*Megillah* 14) that Yirmiyahu brought back the ten tribes in the days of Yoshiyahu. Thus, we should not refer to Yehudah alone as "the tribe" referred to in *parashas Nitzavim*. However, the Tanach itself constantly speaks of Yehudah alone in discussing the final exile, so the above statement seems to be contradicted by the Tanach itself! However, Rashi recognized this problem and wrote elsewhere in the Talmud (*Sanhedrin* 110b) that Yirmiyahu only restored a small number of the ten tribes. Obviously they blended into Yehudah and lost their individual identity, explaining the Tanach's terminology. Thus, the section clarified above from *chumash Devarim* properly meant "Yehudah" when it referred to "a tribe."

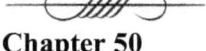

Chapter 50

Here we will show that Yaakov foresaw the idol of Michah in Dan as well as the golden calf that Yeravam established there. He also prophesied about the exile of the ten tribes and prayed for their return. I already noted in chapter 17 some proofs about these items, but here the proofs are expanded further with new insights into the Torah's terminology.

In previous chapters I explained in general terms many matters concerning the kings of Yehudah and Israel and specific items about Yehudah's kings. Now I will delve carefully into the kings of Yisrael.

Yaakov foresaw the sins of Yisrael and the exile of the ten tribes and recorded the specifics of the sin and the location, praying for their ultimate return. Note that Yeravam placed one golden calf in Dan and the other in Beis-El. Tanach blames these actions for the exile of the ten tribes. Regarding the one in Beis-El, I presented in chapter 15 and 16 (and in chapters 79 and 80) absolute proofs that Yaakov had visions of this idol and built altars in Beis-El to pray over them. However, the calf established in Dan was a far greater transgression. Since the calf in Beis-El was close (and meant as an alternative for the people so as not to go to Yerushalayim), and yet they traveled to the distant Dan, the text condemns them for this evil exuberance (*Melachim I* 12:30), as explained by *Metzudas David*. (The *Zohar* quoted in the *Alshich* states that the Beis-El calf was a male idol, and the one in Dan was female.) Where did Yaakov refer to this vision?

In his prophecy to Dan (*Bereishis* 49:16-18) Yaakov sees his son Dan as a snake on a path who bites the leg of a horse "and the rider falls backward. I hope for Your salvation O G-d." Although all commentators agree, rightfully, that this is a vision of Shimshon who collapsed the pillars of the great Philistine temple, killing hundreds of them, I am convinced that this cannot be the only meaning of these verses, because of many questions that can be raised:

1) Why did Yaakov begin by stating that Dan would judge the people, i.e., that he would produce one of the judges, Shimshon. Except for Shimon, every tribe produced at least one judge. Why is this significant for Dan?
2) Why did Yaakov repeat "Dan" in the next verse, since it is understood without repeating his name.
3) Why did Yaakov need two examples of a snake on the way, and an adder on the path, doing the same thing? He could have said "snake that bites the heel of horse" and omitted five words. What difference that the snake is on a path?
4) The parable itself is imperfect. The snake's venom moves slowly through the victim's body until it kills, while Shimshon's action instantly caused the great collapse that killed the Philistines.
5) Why did Yaakov add a prayer in v.18 ("I hope for Your salvation.") for this situation? His descendants faced far

greater crises in their history! If the "salvation" he prayed for here is only for Shimshon, it seems it did not accomplish much. Shimshon himself died, and he killed only three thousand of the enemy.

It therefore appears that there is a second message behind the words of Yaakov, i.e., he was actually prophesying two matters about the tribe of Dan – one positive and one negative. The first verse that Dan will supply a judge like other tribes is indeed a prophecy about Shimshon. The verse about a snake and an adder is a very negative vision. It symbolizes two situations in Dan that blocked people who were "on the road and on the path" to go to the temple for the festivals: a) the idol of Michah which served as a substitute for visiting the tabernacle at Shiloh (*Shoftim* 18:31); b) the golden calf of Yeravam that was established in Dan as a replacement for Yerushalayim. These obstacles are visualized as "biting the heels of the horse." Let us explain the symbol:

From the verse (*Devarim* 32:13), "He makes him ride on the high places of the earth" we gain an image of the earth as a horse upon which we ride. Hence, biting the horse can mean that the kingdom of Yisrael will fall from the land and be exiled due to the idolatry in Dan. We have previously noted the Tanach condemns Yeravam for his golden calves and blames him for the exile. Onkelos and Rashi state that the snake and adder are creatures which, respectively, a) have an incurable venom and b) cannot be charmed. So too, the people refused to listen to their prophets, and never cured themselves from this idolatry. Just as venom moves slowly through the body until it kills, so too, the sin of the idolatry grew through the decades, increasing G-d's fury, until it brought about the exile. This finally explains the special prayer of Yaakov at the conclusion of this vision. He was praying for the return of his children from exile!

Note now how perfect is the parable of the snake/adder biting the heel of the horse. The Torah had warned that if we contaminate the land of Israel by sin, the land would spew us out into exile (*VaYikra* 18:28). The impurity would affect the land to expel the people. In the parable, the sins are the venom of a snake which bites the horse (the land) causing it to throw off the rider (the people) to fall backwards (into exile). This is caused by Dan and its golden calf. Since Dan is at the northern border of the land, the venom starts at the *heel* of the horse, making its way through, and affecting the spiritual status of the entire kingdom of Yisrael.

Now we also understand the repetition of the term "Dan." Yaakov begins: *Dan shall judge his people.* This refers to Shimshon who will gain this status despite the idol of Michah in the tribe's territory. *Dan shall be a snake...*refers to the idolatry in Dan, hence the term required repetition. We have already explained "snake/adder "as representing two aspects of Dan, i.e., Michah's idol, and the golden calf, both in Dan. The snake is *"on the road"* (a term used for wider roads), pointing at Michah's idol. I.e., although the road to Yerushalayim was open, this idol stopped many from going there. The adder is *"on the path"* (a term used for a narrow way), referring to Yeravam's calf. These "official" golden calves were a major deterrent for pilgrimages to Yerushalayim, hence only few people made the attempt on a "path" to Yerushalayim. As the major cause of the exile of the ten tribes, this vision of idols and the tragic results compelled

Yaakov to call for G-d's salvation.

Thus, this vision of the future conveys an unhappy image, just as Yaakov said negative statements to Reuven, and to Shimon/Levi. The "blessings" of Yaakov are primarily visions of the future, including good and bad.

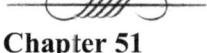
Chapter 51

It is found in the Torah that from Moshe would emerge a great nation, and so it happened! We will also explain how Gershom Ben Menashe was a priest for the tribe of Dan with the idol of Michah.

R. Yochanan states (*Berachos* 7a) in the name of R. Yose, "Every good promise that emanated from the Holy One, even a conditional one, was not withdrawn, as we see with Moshe, to whom G-d said (*Devarim* 9:14), 'Let Me be and I will destroy them [for worshiping the golden calf]... and *make you into a greater nation than them.*'

Although Moshe pleaded for them and the decree was rescinded, the promise to Moshe was fulfilled, as found in *Divrei HaYamim I* (23:17), 'And the sons of Rechavia [son of Eliezer Ben Moshe] increased greatly', to which Rav Yosef added, 'more than 600,000'."

I believe that Moshe's being progenitor of so many is clear from the Torah itself. In G-d's angry threat (above), there was a threat of destruction of *am Yisrael*, and a good promise to Moshe. When Moshe's pleas succeeded, the Torah records (*Shemos* 32:14) that G-d (only) reversed "the evil that He had spoken of doing to His people," but *nothing else*. Otherwise, the text should have simply been "And G-d reversed His words." Our text, and the historical fact that Moshe's descendants did increase greatly, together show the precision of the verse in *Shemos* (32:14), as we would expect from the Divine author of the Torah

Let us go a step further. In addition to having hundreds of thousands of descendants, Moshe was also, tragically, the grandfather of Gershom's son Yehonasan, who served, and his sons after him, as the priest for the idol-worship of the tribe of Dan until the dispersion of the ten tribes. It is astonishing to hear such a calamity occurring through Moshe's descendants! I wish to offer my thoughts about this, with an introductory parable:

A king relates to his primary chief advisor that a certain officer had committed an ugly and rebellious act, and he has decided upon an appropriate severe punishment. A sagacious advisor would back up the king completely and perhaps even suggest a harsher punishment for this renegade's abuse of the king. However, imagine that the advisor pleads with power and eloquence for leniency and total forgiveness. Would this not constitute his own abuse of the king's honor?

Moshe faced this logical dilemma. HaShem had told him that the people were worshiping a golden calf in his absence. What was Moshe to do? If he agreed that they should be destroyed, he would no longer be the great lover and defender of the Jewish people. If he would plead that they should be forgiven, he would be desecrating, rather than honoring, the glory of the Creator! But Moshe, with his holy spirit, found the wise solution. He argued that by not destroying them the glory of G-d would be elevated. For if they were annihilated, the nations would say [as

Pharaoh had stated to Moshe that they faced an evil star ("ברעה")] that G-d had taken them out only for the purpose of destroying them. By sparing them, the world would acknowledge that He is truly a G-d of mercy and compassion. G-d accepted this argument (and had hinted in advance that He sought a defense for them when He said to Moshe (*Shemos* 32:10), "And now allow Me...") and thus Moshe saved 600,000 families of *Am Yisrael*.

Now a double "measure for measure" took place. A) Having saved hundreds of thousands, he became the ancestor of hundreds of thousands through his grandson Rechavia. B) However, as the instrument through whom Jews survived, who had stood by unperturbed as a golden calf was being worshiped, Moshe had a grandson from Gershom who functioned as a priest for an idol. This is my possible explanation of this anomaly.(71)

Chapter 52

By precise analysis of the Torah's terminology, we will see that it foresaw that the idol of Michah would be of silver, and Yeravam's calves would be of gold, as well as in which eras they would be worshiped. It also hints that the copper snake made by Moshe would become an object of worship – that the priest of Michah's idol would be a levite (and his personal identity was known), while Yeravam's calves would not be served by Levite priests. The Torah also saw Naaman from the era of Elisha.

The Torah's vision of Michah's idol and Yeravam's calves emerges from *Shemos* (20:20), "Do not make with Me gods of silver, and gods of gold do not make for yourselves." Many questions are raised by the commentators. A) Why is "with Me" used for silver gods, and "for yourselves" is mentioned with gold gods? B) These two terms are themselves unclear. They become crystal clear, however, once we note what happened in Jewish history when we produced idols in Eretz Yisrael.

Michah's idol was of silver (*Shoftim* 17:4), while Yeravam's calves were of gold (*Melachim I* 12:28). There was another major difference. Michah's idol served in the era that all the people were united as one nation, and the tabernacle at that time was in Shiloh. A Jew might decide to visit one or the other, or even both, as we are told (*Shoftim* 17:6), people did "anything that was right in their eyes." Yeravam's calves were established right after the split into two kingdoms, and he blocked his people from going up to Yerushalayim. Hence the opening phrase: "Do not make *with Me* gods of silver" matches perfectly the case of Michah, in which people might do both: i.e., visit Shiloh, and worship Michah's silver idol *"with Me."* The next phrase, not to make *for yourselves* gods of gold, matches Yeravam's era when his golden calves were served by the idolaters exclusively for themselves, replacing the temple in Yerushalayim. Thus, the text perfectly envisioned this situation.

(Grammatically, when *lachem* (for yourselves) appears, ordinarily it has a simple meaning, e.g., "take for yourselves a beautiful fruit" [that every Jew should have an esrog]. However, when used as a contrast to another pronoun, e.g. (*Shmuel II* 16), "What have I (*li*) to do with you *(velachem)*, it separates *you* from *me*. Here too, "with Me" is distinguished from "for yourselves", implying that any god of gold must not be worshiped when there is no recourse to doing so "with Me" at the same time. By placing silver gods before the golden in this verse, the Torah followed the historical order too, and thus this verse is a marvelous example of G-d looking into the future and condemning idolatry in advance, even describing in detail the respective metal material used for these gods.

Refer also to chapter 17 for other proofs of the Torah recognizing these two periods of idolatry.

This analysis answers the puzzle posed by R.Yitzchak Abarbanel about this verse. He questioned the need for it, since the Torah had already warned in the Ten Commandments, (*Shemos* 20:3), "You must not have any other gods before Me...." – isn't this verse a repetition? However, I clarified in chapter 42 that that verse was directed at King Menashe, who erected his idol in the Holy Temple itself, literally *"before Me!"* Our verse was needed for G-d to direct His commands to Michah and to Yeravam. The holy Torah, as always, is very precise and perfect.

We should note that many verses are found in the Torah about idolatry, each directed at a different situation in our later history. Demonstrations of this fact can be found in the following chapters: chs. 37, 42, 45, 46, 47, 53, 56, 68, 76 and 80.

The Torah foresaw all the methods of idolatry, the three principal practitioners amongst our kings (Yeravam, Achav, and Menashe), and the idols each would serve, respectively, as I shall record in Part Two of this work.

Only silver and gold idols are mentioned since no other metal was used for idolatry in Tanach. The copper serpent that Moshe made was not produced for idolatry but for a good purpose, so there is no warning about a copper idol. I am certain there must be some warning about this serpent too, but I am uncertain where it is. Perhaps, there was a hint in G-d's expression to Moshe, when he was told (*BeMidbar* 21:8-9) to fashion that serpent as a cure for those bitten by snakes, "Make *for yourself* a copper serpent...." This hinted that it was meant only for that time and situation, but not to be preserved for future generations. In fact, centuries later, when it had become an object of worship, while many righteous people were afraid to destroy an object made by Moshe, King Chizkiyahu destroyed it, and the tzaddikim praised him for this act (as stated in the gemara *Pesachim* 56a). He surely understood the significance of the statement, "Make *for yourself*," as explained above.

Marvels of Our Blessed G-d's Torah

I found another marvelous example of a textual hint about a future idol, the one made by Nevuchadnezzar.

The Torah predicts (*Devarim* 4:28) that we will in the future be spread amongst the nations and will worship gods that do not see, nor hear, nor eat, nor smell anything. The Vilna Gaon asked, why did not the list include that it does not speak? However, he answers that Nevuchadnezzar had managed to have his idol speak! The midrash on *Shir HaShirim,* on the verse (7:9) "I will go up to the palm tree...." states that Nevuchadnezzar placed the *tzitz* (plate) of the high priest into the mouth of his idol and it proclaimed "I am your G-d...." Thus, by omitting the item of speech, the Torah foresaw that in the future an idol would speak!

The Torah also had a precise vision of Michah's idol and its production. The description of the idol's manufacture (*Shoftim* ch. 17-18) indicates that it was made by a professional sculptor who was paid a high fee of two hundred silver pieces. It remained in the private possession of Michah in his home. Eventually, members of the tribe of Dan learned about it, burglarized it, and set it up for tribal worship. Thus, in the chapter recording the blessings and curses (*Devarim* ch. 27) that were recited on the mountains of Grizim and Eival, the Torah states, "Cursed be the man who makes an idol or molten image..., the work of a craftsman's hands, and places it in a secret place...." Had the Torah not envisioned Michah's actions, the references to a craftsman, and to a secret place, would have been entirely extraneous! What difference whether it is a professional or an amateur design, and why must it be in a secret place? These additions are another example of the Torah picturing a later event and describing it in detail, as only G-d could do.

There is another dimension to the verse quoted earlier, not to make a silver idol "with Me," which we linked to Michah. As described in *Shoftim* ch.17, Michah found a Levi to serve as his kohen, and this delighted him especially (vs. 9-13). The Torah declares (*BeMidbar* 3:12) that the Leviim belong to G-d, to serve Him. Hence, the term "with Me" may also be understood to mean not to utilize one who is reserved "with Me" to make and serve silver gods. In contrast, the Tanach emphasizes (*Melachim I* 12:31) that Yeravam chose people who were not of the tribe of Levi to serve as his priests, thus we do not find "with Me" in the reference to golden idols in that verse. This additional insight goes hand in hand with the earlier one and complements it.

I find another Torah reference which hinted at Michah's idol and his Levi-priest. We read in *Devarim*,18:1: "The Kohanim–the Leviim, the entire tribe of Levi, shall have no part nor inheritance with Yisrael; the fire-offerings of G-d and His inheritance they shall eat. He shall have no inheritance among his brothers; G-d is his inheritance as He spoke of him."

Apparently, the first half of the second verse repeats the first verse! What was its purpose?

However, the term "inheritance" as used in these verses clearly can mean two different things. 1) Ownership of land in Eretz Yisrael, as in the second verse. 2) The sacrifices that the kohanim eat from, as in the first verse, which further differentiates between actual sacrifices (fire-offerings) and "his inheritance" (other offerings like the *terumah* and *maaseir*).

Seeing into the future all the machinations of Michah and his "kohen", G-d writes, "The Kohanim-Leviim, the entire tribe of Levi, will have no share or inheritance in the *land* of Israel; they receive/eat from the fire-offerings and the "inheritance" of *terumah-maaseir*. And this "inheritance" of holy things he shall not have among his brothers (i.e., far from the holy temple, living among the people with his private idol in Dan) for his inheritance is G-d (i.e., with G-d, in His holy place, in Shilo or in the *beis haMikdash*). How perfectly, the second verse switched from the plural to the singular form, for it was referring to the Levi-priest who served Michah's idol! Even the extraneous term "the priests-the Leviim" (since it is followed by "the entire tribe of Levi") may be seen as a hint to a particular Levi who served as a Kohen, who is then addressed in the next verse.

A few verses further (18:6-8), the Torah presents three verses to describe a Levi who may come from anywhere in the land, and directs him to proceed to the place chosen by G-d and serve there with all his brother-leviim and share with them equally in their portions. I believe that this section may also be directed to that Levi who passed Michah's abode and (*Shoftim* 17:9) described himself as one looking for some place to stay. Thus, the Torah states that any such a Levi should go to G-d's appointed place, not find a substitute and profane place to settle there when he could have a holy share with his brethren in a holy environment.

Eventually, (*Shoftim* ch.18) members of the tribe of Dan robbed Michah of his idol, taking it and his "kohen" with them, and established it in their own territory, where the kohen and his children continued to serve it until the exile. His name is Yehonasan Ben Gershom Ben Menasheh. Chazal note that the *nun* in Menasheh is lifted above the line, because it is really Moshe, whose grandson served this idol! Out of respect to Moshe Rabbeinu, this *nun* covered up part of the shame of Moshe. Amazingly, in the Torah's verse warning us not to make silver gods, which we already explained referred to Michah's idol, the term to [not] "make" is written with an extra "final *nun*" - תעשון - followed by a second identical verb in that verse without the extra letter. I am convinced that this is a marker to the "nun" in Shoftim, connecting Yehonasan, grandson of Me*na*sheh, to this verse describing Michah's silver idol that he served. This is another example of G-d, writer of the Torah, linking it to the later events of Jewish history, as recorded in Nach.

I have already noted that the second phrase about not making golden idols refers to Yeravam's idols. The very next verse (*Shemos* 20:21) states, "Make for Me an altar of earth, and sacrifice upon it your burnt offerings ... and your oxen; in every place where I record My name, I will come to you and bless you." This entire verse is an enigma! What is it doing here in *Shemos,* when altars are discussed later in *Parashahs Terumah*, and all sacrifices are not discussed until *Chumash VaYikra*! How is this verse connected to a verse forbidding false idols? Rashi's comment on the altar of earth does not answer these questions.

However, we find (*Melachim* 5:17) that when Naaman, general of Aram, was leaving Elisha after Naaman was cured of his leprosy, he requested permission to take a large load of earth on his oxen, obviously to build a special private altar for him to serve G-d (as Ralba'g explains), for he would no longer offer sacrifices to his false gods. Chazal explain that he would consider himself a *ger toshav*, observing only the seven Noahide commandments.

We know that once the *Beis HaMikdash* was built, no sacrifices could be brought anywhere else ever again.

The explanation of how Eliyahu could sacrifice on Mt. Carmel is
well-known, as an exceptional allowance in an exceptional situation, as documented in the Talmud. But how could Elisha permit Naaman to continuously offer sacrifices in his foreign residence to G-d? He must have had some proof from the Torah to allow it! It is surely this verse of making an altar of earth [written in the singular form] that allows this man to do so. It is recorded here in the perfect place! After warning the Jewish people not to make or worship idols of silver or gold (and as explained regarding the golden calves of Yeravam, it meant to do so away from the appointed place of G-d), it adds that one Gentile person will be allowed to make himself an earthern altar to worship G-d in his land. Thus, the earlier warning was in the plural form, while this verse, addressed to Naaman, is in the singular!
His actions took place in the period when Yeravam's idols were still being worshiped, hence it is a most appropriate location for this verse.

Now the verse concludes: "In every place that I will record My name (better: that I will cause [or allow] My name to be mentioned), I will come to you and I will bless you." Having just concluded with Naaman's altar of earth which he erected in Aram, the Torah adds that in *any place* that G-d would allow His holy name to be pronounced, even in Aram, He would come to bless the man who sacrificed to Him, i.e., Naaman. Nevertheless, since the text states "the place" [בכל המקום] rather than "any place," we also understand it as a reference to Yerushalayim as well, giving it a double meaning. If Naaman is implied here, the expression "I will come to you" makes good sense, for if it only meant the Holy Temple, where G-d is present always, the expression seems to be meaningless!

Reviewing all the above, it appears convincing that this verse was meant for the unique case of Naaman, placed here by the foresight of G-d, (looking into the distant future), and recorded it with His Divine pen of fire.

Marvels of Our Blessed G-d's Torah

Chapter 53

Here we will show that the Torah foresaw Yeravam's actions of making his molten idol and creating a new eighth month in the Jewish calendar.

The text in *Melachim I* (12:32) describes how Yeravam ordained a feast on the fifteenth day of the eighth month imitating the festival of Sukos that had been celebrated a month before in the *Beis HaMikdash*. He did not do anything about that month before the day of his festival, such as proclaiming it as the seventh month.

Let us now note the seemingly extraneous words in the Torah in describing the holiday of Sukos (*VaYikra* 23:34-36, 39-41): "...On the fifteenth day of *this* seventh month will be the holiday of Sukos for seven days unto G-d....(v.36)You shall do no servile work. (V.39) But on the fifteenth of *the seventh month*, when you have gathered the produce of the land, keep the feast of G-d seven days; on the first day [observe] a sabbath, and on the eighth day [observe] a sabbath. [V.40 presents the mitzvah of the four species, to be observed for seven days.] (V.41) You shall keep it as a feast unto G-d for seven days in the year; it is a statute forever for your generations, *you shall celebrate it in the seventh month*." Having first written "*this* seventh month" followed by "*the* seventh month," it is clear that the Torah meant every seventh month of all years to come. Why then did the text repeat the final phrase of verse 41, emphasizing once again the seventh month? Although the first half of that verse also seems repetitious, this is answered in the Talmud, as dealing with rules for one who missed bringing his *shlamim* sacrifices and how long he can make it up – but the final phrase seems a clearly extraneous repetition! If we were to suggest that this final verse is simply a last summary of the subject, it should have also repeated that it takes place on the fifteenth of the month! Why the month but not the day?

No human writer – only G-d alone – could have foreseen that a future king would commit this strange folly of inventing a new holiday on *the same day of the Torah's Sukos, but in a different month.* Thus, the final phrase is a warning to Yeravam not to create his new holiday in the incorrect month even if he keeps the fifteenth day intact!(72)

Two powerful proofs to the above argument

1) Reread v. 41 in the last paragraph, and notice that "it is a statute forever for your generations" was placed after phrase one, before phrase three. Logically it should have been placed at the beginning [or the conclusion] of the verse, if it applied to both phrases. It can be understood perfectly, however, if directed at Yeravam, who came generations later and tampered only with the month, not the days. It states, in effect, [remember, Yeravam!) that it is an eternal law to observe this holiday in the seventh, not the eighth, month!

2) In this very chapter, there are three other statements (vs. 14, 21, 31) declaring "a statute forever for your generations." However, they all add "in all your dwellings." In our v. 41, it is omitted. Obviously, since it was intended as an admonition for Yeravam, it would

have been inappropriate, for it was unnecessary for the people in Yerusahalayim. (It is interesting to note that near the beginning of this chapter, the laws of Pesach conclude with this phrase entirely omitted. I might suggest that this could be a hint at the future action of Chizkiyahu, (*Divrei HaYamim II* 30:2) who instituted a Pesach celebration in the second month of the year, when it had been impossible to do so in Nisan. Thus, this verse could be an indirect approval of his decision.

Although the Talmud records that the Torah scholars of his time were upset about his action, the text itself clearly indicates that great and positive results came from this belated celebration.

I believe that these two arguments clearly confirm the thesis that verse 41 was a message to Yeravam in a future era, which only our great G-d could have foreseen and recorded in this precise manner.(73)

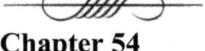
Chapter 54

We will see through the window of the Torah that it foresaw the site for the splitting of the Jewish people into two kingdoms to be Shechem. (Although this was already reviewed in chapter 3, here we will add many additional and worthy points.) The Torah also saw the time period in which this would occur.

Let us ponder why the Torah chose a site near Eilonei Moreh for the ceremony of the blessings and curses on Mt. Grizim and Mt. Eival (*Devarim* (11:30), which as we know is another term for Shechem (*Bereishis* 12:6), and as is well-known to all who visit Eretz Yisrael and see these mountains near Shechem. There were certainly other sites available, closer to the Jordan River, where they crossed over it into the land!

Imagine a human emperor passing an important edict for all his citizens. One brazen individual openly abrogates this decree. The king would order his execution to take place in the city where he dared to commit this rebellious deed, to teach its citizens a powerful lesson. However, the decree would have been issued in his capital city, for he could not have foreseen where this rebellious act would occur. Only our Creator, standing above time, could see that Shechem would be the location for acts of sin and rebellion, and therefore could choose in advance these warnings to be issued at the site of future actions.

It was in Shechem (*Melachim I* ch.12) that Rechavam issued his nasty response to the people, leading to the split of the kingdom and the rise of Yeravam with his establishment of idolatry in the kingdom of Yisrael, and the eventual exile of the ten tribes. The establishment of the separate kingdom of Yisrael is directly linked to the exile by the verse (*Melachim II* 17:21-23) that describes the steps from that split through the idolatry of Yeravam to the exile. Thus, the curses pronounced on Mt. Eival, beginning with idolatry, unfortunately came to pass at that site, properly chosen by HaShem in advance, for the articulation of these curses. Indeed, the fact that the tribes were told to break into two groups on two mountains is itself an indicator that due to events that would occur later in this area, they will split into two kingdoms!

Amazingly, the choice of tribes for each mountain is itself highly significant!

In my opinion, the six tribes who were stationed on Mt. Eival (for curses) were the primary tribes of the "ten" driven into exile: Reuven, Zevulun, Dan, Naftali, Gad, and Asher. On Mt. Grizim stood Yehudah and Binyamin, the two major tribes of the kingdom of Yehudah; Ephrayim and Menashe (combined as "Yosef"), and Shimon, who are recorded (*Divrei HaYamim II* 15:9) as having moved in very large numbers to the kingdom of Yehudah, under King Asa, whom they viewed as being especially blessed by G-d; and Levi, who flocked to Yehudah soon after the split into two kingdoms, since Yeravam had deprived them of serving in Yerushalayim, as stated clearly in the text (*Divrei HaYamim II* 11:13-14). The final tribe on Mt. Grizim is Yisaschar, for whom there is no statement to indicate that they joined Yehudah. However, as the tribe known for their dedication to the Torah, and to fix the Jewish calendar (*Divrei HaYamim I* 12:22), and the fact that they were geographically next to Ephrayim, strongly supports the logical presumption that many of them decided to live in the kingdom of Yehudah with its holy temple in Yerushalayim, rather than in the godless kingdom of an idolatrous Yeravam. Thus, the least meritorious tribes stood on Mt. Eival, heard the terrible curses that began with the sin of idolatry, ignored the warnings, and were the first to be exiled. How fitting that this ceremony was conducted at Shechem, the location from which the split into two kingdoms occurred.

Interestingly, Yehoshua also chose Shechem (Yehoshua 24:1) as the site for his final address and exhortation to all the people. After his powerful address, the people entered into a covenant to observe the Torah faithfully, and that verse (25) ends with "he set for them a statute and an ordinance in Shechem. " Why was Shechem repeated here? Surely, Yehoshua saw the future downfall that would start at Shechem, and established this statute in the hope of preventing it, as he emphasized later (after raising up a great stone as a testimony to the proceedings) in verse 27: And Yehoshua said, "This stone...shall be a witness unto you, lest you deny your G-d."

At Shechem Moshe spoke by G-d's instruction, and now Yehoshua responded with his own voice at Shechem.

Additionally, we may now understand a puzzling description of the area in the text of the two mountains (*Devarim* 11:30), "opposite (מול) Gilgal, near Eilonei

Moreh." What is the purpose of adding Gilgal? Amazingly, Rashi claims that here the term *mool* means "far from Gilgal." This compounds the mystery! Even if we accept the opinion in the Talmud (*Sotah* 33b) that it means *near* Gilgal, the fact is that it still seems an unnecessary addition. Once we know these are the two mountains near Shechem, Gilgal adds nothing!

However, the term Gilgal was invented by G-d for the site where Yehoshua carried out a great circumcision ceremony for the thousands of uncircumcised Jews who left Egypt (*Yehoshua* 5:9), with the statement "I have *rolled away* (galosi) the disgrace *of Egypt* from you." Why Egypt?

In *Chumash Shemos* (10:10) when Pharaoh almost yielded to release the people, but then hardened himself against it, he warned Moshe, "See, that evil (רעה) is before you." Later, when Moshe was pleading for G-d to forgive the sin of the golden calf, he said (*Shemos* 32:12), "Why should the Egyptians say 'He brought them out for *evil* (רעה) to slay them in the mountains...'" Finally (v.14) "G-d repented over the רעה that He planned to do to His people." The blood that would have been spilled was converted to the blood of the circumcision at Gilgal, as Rashi records from a midrash on the verse above (10:10). Thus, the "disgrace" of Egypt (had it occurred) was "rolled away" by the redemptive act of circumcision. Hence, Gilgal is a site of blessing for the Jewish people, including the fact that it became the location of the ark and the "tent of meeting" (*ohel moed*).

In contrast, Shechem is a site of evil and sin, as previously outlined.

Thus, as the Torah introduces the ceremony that would take place on the two mountains – curses and blessings – it presents two locations as markers; Gilgal (a blessed site) and [Shechem] Eilonei Moreh (a sinful site) as geographical indicators, even though Gilgal was some distance away. Since the term Gilgal was created only in Yehushua's time,(75) it is crystal clear that G-d looked ahead to the blessings that would be manifested there, and to the evil that would emerge from Shechem. (We find that *Hoshea* (4:15) mentions Gilgal as a site for idolatry! This might have occurred in a later era, or it may be a second city with that name, as has indeed been suggested. See the discussion in the early section of Chapter 33.)

Earlier in this volume, I already discussed Shechem in great detail.

Further support for the above analysis

We must also explain why Moshe mentioned the ceremony on these two mountains, and their location, in *Parashas Re'ei*, rather than as the introduction to that section of curses and blessings in *Parashas KeeTavo*!

However, looking back to the concluding verses of *Parashah Eikev*, we find (11:24), "Every place whereon the soles of your feet shall tread will be yours; from the wilderness and the Lebanon, from the Euphrates River to the uttermost sea shall be your boundary." This promise came to fruition in the days of Shlomo. Then *Parashah Re'ei* begins and spells out a blessing and a curse. The blessing if we heed the word of G-d, took place in Shlomo's era, with the above expanded boundaries. The curse followed immediately after his death with the split into two kingdoms. Hence, after describing this massive territory and presenting the idea of blessings and curses, the text inserts the location of the ceremony near Shechem, which was the site from which the curses began. In contrast, the description in *Parashas Kee Tavo* speaks only of the entry into the land and the mitzvah of establishing the law of the Torah by means of a special ceremony on the two mountains. This took place after the conquest of the city of *Aay* (*Yehoshua* ch.8), unlinked to later historical events. Hence, the insertion in *Re'ei* is given as a historical reference to follow the period of the great expansion of Jewish territory in Shlomo's era.

Thus, the Torah foresaw the splitting of the tribes at Shechem, and decreed a symbolical splitting of the tribes beforehand on the mountains at Shechem. Eventually, Shechem was the site that started the process leading to the exile of the ten tribes. Earlier in this volume, I reviewed the chain that began with the sale of Yosef near Shechem, and the earlier erection of the altars at Shechem by our forefathers, which all served to connect this city to the tragedies that emerged there.

Chapter 55

This chapter points to the place in the Torah which clearly indicates that the tribe of Binyamin would join forces with Yehudah even when the other ten tribes would rebel against David's dynasty. So too, they would remain in the land even when the other tribes would be exiled.

Moshe says of Binyamin (*Devarim* 33:12), "The beloved of G-d, Who shall dwell [ישכן] for security over him; He shall hover over him all day, and He shall dwell [שכן] between his shoulders." What does G-d's dwelling over him connote? The root sh-ch-n, used twice in this verse, rings with the verse (*Shemos* 25:8), "And they shall make Me a sanctuary and I will dwell [ושכנתי] among them." Clearly, G-d dwells on earth in His holy sanctuary in Yerushalayim. In discussing the site of the Beis haMikdash, the Torah [which kept its location secret] states (*Devarim* 12:14), "In the place that G-d will choose, *in one of your tribes,* there you shall offer your burnt sacrifices...." Surely, the "one" is Binyamin, in whose territory the altar stood and the sacrifices were brought. We must now understand how G-d hovered over him "all day."

The navi Yirmiyahu (15:9) speaks of the exile of the ten

tribes [according to most commentators], and describes its setting "sun" (downfall) as taking place (בעוד יומם)" while still in daytime." Although exile and doom is usually viewed as night/darkness, here it can be understood as contrasting with the kingdom of Yehudah, which continued to exist for a long time. Therefore, G-d's protection as He hovers over Binyamin "all day" is easily understood as representing Binyamin's continued existence in the land until the final exile of Yehudah, which finally brought the "night." To my mind, this is the simple interpretation, not some esoteric expedition into terminology. It is quite clear that the Torah foresaw Binyamin's partnership with Yehudah, leading to its continued existence after the exile of the ten tribes, until Yehudah itself was exiled at "nightfall." So too, the hint of "all day" echoes the fact that the other tribes would have been exiled earlier "during the day," as Yirmiyahu stated Here again we see the evidence of the Torah coming to us directly from G-d.

I explained in ch. 36 that the phrase (*Bereishis* 49:10) "The staff shall not depart from Yehudah,' referred to the era of the first Holy Temple. However, since "staff" [שבט] may be translated "tribe," it may be a hint that the tribe of Binyamin will never depart from its attachment to Yehudah, as occurred in history! I discussed this at length in ch. 20.

I believe that when Yaakov called his youngest son "Binyamin," it meant (as Rashi states there) 'son of the south," based on the fact that "yamin" can mean south. Since Binyamin's great geographic asset in later history was the altar in the *beish hamikdah* in Yerushalayhim, viewed in the Torah as being in the south of the country (as in Rashi, *Bereishis* 12:9). This would be a manifestation of the holy spirit in Yaakov.(75)

If a "day" is period of history, I think that when Yaakov bought the birthright from Eisav (*Bereishis* 25:33) saying, "Sell me your birthright *kayom* (usually translated as "today", as if it reads *hayom*), it may be understood quite differently. Perhaps Yaakov foresaw the eternal battle of Eisav vs. Yaakov that would culminate in his victory when Mashiach comes, but wanted to acquire "a day's worth" of supremacy in this world, with his mind visualizing the first *Beish haMikdash*. The letter כ in כיום may be understood as "approximately a day," since a large part of Yaakov's family (the ten tribes) were exiled before the rest of the tribes, so the day was not a complete one. The second temple cannot be viewed as a "second day" since they were under the thumb of enemies, especially the Romans, for the most part.

Chapter 56

Here we will show that the Torah foresaw the lust of Achav for the vineyard of Navos, how he plotted to gain it for himself, and the part played by the false witnesses and the elders in this terrible act

There is a difficult verse in the Torah about following a majority (*Shemos* 23:2), "Do not follow the multitude for evil, and do not testify (*taaneh*) in a dispute to turn aside after a multitude to pervert justice." [There are many differing renderings of this verse because of the confusion of terms and endless possibilities of translation. The one given is only one such translation.] I offer the following interpretation:

It is human nature for people to follow the opinion of the many. Frequently, they will even quote a popular opinion in a way that implies that they personally know it as an established fact. Yet, it may have begun as a statement of one individual, perhaps even basically true but including an incorrect element which could uproot the entire "fact." Hence the entire verse directs us not to make any claim based on statements of others that we did not personally verify. The Hebrew verb *n-t-h* (נטה) used twice in this verse (for "testify" and "pervert justice") implied accepting an attitude based on improper considerations, such as outside influences, or illogical, emotional leanings. Thus, "Do not testify in a dispute by making a claim improperly, e.g., by relying on the multitude's opinion." Since "dispute" (ריב) is spelled in this verse without the *yud* (רב), the gemara adds an additional idea of not relying on the words of a greater scholar (רב) in giving your personal testimony, but only on what you know yourself. It is obvious that the verb *taaneh* in this verse meant to give testimony, since the phrase immediately preceding ended with "do not join your hand with the wicked to be an unrighteous witness."

We might also render this verse as above, without the final three words, separating them into an independent phrase which states that, when unrelated to matters of testimony, it is generally a proper principle to "rely on the majority opinion," e.g., a court may issue an enforceable opinion based on a two-to-one agreement.

We will now show that these verses are related to Achav and Navos. In that terrible event, the elders in the area of Navos were ordered by Izevel, Achav's wife (although they thought is was sent directly by Achav, since it came with his seal), to hire two false witnesses to testify against Navos, causing his execution, and allowing Achav to take over his fields. The Torah begins the statements about bearing false witness as follows (*shemos* 23:1), "Do not raise a false report; do not join your hand with the wicked to be an unrighteous witness." There is a puzzle here. The first phrase is universally understood as referring to those who gossip, spreading evil rumors about others, even true reports (*lashon hara*). How does this connect to court testimony in the same verse? Shouldn't this opening phrase itself been clarified further, since it could mean many things (e.g., instructions to ordinary people, or to judges not to accept testimony based on hearsay, or not to listen to one side without the other present, etc.)?

As one verse, it must be saying that we must not hear a false report that *will lead* to our joining hands with the wicked for false testimony. And, how does this lead to the next verse of not following a majority for evil reasons? Furthermore, since the Ten Commandments already stated clearly that we must not bear false witness, why were these repetitious verses needed?

We have already mentioned several times the vast difference between the Torah and human laws. The latter type record ordinances and decrees in general terms, oblivious of who will or will not ever break them, or when, and how they may occur. HaShem knows the future events To which these laws will relate, and records them in terminology reflecting those occurrences.

Regarding the Navos event: both the elders, and the false witnesses, might have rationalized their behavior. The elders could have thought that it is possible that Achav knows whereof he speaks (the message had been signed with Achav's seal), and that Navos indeed was guilty of blasphemy, and a death penalty, but there weren't two kosher witnesses to testify. Even if it was false, they themselves were not testifying, and the guilt for such testimony would be the witnesses', since the Torah rule is not to listen to people and lie, but only to G-d's law. The witnesses could justify their agreement by thinking that they are nobodies compared to these elders, so who are they to stand up against them, for they probably know that this is a true report and their testimony is somehow a justifiable act. Hence, the Torah here speaks to all the actors in this situation.

First it speaks to the elders: *Do not raise a false report* -- which includes spreading a report one has not confirmed as a verified fact. Hence they had no right to accept the command of the message which had been signed with Achav's seal. [It surely also addresses Izevel, the originator of the false report.] *Do not join your hand with the wicked* – speaks to 1) Achav, who certainly knew that his wife was going to do some evil (21:7); 2) to Izevel, not

Marvels of Our Blessed G-d's Torah

to join hands with her evil husband, by planning her horrible scheme for his sake; 3) to the elders, *to be an unrighteous witness* – also not to hire unrighteous witnesses, with your hand right in middle of the plot. (Next verse) *Do not follow a multitude for evil....* – speaks to the false witnesses. Whether they sensed it was a false report (as is mostly likely) or even if they thought that it might be possibly true, they were forbidden to testify to a lie (for they had not heard anything from Navos), to follow the multitude of elders to do their bidding. It is also noteworthy that after Navos was stoned, the elders sent the news to Izevel, not Achav. This shows that, despite Achav's seal on the letter they had gotten, they sensed that this was actually a cunning act of Izevel, and clearly false.

How perfectly the Torah preceded these verses with an admonition (23:27) not to curse G-d (*elohim*) or a ruler. This was precisely the testimony against Navos (*Melachim* 21:13), that he blasphemed G-d and the king! Thus, the Torah followed up this admonition with the proviso that testimony about such a terrible act must be absolutely true, and based on personal knowledge through two proper witnesses. The verses detailed above speak to all the actors in the tragedy of Navos, as we have shown in many other cases in this volume. We now understand why in addition to the command in the Ten Commandments about falsely testifying, the Torah recorded these verses to point a finger at the tragedy of Navos centuries later.

A few verses later (23:7), the Torah combines two seemingly unrelated matters in one verse: Distance yourself from false words – and do not kill the innocent and the righteous, for I will not justify the wicked. How are these topics related? [Apparently, the implication is that sometimes a lie may lead to an innocent person being killed.] With Navos, all the perpetrators combined their lies to execute an innocent man."I will not justify the wicked" could imply that Achav, identified in Tanach as wicked, would never be forgiven for having started the process by cleverly passing the entire procedure into the diabolical hands of his evil, sinister wife Izevel.

Another amazing point related to the above

Regarding the son of Shelomis, who cursed G-d, Moshe placed him in detension to await the verdict from G-d. Moshe was commanded (*VaYikra* 24:14), "Bring forth the blasphemer outside the camp... and the entire congregation shall stone him." After explaining this ruling, HaShem adds (v.17), "And if a man kills any person, he shall be put to death." Why is this law placed together with blasphemy? In the other case of the man who profaned the Shabbos and was incarcerated since the punishment was not known (*BeMidbar* 15:32-36), G-d gave His verdict, but no additional laws were mentioned there!

This too may be a hint at the Navos incident. It was through the law of cursing HaShem that Navos was victimized by false witnesses. The Torah therefore warns that he who (by these means) strikes dead a human being shall be put to death. G-d carried out this retribution by having Achav, the original instigator, killed in the territory of Navos's vineyard (*Melachim I* 21:19).

The Torah uses two adjectives for false witness – *shov* and *sheker*. The latter is clearly an absolute falsehood. *Shov* also means "in vain," or nothingness. The phrase recorded earlier "do not raise a false report" uses the term *shov*. This is especially appropriate for the elders who accepted the command to find false witnesses. They had an additional justification, for they could have presumed that the king, with his absolute power, could always find another way to get Navos out of the way. Hence, they were contributing little to the entire process, and the guilt is totally upon Achav or Izevel. In the total scheme their action was really nothing of significance. Hence the Torah warned here not to raise a report of *shov* - even one that seems to be in vain must not be spread about.

Note an amazing point. In the command not to covet the possessions of others, the list in the second set in *Chumash Devarim* adds "his field," which is not in the original list in *Shemos*. In the second set, the prohibition of not bearing false witness used the term *shov* while in *Shemos*, "*sheker*" is used. How sublimely perfect! We may say that the second set looked at Achav and the corrupt elders. Do not cause witnesses to testify, that you think are in vain anyway, due to the unlimited power of the king, who can get anything he wishes one way or another – in order to get *the field* of another man that he covets!

I add parenthetically – we may understand "Do not raise a 'false' report" literally as an "in vain" report - to mean: Do not just talk for talking's sake of things that are irrelevant and a waste of time, since *shov* does not mean *lashon hara* or false gossip. Talk only about important things such as Torah and mitzvos.

Chapter 57

Here we will show how the Torah foresaw the drought in the era of Eliyahu and Achav -- the use of the ravens to bring bread and meat to him while he hid from Achav – a hint of the name Tishbi in the chumash - and why the dove brought to Noah specifically an olive leaf.

When Noach sent forth a raven to test the ground after the flood, the Torah states (*Bereishis* 8:7) that it went forth and returned [quickly] "until the waters would *dry up* (*yevoshes* – יבשת) from the earth." Rashi quotes the midrash that the raven returned until it got its next assignment during the drought period in Eliyahu's time, when ravens brought bread and meat to him. I know people can ask how this can be any sort of proof, when the verse has a simple meaning with no problem. Besides, the ravens brought Eliyahu food *during* the dry drought years, not up until the time of the drought, which would mean that with the arrival of the drought they stopped! What that midrash meant is clear, but not from the terminology of this verse, hence these words do not demonstrate the usual argument in this volume that the written Torah speaks of future events.

However, the terms for "went forth and returned" in the Hebrew – *yatzo vashav* - are in the infinitive form, not the past. This form is very flexible in Tanach, and can be past or future, present or command form as all Torah students know. (For some examples, see *BeMidbar* (30:3) – future; *Yehoshua* (6:9) –present; (*Yirmiyahu* 14:5) – past; (*Shemos* 20:8) – command; etc.) Thus, in our verse, these verbs may also be seen as implying a future act of going out and returning. So too, the other problem is not one at all. The ravens brought him meat and bread, while he drew water from a nearby brook, until the *brook dried out.* (*Melachim I* 17:7). This is the water that the verse in Noach refers to, for when that happened, the work of the ravens ended and he was told to move on elsewhere! How interesting that the Hebrew term *yevoshes* contains the precise four consonants of Eliyahu's title, the *tishbi* in reverse! Note also that the ravens of Eliyahu are described as "*the* ravens" implying some known birds from a previous description, as "the" usually implies. (Possibly, the original ravens of Noach were preserved throughout centuries for this assignment, and the singular use in *Parashas Noach* of "the raven" refers to the species, not a number, which may have been two ravens.)

A further demonstration that the water referred to in *Noach* is regarding the brook, and not the flood waters, for if it means the flood, the verse should have stated, "until the land dried up," as it does later (8:14). Referring to the brook, the term "the water dries up" is exactly correct, for this is what forced him to move elsewhere.

Why did G-d choose ravens to feed Eliyahu? I suggest the following: *Bnei Yisrael* are called G-d's children. Why did He bring starvation upon the people? Surely, because they did not follow His Torah. The raven is known as acting cruelly with its little offspring, who are born with no resemblance to the father. Once they are mature, he recognizes them and deals mercifully with them. In contrast to the people of his time, Eliyahu was, of course, very righteous. Thus, when the ravens fed him, it served as a reminder that those who act righteously will receive mercy and blessings from their Father (in heaven).(76)

I saw the following idea in the volume *Gur Aryeh* (by the Mahara'l): Ravens do not bring good news. This is why Noach's raven did not go out to seek signs of dry land. He was ready for "another assignment," to feed Eliyahu, helping the one who brought a drought to the world.

The Talmud (45a) relates that Rav Ilish was held in captivity, along with the daughters of Rav Nachman, who he considered to be holy women. [Eventually, he left the women in captivity because he overheard them indicating that they were satisfied to remain in captivity with their "new husbands."] Another captive understood the language of birds. A raven passed by with shrill sounds. The man told the Rav that they said "Ilish, flee! Ilish flee!." He refused the attempt and said that they are liars. The Maharsh'a writes that this is the evil nature of ravens, as they showed with Noach. If one might ask: Weren't they good messengers with Eliyahu? The Mahara'l's comment answers this question, for they were only willing to assist the man who brought drought. Hence R. Ilish felt justified not to trust them. When doves passed by with the same message, Rav Ilish succeeded to escape, while the other man was caught and killed.

However, my holy and righteous ancestor, Rav Mordecai Yafeh, author of the *Levush*, questions the original premise of the Maharal. He argues that, on the contrary, Noach's raven should have been happy to go forth and return with the *bad news* that they could not disembark from the ark.

However, we can also claim the opposite. The "other assignment" that the raven was reserved for was his help to Eliyahu, and since a good messenger (*saneigor*) should not be used for evil reports (*kateigor*), he could not go forth for Noach to inform him of the bad news that water covered the earth! But if this is so, why did Rav Ilish call the raven a lying bird, for it was helpfully encouraging Rav Ilish's escape, just as it helped Eliyahu survive. It is also difficult to understand how the dove, presumably a good bird, first brought back to Noach a bad report, but with Rav Ilish it brought about his escape. Apparently, it can do both good and bad actions.

Actually, my great ancestor added the conclusion that G-d determines by His own considerations who and what to send for any assignment, sometimes an angel and sometimes a living creature of His choice. (76) This entire subject requires further intensive examination.

I found in the *sefer Maasei HaShem* [by Rav Eliezer Ashkenazi] that unlike doves, a raven cannot find its way back after a flight [which is why it instantly returned to the ark when it saw the water covering the earth].

Doves can be trained to return to its home location, as was done frequently in previous centuries before modern communication techniques were developed. He also wrote that doves are the only bird that keeps one mate faithfully, while ravens and others mate with any member of their species. This is why the Jewish people are compared to doves (*Shir HaShirim* 5:2). I believe that in sending ravens to Eliyahu, G-d showed that although these are promiscuous creatures (just as the Jewish people at that time were worshiping other gods), and ordinarily cannot find their way back to their previous location, the ravens carried out their assignments properly and found their way back home to the palace. The message: It is time for *bnei Yisrael* to abandon their idols and find their way back to G-d.

In the first verse that Eliyahu is introduced to us, he predicts the drought that would dry up the land. In that verse, he is called *the Tishbi* (התשבי), which we have already noted is "dry" (יבשת) backwards. This title is only used five times in Tanach, although Eliyahu is mentioned over sixty times. Perhaps Eliyahu noted this fact when he predicted the great dry spell that would overtake the land for years.

Chapter 58

In the great war at Ramas Gilad in which the two Jewish kings (Achav and Yehoshafat) joined forces, the holy Or HaChayim shows how the entire event was foretold in the Torah, including the role of the true prophet Michayu Ben Yimla.

The Torah instructs us about recognizing a false prophet with the following verses (*Devarim* 18:20-22):

But the prophet who will *dare to speak* a word *in My name* which I did not command... that prophet shall die. And if you will say...how shall we know?.... When the prophet will speak in the name *of G-d*... and it will not come... *that is the word* that G-d has not spoken... do not fear him [the prophet].

The *Or HaChayim* poses four questions on these verses, and writes as follows::
1) Why did this section begin with "but," and why "dare to speak" rather than "who will speak"?
2) If the prophecy does not come true, it is obvious that it was false, so why talk of such a scenario?
3) Why use "in My name" in v. 20, and "in the name of G-d" in v. 22?
4) What is the significance of adding "that is the word" in the last verse? We know what word is discussed!

In the description in *Melachim I* (ch.22), kings Yehoshafat of Yehudah and Achav of Yisrael agreed to make war with Aram, having been guaranteed victory by four hundred prophets. Yehoshafat asked Achav if there was any other prophet and he admitted that there was one more, Michayu Ben Nimla. When he was summoned he said the same words as the others, but when Yehoshafat got suspicious [for he did not say "Thus said G-d"], he demanded that he speak again. Michayu then predicted that Achav would die in battle. He explained how he had received a vision of heaven, in which G-d came permission to a certain spirit (Navos) to convince these prophets by a false spirit that Achav would be victorious, when in fact he would die in battle.

However, they went to war anyway and Achav was killed.

In my writings on *Neviim*, I questioned why Michayu first agreed with the false prophets, apparently also affected by the spirit of Navos, and only in his second pronouncement proclaimed G-d's message, unaffected by Navos' spirit. Also, why didn't the spirit of Navos accomplish his total mission, since Michayu revealed the real truth? Furthermore, why did Michayu potentially nullify G-d's plan by revealing the truth? Had Achav become frightened by the truth and refrained from going to battle, he would not have been killed!

However, we may now answer the four questions posed above. The Hebrew word for "but" (lt) is a limiting word, and combined with the phrase "who will dare to speak" implies that a death penalty is only given to a prophet who consciously dares to fabricate a false prophecy, but not one who is tricked by the will of G-d to deliver a prophecy he was fooled into believing, such as that of Navos' spirit. These four hundred prophets were not guilty of a capital crime. Even Michayu, also affected by the spirit of Navos in his first utterance, agreed with them at first. Although the Talmud (*Sanhedrin*) states that one false prophet, Tzidkiya Ben Kenaanah, was guilty of a capital offense, it explains a special reason. There is a well-known rule that two or more prophets do not speak in the same precise language. Since these hundreds all said the exact same words, they immediately realized this problem and ceased speaking, and only Tzidkiya persisted. Thus, he was fabricating a false prophecy, and compounded his guilt by his physical attack on Michayu (v.24).

However, when Achav demanded that Michayu speak the truth *in the name of G-d* (obviously suspicious that he had not prefaced his statement with "thus says G-d"), the navi was forced to state the truth, for a true prophet cannot say a lie in the name of G-d. Nevertheless, the spirit of Navos prevailed anyway, since the king did not accept the warning of Michayu and went forward to his death in battle.

How perfectly the Torah clarified the definition of a false prophet who deserves to die, declaring (*Devarim* 18:20, 22), "the navi who dares to speak a word *in My name* that I did not command - (v.22) who will speak *in the name of G-d*, and it will not come...." These expressions absolve a false prophet from a death penalty if he omitted the name of G-d, but was influenced by a false spirit that spoke through him (e.g. Navos) with G-d's approval. Once again, the Torah's expressions show that the events in Achav's life already were known to the

Creator who stands above time and records the Torah for us.)

Chapter 59

We will search the Torah to find where it saw the miracle of Elisha with the bottle of oil for a poor woman.

[We read in *Melachim II* (chapter 4) how a poor widow cried to Elisha that due to a heavy debt, her children were to be taken from her as servants to the debtor. Taking a pot with some oil in it from her, he proceeded to fill many borrowed containers with precious oil, settling her debt and leaving her with a large surplus.]

I find the hint for this event in *Devarim* (32:13) where Moshe states that G-d provided "oil from flint-rock" for His children. Regarding the prior phrase about "honey from a rock," Rashi found a midrashic story to confirm this prophecy, but there seems no good source from oil from any rock in Tanach. [While Rashi connects this phrase with the great abundance of olive oil found in Gush Chalav, it does not explain the reference to "flint-rock."] I believe that this miracle of bringing forth oil from a pot is the reference in the chumash. This pot (*asooch*) is made of crushed pebbles and can be envisioned as flint-rock. As I will discuss in the coming chapter, all the miracles done by our holy prophets have clues in the Torah itself, and this tale of Elisha comes closest to the phrase in the chumash.

Marvels of Our Blessed G-d's Torah

Chapter 60

This chapter provides a general overview on the concept that the Torah foresaw thousands of details of events of the future. Thus one can understand that it looked ahead to the end of the generations. I will explain some of them and every reader can then proceed to understand the others.

Here is a new way to see that the Torah saw everything to the end of all generations. A complete volume would be needed to clarify every detail of this thesis, so I will record only a little here, while readers will be able to understand the rest, for they are quite obvious and easily understood.

Note that the Torah promised Yehudah (*Bereishis* 49:10) that the kingdom would come forth from him, and we see that it was so, for David and his descendants ruled. Before he gained the throne, Shaul attempted several times to kill him, but he was always saved in miraculous ways For example, when he found himself surrounded on a hill by Shaul's men (*Shmuel I* ch. 24), a messenger ("*malach*" - angel?) came to tell Shaul that the Philistines had invaded the land, and he withdrew quickly. These miracles include his victory over Gulyas, for in all of these events, the hand of G-d protected him in fulfillment of the promise to Yehudah. The reader might object and say that had David been killed, the promise could have been fulfilled by another descendant of Yehudah. Even so, the fact is that G-d had chosen David as the king and protected him in spectacular ways to keep that promise.

This is only one outstanding example of the phenomenon that all the promises and prophecies in the Torah become fulfilled despite all possible hardships and stumbling blocks that are raised to nullify them. Let us examine more closely the prophecy for Yehudah as king, and make some observations.

Many years of exile and servitude for the people in Egypt remained at the time Yaakov promised the kingdom to Yehudah. How many potential obstructions might have nullified that prophecy!

1) Couldn't Yehudah's five sons have died without children?
2) Couldn't they have assimilated into the Egyptian population and vanished from Jewish history?
3) Couldn't all the Jewish people have intermarried among themselves and eventually forgotten from what tribe they descended? (Instead, family lines of descent were carefully recorded and remembered, as we find at the end of *Megillas Ruth*, the complete list of the line from Yehudah's son Peretz, through Boaz, to David.)
4) What if the Jewish people had not been able to leave Egypt at all?
5) What if they had not been able to conquer Eretz Yisrael and would have remained without a country?
6) What if the people who chose Shaul would have insisted that his tribe remain the kings forever?
7) What if David or one of his royal descendants would had been deposed and the kingdom might have passed to

someone from another tribe?

Thus, G-d intervened again and again to prevent any of the above scenarios, and many more, to guarantee that the Torah's promise would come true and remain so. Hence, Yaakov's prophecy foresaw those many centuries of Jewish history, recorded by the Creator who stands above time and knows all the outcomes in advance.

The promise that Yehudah would keep the staff of the kingdom in his hand which held true until the destruction of the temple, was accomplished by many intercessions by G-d throughout the centuries, e.g.:
A) When Asalyah assassinated all the descendants of David (*Melachim II* ch.11), the baby Yoash was saved by his sister and eventually was placed on the throne to continue the prophecy of Yaakov.
B) This prophecy stood like a great wall of protection in all the wars that the kingdom of Yehudah had with other nations, as well as with the kingdom of Yisrael, to guarantee that Dvid's progeny survived to continue the rule of his family.

Thus, Yaakov surely foresaw all of these centuries of Jewish history. So too when the angel of G-d went forth to smite in one night 185,000 soldiers of Ashur, and saved King Tzidkiyahu from annihilation, this prophecy was the ultimate weapon of victory, guaranteed centuries before by the Torah.

Note also that the Torah promised about Pinchas that (*BeMidbar* 26:13) "he shall have, and his seed after him, a covenant of an eternal priesthood...." I explained elsewhere in great detail that this meant the High

Priesthood, and so it was. In the most beautiful location, the Holy Temple in Yerushalayim, we find (*Divrei HaYamim I* 5:30-36) that the twelfth generation from Pinchas was Azaryah, who (v.36) was High Priest in the temple of Shlomo. We must remember that Pinchas was the son of Elazar, and the High Priest (Eili) descended from Isamar, Eliezer's brother. His descendant was Evyasar, the High priest driven out by Shlomo, and replaced by Tzadok, a descendant of Pinchas. The list continues until Yehotzadok, who was High Priest at the time that Nebuchadnezer destroyed the temple (v.41). Hence, when G-d made that promise to Pinchas, He looked ahead and saw that this lofty position would be transferred by Shlomo from Isamar to Elazar. Looking into the future, G-d saw that Evyasar would join Adoniyahu in his aborted attempt to take the throne of David, and this would cause him to lose his position. All of history stands open and revealed to our Holy Creator, who can therefore predict and inform His prophets, and us in His Tanach, about events that will occur, centuries in advance.

I will also show in the next chapter that the Torah foresaw the precise location of the Holy Temple (on the mountain purchased from Aravnah the Yevusi) in the territory of Binyamin, as predicted by Moshe in his message to Binyamin (*Devarim* 33:12), "He shall hover over him all day, and He shall dwell between his shoulders."

I already explained at length in chapters 34, 35, 36, and 37 the many details in the lives of the judges and the kings that the Torah saw long in advance, standing above time and recorded by G-d.

So too, we clarified in chapter 38 that G-d's promise to Yaakov that kings would descend from him in the future referred to Ephrayim and Menashe, who were not yet born at that time. Eventually, kings of Yisrael included Yeravam of Ephrayim, and Yeihu of Menashe. Thus, in effect, G-d saw exactly how these kings would descend from the as yet unborn Ephrayim and Menashe and attain the throne, presenting these prophecies to us centuries in advance.

Observe how the Torah warned in the second chapter of the krias sh'ma (*Devarim* 11:16-17), "Beware let your heart be deceived and you will turn and worship other gods.... And G-d's wrath will be kindled upon you and He will seal up the heavens and there will be no rain...." – and so it happened in the days of King Achav. In coming chapters (63 and 68) I will demonstrate that the Torah saw King Achav, and Eliyahu on Mt. Carmel. All these future situations were already previewed in this warning about holding back the rain.

Equally astonishing is the gift given by HaShem to fashion the *Urim VeTumim* instrument, through which He communicated with the prophets and the High Priests in various crisis situations throughout the Tanach. Indeed, He prepared us to revere our prophets by announcing in the Torah (*Devarim* 18:15,18) that He would raise up prophets for us whose messages from G-d we are commanded to heed. Obviously, G-d already saw the holy prophets who would speak to us centuries later, and had prepared them for their appearances in the designated era that they were destined for. Thus, all forty-eight prophets, and the seven female prophetesses, were visible to G-d when He told us in the Torah that they would be provided for us in times of need. We may presume that Moshe, in presenting this promise of G-d to us, also foresaw the advent of these holy people and the periods of history in which they would function.

The Torah promised (*Devarim* 7:24) "And He will deliver their kings into your hand, and *you shall destroy their name*... no man will stand up before you until you have annihilated them." This occurred precisely when Yehoshua fought five kings (*Yehoshua* ch.10) whose armies were smashed and they fled and hid in a cave. Soon after they were found and executed by Yehoshua. [Their personal names are never mentioned in the story!] Once again, the Torah looked ahead to this event and saw that these anonymous kings would survive the battle only to be handed over to Yehushua for execution.(77)

Note also that G-d showed Moshe the entire land of Eretz Yisrael "up to Dan" (*Devarim* 34:1). Eventually the boundaries of the land stretched from "Dan to Be'er Sheva". However, we find (*Shoftim* 18:27-29) that the tribe of Dan conquered the city of Layish and renamed it Dan in honor of the patriarch of their tribe. Hence, the Torah saw the future events that fashioned this name decades later.

The Torah made a marvelous promise that when all the people would come to Yerushalayim three times a year "no man shall covet your land when you go up to appear before your G-d...." We find in the *Yerushalmi Talmud* (*Peah* 17b) several tales of miracles by which Jewish property was protected during these pilgrimages. The most notable concerns two brothers from Ashkelon who had non-Jewish neighbors. These people plotted to empty the home of the brothers of all valuable objects while they were in Yerushalayim. When the brothers left, HaShem provided angels in human form who inhabited the home during the pilgrimage season. Upon their return, the gentiles asked them who these people were, but the brothers indicated that they had no idea whom they were talking about.(78) G-d perceived the future centuries and could promise absolutely that no damage would occur when His people would go up to Yerushalayim for the festivals.

I previously clarified (ch. 35) how the Torah [Yaakov] foresaw the entire era of Gideon - the miracles that gave his the fortitude to go forth with a small army and win a great victory over a huge army. This event was a small part of the period we call the "Judges" during which the Torah had promised (*Shemos* 23:30-31) that
we would drive out the nations from land in a slow promise until our boundary would stretch from the Reed Sea until the [Euphrates] River. In this prophecy the Torah envisioned the entire period of the judges and beyond to make such a binding promise. Yaakov, too, saw the emergence and life story of Shimshon, the only judge from the tribe of Dan, so that he could promise (*Bereishis* 49:16) "Dan will judge his people...."

Moshe commanded the leviim to place his *Sefer Torah* next to the Holy Ark, and foretold that it will serve as a witness to the future centuries when the people will turn away from G-d and will therefore suffer many misfortunes. This command served as a protection for the ark to be preserved throughout the centuries from being destroyed by our enemies. Despite many harrowing adventures, it indeed survived up to the destruction of the Temple, [and will be restored from its hiding place with the advent of Mashiach]. The Torah's promise is a greater protection that an army of thousands with advanced artillery.

I detailed in several previous chapters how the Torah predicted that Binyamin will provide a king in Israel. It thus previewed all the incidents leading to Shaul's choice, his meeting with Shmuel, as well as Binyamin's survival from the great war (at the end of *sefer Shoftim*) that reduced Binyamin to six hundred men. Had they been annihilated, the prophecies of Yaakov would have become false, for there would not have been a Shaul!

I explained in ch. 45 the unusual wording of a verse in *Shemos* (21:14) which can only be understood as a prophecy of the execution of Yoav by orders of Shlomo. Here too the Torah foresaw an event centuries before it occurred, and surely knew of the many events that led to this execution.

The prophecy of Moshe to the tribe of Levi in *Devarim* (49:8-10) speaks of the glorious spirituality of that tribe. Suddenly, Moshe adds v.11 depicting Levi as a powerful adversary who destroys his enemies! Nowhere in Tanach is Levi engaged in military pursuits! However, as I shall demonstrate in ch. 72 with several proofs, this verse is a prophecy of the great victories of the Chashmonaim under Mattisyahu and his sons against the vast armies of Antiochus. He, more than anyone else in ancient history, desired to totally disconnect the Jewish people from their Torah and mitzvos. His defeat confirmed the vision of Moshe (*Devarim* 31:21) that the Torah will be the eternal witness "that it shall not be forgotten from the mouth of his seed" [to this day!] So too the powerful promises (*Devarim* ch. 30) that after many centuries of Jewish trials and tribulations G-d would restore us and gather us from all over the earth to our ancient homeland is the guarantee of our eternal existence.(79)

Now, reflect as well that the Torah (*VaYikra* 26:34) indicated an exile of seventy years as punishment for the seventy years that the *shemittah* was not observed. Many centuries later, the Persian ruler *Koresh* [Cyrus] allowed the return of the Jewish people to Yerushalayim to rebuild their temple, precisely seventy years after their dispersion. In fact, the navi Yirmiyahu specifically noted the number seventy in his prophecies (*Yirmiyahu* 29:10). Thus, this promise guaranteed the defeat of Haman in his attempt to destroy the Jewish people.

All the discussions in this chapter are only a tiny example of many dozens of further indicators that G-d's Torah previewed all the events of the eternal Jewish people and presented prophecies of our future to the end of days. The glorious promises in ch. 30 of *Chumash Devarim* that G-d will bring us forth from the corners of the earth and restore our eternal people to its eternal land remain to be fulfilled - speedily in our days. As we say in our daily prayers, "May our eyes see the return of our holy G-d to Zion with loving mercy."(80)

ותחזינה עינינו בשובך לציון ברחמים

Footnotes

Chapter 1
(1) Note that this is not a rule for the entire Tanach. There are numerous references to "amim" in terms of the gentile nations of the world, as early as in Bereishis (27:29): "nations will serve you," and in the shirah (Shemos 15:14), "The nations heard and trembled."
(2) It should be noted that many commentators do not follow this interpretation - apparently unsatisfied that David should be pictured as a kind of vulture. See Ramban, Radak, Ralbag, and others.
Chapter 5
(3) - Although it is ordinarily not the goal of a translator to insert personal opinions, I find it difficult to avoid this one comment, the only one in this volume that disagrees with the brilliant author, and insert a

differing analysis. In my volume on Bereishis, I presented an original analysis of the oath of Avraham to Avimelech, and convinced myself that it became null and void when Avimelech drove Yitzchak out of his territory I tried to prove, based on many cogent hints, that in chapter 26, Yitzchak did not renew this covenant with Avimelech, but rather got him drunk to the point that Avimelech only presumed that there was a covenant made. This is not the place to rewrite that entire analysis, but I will add the most powerful evidence here. That incident concludes with the fact that Yitzchak's shepherds found a well on that day, and therefore the name of that site is "Be-eir Sheva." The Seforno and others point out that this was the seventh well that Yitzchak had found. Thus, that place is named "Well Seven." However, if Avraham's oath remains binding, and confirmed by Yitzchak in a renewed one, why must the Torah invent a new reason for this name, which was given by Avraham years before? If my thesis is correct, the Torah "apologizes" for not changing the name, and offers a new reason for keeping it, but negating any reference to any covenant. I encourage the reader to see my volume ("There Shall Be Light") and find some powerful supports to this thesis in that chapter.

Chapter 9

(4) In Melachim I (22:48), both Rashi and the Metzudos indicate that Edom lost its monarchy only with David's conquest of them. This would interfere with the author's precise number of eight.

Chapter 11

(5) There are authorities who insist that there is a higher level of sanctity for the land west of the Jordan. See the marvelous discussion of Rav Yochanan Zweig about this topic that I recorded in my volume on Chumash BeMidbar, Parashas Mattos.

Chapter 13

(6) Ramban's problem is answered by the Targum, and Metzudos, who treat "Ramah" as an expression for the high Heavens!

(7) May I dare suggest that this is part of her great weeping in Yirmiyahu, "over her children for they are not [alive]." If there are two reasons for her weeping, this could be indicated by the repetition in that verse of the expression "over her children!"

(8) I note that in the other references, the combination of tachas asher produces the meaning of "because." I could not locate such a meaning when tachas or mitachas is used.

Chapter 17

(9) The author did not take Onkelos in account about this city. Onkelos states that Chovah was north of Damascus, hence it could not be Dan. The ancient concept saw east, from whence the sun arrived, as the top

of the world, hence left and right in Chumash must mean north and south. In response to the author's problem, Onkelos would say that because Chovah is never again mentioned, the Torah gave us its geographical location, outside of Eretz Yisrael, to show how far the enemy was pursued beyond the Jewish land.

The author does have a response to this point. Since Avraham chased the enemy as he came from the south, it is true that Dan is left of Damascus, as viewed from the physical body of Avraham running northward, for Dan is to his left and Damascus to his right!

(10) However, in our case, Avraham arrives at Dan, fights a victorious battle, and pursued the enemy to Chovah. The simple reading implies a pursuit to a new location. Rashi must read these two verses as the Torah first mentioning the final end of the pursuit, and then returning to explain how they got there, in flashback style. This is not the simplest reading. However, the author has accepted it as the true explanation.

(11) It is perfect according to Onkelos, for in his interpretation Avraham did reach Damascus and even slightly north of it to a town named Chovah!

(12) Of course, this remark is irrelevant to Onkelos, for only Chovah needed such a marker to identify a city never found again in Tanach!

Chapter 18

(13) The author left out the obvious implication that our tradition has unanimously accepted: Edom = Rome = the Catholic Church.

This is especially powerful in the vision of Ovadiah which contains many hints about the church, and concludes that Mt. Eisav will finally be judged and the kingdom will return to G-d (alone, rather than a "trinity").

Chapter 21

(14) Rashi's interpretation that Yaakov refers to G-d, whose Shechinah "rose upon my bed" can also fit with the general approach of the author. Thus, Yaakov feels that after Reuven's act, the Shechinah will never again visit, and he will cease hoping for any more sons.

(15) I find one reference mentioned daily in the Shacharis difficult - Nechemia 9:8 – and have no way to explain it. Here the Girgashi is mentioned last in a list which omits the Chivi!

(16) Actually, there are two references that include the Prizi (Shemos 3:18, 3:17), while none include the Girgashi. I suspect that perhaps the Girgashim were the only group who fled without a fight, because they had the least to lose. Unless the Prizi's territory was not as good as the other five, but better than the other area, placing them in the middle, I cannot explain their inclusion twice and omission once.

(17) I note that in the second series, the expression "and He will give it

to you" is used, while in the first it says "to give to you." I think that the second phrase has a more final ring to it, in keeping with the author's suggestion..

Chapter 26

(18) Nevertheless, the next two verses again repeat that the choice is ours. The prediction is made, but it is not preordained and our free will still operates. We can avoid this terrible consequence, and v. 18 will then be reinterpreted as the conclusion of v. 17 rather than as a vision of the future.

Chapter 27

(19) I believe we may presume that had the Givonim avoided the deception and simply come for peace, the law of the Torah that they serve us with taxation (Devarim 21:11) would have been far more lenient than the low subservience they were subjected to, (due to their deviousness.) When the Torah speaks of conquering distant cities it only demands (Devarim 20:11) that they be subjugated into servitude. It does not add that we must destroy their idols, or order them to observe the Noahice commandments. While there are other opinions on this subject, Rav Shlez can argue his views here.

Chapter 29

(21) This does not appear a very strong hint, since it describes Kalev during his spying journey, not forty years later. However, I think it might be interesting to use the term אשר as כאשר ("Just like"), and then the phrase would translate as "I will give him the land (just as he was when) he trod upon it."

Chapter 30

(22) Here the author discusses at length what is evident to anyone with a current map of Israel. I have therefore left out a large paragraph on page 132 of his discussion.

(23) The Biblical maps all show that the border between Binyamin and Ephrayim is north of Yerushalayim. Hence, this interpretation would place Rachel's grave north of Yerushalayim - an impossibility.

(24) I omitted here a good part of page 134, where the author attempts a complicated analysis to justify Yaakov's vision that she was buried at the border of Binyamin. All maps of ancient Israel show her burial as being far from Binyamin's border.

Chapter 33

(25) Note that only once does the Tanach refer to "Gilgal." All other references are to "HaGilgul."

(26) I am puzzled by the author's ignoring the early reference to Dan in Chumash Bereishis (14:14)! In fact, Rashi notes there that this is a case of naming a site on the basis of the future.

Chapter 34

(27) A fourth name not mentioned by the author is Arnan, found in Divrei HaYamim II, 3:1). I might be bold to suggest that the double nn form completes the root rnn, which means in Hebrew "song/rejoicing." Perhaps after having contributed his field for such a holy purpose (and he offered it to David for no price, only to be refused), the Tanach converted his name to a joyous meaning.

Chapter 35

(28) Probably Rashi inserted this additional interpretation to explain the use of כאחד in place of כשאר. (Yaakov could not use ככל, because Shimon was excluded!) Nevertheless, it is far-fetched to imagine that Rashi considered his comment to be the simple meaning of this verse, as the author correctly concludes.

(29) The Or HaChayim specifically states that all the tribes contributed at least one judge, but ignores the fact that Shimon is excluded! While I cannot explain this oversight, I think one can argue that this is hinted by the absence of "all" [כל] in this phrase.

Chapter 37

(30) See also the kabbalistic mystic explanation of Ramban about the name of Zerach, the twin of Peretz,

(31) I wonder if it might be logical to suggest the possibility that Bas-Shua, who should have been the mother of Peretz, was herself reincarnated as Bas-Sheva, and produced Shlomo, part of the ancestry of Mashiach.

(32) Just as Onan refuses to give Eir eternity thru yibum, so too Shaul (Onan) seeks to destroy David (Eir)!

(33) I wonder if Rav Shlez realized that if understood this way, the final expression that there is a war of G-d with Amalek no longer means that G-d will conduct the war Himself, but only through Mashiach. Hence there is no contradiction to the phrase in Chumash Devarim that we must remember to wipe out Amalek. In both sections, it is our responsibility! Also this is a hidden prophecy that Shaul will not succeed to totally erase Amalek from the world, which becomes apparent only after the fact!

(34) Although the verse says that this happened "on the road to Timnah," it is noteworthy that Timnah is mentioned three times within three verses, at least one of which could easily have been left out, as any reader can confirm.

(35) This geographic statement is not necessarily accepted by many commentators.

(36) I wonder if this might help explain why Moshe is told to write this message "in the book, and place it in Yehoshua's ears." It appears that

G-d did not want the people to hear this message at that time, for it would discourage them from any attempt tp wipe out Amalek. But this truth was recorded for us to realize in the future that, when we failed, it was foreseen already in the Torah.

(37) There is a debate in Rishonim whether this is really accomplished [majority opinion], or whether it is a false trick which these people can train to do. Either way, the Torah forbids going to them. In the Torah (Vayikra ch.20) it is mentioned right after Molech worship, implying that it is a form of idolatry.

(38) Several commentators (e.g., Rav Yaakov Kaminetsky) are certain that Yosef indeed had other sons. See my analysis of this topic in my volume on Bereishis (*There Shall be Light*) pp. 345-347. (Second printing:338)

(39) Perhaps this was reinforced by the last phrase in the verse: "Luz which is Beis-Lechem."

Chapter 39

(40) Since the 18 amos of Yachin represent a time period, it is easy to understand why the height of Boaz was omitted. The crown of Torah has no time limit – it is forever and ever.

(41) The significance is, perhaps, that as a "reward" for our forefathers faithfully spending time in the promised land as strangers only, their descendants gained matching years living there as the true owners.

(42) This secret of the lunar month was known throughout the centuries by the Jewish people. Various Greek astronomers tried to calculate it and were off by significant amounts. Using the above calculation, our lunar month equals 29.53059 days. In recent times, the government, with the latest advanced computers finally discovered the precise number: 29.530588! See the encyclopedia "Nachalei Limud" by Rav Yosef Bagad, p.100. [Probably the computer is off by - .000002!]

(43) The kaballah has its own mystic explanation of this "extraneous" chapter, i.e., that it alludes to major periods of history preceding the arrival of Mashiach, "king in Israel."

(44) This list of fifteen includes Asalyah, who usurped the kingdom by wholesale murder. The fact is that she did rule. If one wishes to exclude her, we could add Tzidkiyahu as the fifteenth king, since he did rule for eleven years before the destruction

(45) Some meforshim had trouble in making this count. But Maharam miRutenberg worked out an excellent count, as recorded in the commentary of the Aderes, in the Feldheim edition of the Baal haTurim, 5753, Yerushalayim.

(46) I am astounded by the inclusion of Avimelech in this list of righteous judges. Chapter 9 of Shoftim clearly identifies him as a brutal

murderer!

(47) I considered omitting this final point! The fact is that the verb *moshel* is always followed by "b", not "al,." with only one or two rare exceptions!

Chapter 42

(48) So too, two of Yoshiyahu's descendants sat on the throne for three months. Yehoyakim reigned for eleven years. However, while this is not the place for a lengthy discussion, the indications are that in his early years he was still righteous enough and turned to evil ways much later in his reign. The reader who owns my set of "Great Torah Lights" may refer to the appendix in BeMidbar, and read Ch.26 of Yirmiyahu to recognize this real possibility.

(49) It seems clear from the final chapters of Yirmiyahu, that Tzidkiyahu feared G-d, and consulted with the navi, but had a very weak personality and did nothing against the wicked wishes of his officers. Perhaps that is why he did last eleven years compared to the three others mentioned in this section. G-d may have waited to give him time to repent and act properly.

Chapter 43

(50) These two statements refer only to the battles at Shushan. In the earlier battles across all of Achashverosh's provinces, it is not mentioned. Probably, Mordecai did not have control over the entire kingdom to control the people's desire for spoils.

(51) The reason Binyamin was chosen is not clear in chapter 37. Many commentators explain that Binyamin was the only tribe not guilty of unprovoked hatred (selling Yosef to Egypt) and thus takes revenge against Amalek, who attacked without provocation. Perpetrators of *sin-as chinam* are defeated by those who are innocent of this ugly aggression.

(52) I found that the only other time this verb was used with the practice of *Ov is in Divrei HaYamim I,* (10:13), also dealing with Shaul!

Elsewhere, other verbs are used, e.g. poneh, oseh, and doresh.

(53) There is a strange error in the text of the volume. I cannot believe that the author made it. It speaks of Shaul's haste to ravage *Amalek,* rather than his haste in bringing the sacrifices before Shmuel's arrival. This must be a printer's error. "Amalek" is not found in the original Or HaChayim statement.

(54) I find this to be a magnificent hint to the permission given to Esther, after much debate by the wise men of her time, that the Purim events may be recorded in a volume as part of the Tanach!

(55) The preceding phrase is "his hands were steady until...." The term

steady is rendered by "emunah" which usually means faith. I think it hints at the idea that he gave the Jewish people faith throughout the ages as they saw Shaul, then Mordecai, successfully combating Amalek. This gave them the faith to know that Shiloh will finally arrive to complete the command of G-d.

(56) This analysis was made possible only because the verse changed from the plural *resha-im* to the singular *tzaddik!* This change seems unusual to me, but by this analysis it becomes justified!

Chapter 44

(57) Of course this cannot be seen as a literal interpretation, since when it is used in the sense of admitting, it is always follwed by a k and never by a direct object pronoun.

(58) the church especially - see the disputation of the Ramban before the king of Spain.

(59) Apparently, Rav Shlez was convinced that Yaakov would not use four phrases to bring out one point!

(60) Meforshim presume that "Avimelech" is a general term for Plishtim kings, while Achish was his personal name.

(61) In that account (Shmuel I, ch.17), David's "hand" is mentioned four times from v.40 through v.49!

(62) I am uncertain as to how this interpretation is similar to the previous one. The author also does not continue in this interpretation to the next verse. Apparently David then says that in his haste and fear he felt that all of mankind is deceitful - however, he then proceeds to thank G-d for sustaining him and continues in this fashion for many verses forward.

(63) I believe the unusual verb *karkar* may be related to *akar* (uproot) and/or *makor* (a root), thus meaning to uproot. This would fit perfectly with Chazal's opinion about Sancherev. However, the author does not clarify how a phrase about Sancherev entered a verse which speaks about a star rising from Yisrael! The Panim Yafos apparently meant that the entire verse speaks of Mashiach's times, when the world will be judged harshly, and thus Moav is separated as the one nation that was not involved in the mixing of the people by Sancherev. However, we might then wonder: who are they indeed?

Chapter 47

(64) In fact, even in *Divrei Hayamim* (3:12) in a list of genealogy, he is referred to as Azaryah. Thus only in connection with his sinful act of the incense is his name changed to Uziyahu.

(65) At first glance, it seems that this double name was switched incorrectly! Would it not have been more reasonable to use the "r" in the section where he offers the incense as a "zar"? Perhaps, dropping it

there reflects on his thinking that as king of Israel he has special prerogatives and would not be considered a zar, so he can bring incense to the altar. Thus, the author's point is still valid.

Chapter 48

(66) My only problem with this analysis is that Achaz did not suffer the punishment of *kareis* (spelled out in verse 2) since the line of his descendants continues down to the destruction of the *Beis haMikdash*.

(67) I could not locate this midrash, but the Yalkut Shimoni has one very similar, leaving out Asa.

(68) In Asa's prayer to G-d he said, "It is nothing for You to help, whether there are "many" [cr] or helpless.... the term used in this phrase!

(69) In my humble opinion, a better case for Dan could be the idol of Michah that the tribe of Dan set up and worshiped as described in detail in *Shoftim* ch. 18.

Chapter 50

(70) [Nevertheless, the standard interpretation of Shimshon causing the death of countless Plishtim as he died remains as a second correct meaning for this verse. While the author does return to this point clearly, he opened the entire discussion by stating that "there is another concept here" implying that both are correct.]

Chapter 51

(71) See in my volume on Shemos (in the Great Torah Lights set, p.27) the essay "Moshe's Oath" for a brilliant analysis by Rav Yechezkel Livshitz on the "error" of Moshe in raising Gershom, for a further insight into this tragic result.

Chapter 53

(72) R. Zalman Sorotzkin (*Oznayim laTorah*) also made this point, apparently unaware that he was preceded by Rav Shlez in this volume.

(73) I omit the final section of this chapter, because there is a glaring and obvious fault in the author's argument. Any interested reader can look it up in the Hebrew volume (Ps. 232-3) and find it with some concentration.

Chapter 54

(74) In fact, this is the only "Gilgal" found in chumash!

Chapter 55

(75) This seems to me to be a weak argument. The source of Rashi from ch.12 refers to Avraham traveling from a northeast area into Eretz Yisrael, hence he approached Yerushalayim as he headed southward. But in the land itself, it is hard to think of Binyamin as being in the south, when the entire territory of Yehudah was south of Binyamin, and as one looks at the map of the land today, Yerushalayim seems only a

little below the center of the country.

Chapter 57

(76) I recall once finding an interesting variation on this question. According to Chazal the food came from Achav's palace which was kept kosher by his faithful servant Ovadyahu. Since Achav was searching high and low for Eliyahu, he might have suspected that birds were feeding Eliyahu in a hiding place. But he would never suspect the cruel ravens of doing kindness to anyone.

Chapter 60

(77) I made an interesting discovery here to support the connection between the verse in *Devarim* and the story in *Yehoshua*. In *Devarim*, the Torah uses the singular "in your *hand."* In *Yehoshua* (10:8) G-d promises that the kings would be given into his "hands" - but the *mesorah* tells us to read this word as if there is no plural form, as "hand," matching precisely the text of *Devarim!*

(78) There is a notable absence of any record of actual invasions by other peoples during the three holiday seasons. The story in the *Yerushalmi* appears to be a rare exception of some people who "defied" the Torah's promise, but were foiled by G-d's intervention.

(79) What would the author have said had he lived to see the return of millions of Jews to the land of our forefathers, and the beginning of the unfolding of the promises in chapter 30!

(80) The author's comment in this volume published in 1879-80.

This concludes Part One of this volume.

It is my hope and prayer, with G-d's help, to proceed with Part Two after Part One is completed.

www.ingramcontent.com/pod-product-compliance
Lightning Source LLC
Chambersburg PA
CBHW050248170426
43202CB00011B/1599